Beyond the Muse of Memory

Beyond the Muse of Memory

ESSAYS

ON

CONTEMPORARY

AMERICAN

POETS

Laurence Lieberman

UNIVERSITY OF MISSOURI PRESS
Columbia and London

Copyright © 1995 by
The Curators of the University of Missouri
University of Missouri Press, Columbia, Missouri 65201
Printed and bound in the United States of America
All rights reserved
5 4 3 2 1   99 98 97 96 95

Library of Congress Cataloging-in-Publication Data

Lieberman, Laurence.
    Beyond the muse of memory : essays on contemporary American poets /
Laurence Lieberman.
        p.   cm.
    Includes index.
    ISBN 0-8262-1027-9 (cloth : alk. paper).—ISBN 0-8262-1047-3 (pbk. :
alk. paper)
    1. American poetry—20th century—History and criticism.   I. Title.
PS325.L48   1995
811'.509–dc20   95-36753
                                                                        CIP

♾ This paper meets the requirements of the
American National Standard for Permanence of Paper
for Printed Library Materials, Z39.48, 1984.

DESIGNER: ELIZABETH K. FETT
TYPESETTER: BOOKCOMP
PRINTER AND BINDER: THOMSON-SHORE, INC.
TYPEFACES: FORMATA & MERIDIEN

Frontispiece illustrations by Dee Clark:
Robert Penn Warren *(top left)*, Robert Lowell *(top right)*,
John Berryman *(bottom left)*, James Dickey *(bottom right)*.

for

Frederick Morgan

and

Theodore Weiss,

eagle minds

Books by Laurence Lieberman

POETRY

The St. Kitts Monkey Feuds (1995)

New and Selected Poems: 1962–92 (1993)

The Creole Mephistopheles (1989)

The Mural of Wakeful Sleep (1985)

Eros at the World Kite Pageant (1983)

God's Measurements (1980)

The Osprey Suicides (1973)

The Unblinding (1968)

CRITICISM

Beyond the Muse of Memory: Essays on Contemporary American Poets (1995)

Unassigned Frequencies: American Poetry in Review (1978)

The Achievement of James Dickey (1968)

Contents

ix

Part III. Stephen Berg

Part IV. From *Unassigned Frequencies*
Selected Essays

Postscript

Acknowledgments

The author gratefully acknowledges the editors of the following magazines, in which these essays first appeared:

The American Poetry Review: "The Glacier's Offspring: A Reading of Robert Penn Warren's New Poetry"; "Corkscrews of the Eternal: Three Essays on Robert Lowell's Later Poems" ("Two Marriage Poems," "Dark Smiles of the Terminal Ward," and "Inextinguishable Roots")

The Antioch Review: "Theodore Roethke"

Denver Quarterly: "Stephen Berg: The Passion of Mourning"

The Hudson Review: "James Dickey: The Worldly Mystic"; "A. R. Ammons: Of Mind and World"

John Berryman Studies: "Hold the Audience: A Brief Memoir of John Berryman"

Poetry: "Jean Garrigue: The Body of the Dream" (review of *New and Selected Poems*); "James Wright: Words of Grass" (review of *Shall We Gather at the River*); "Mark Strand: The Book of Mourning" (review of *The Story of Our Lives*); "A. R. Ammons" (review of *Selected Poems*)

The Sewanee Review: "The Knife-edge of Supernal Being" (formerly titled "Exchanges: Inventions in Two Voices")

The South Carolina Review: "Erotic Pantheism in James Dickey's 'Madness'"

Southwest Review: "Beyond the Muse of Memory: Robert Lowell's Last Face"

The Texas Review: "The Long Cry: James Dickey's 'Mercy'"

The Yale Review: "Derek Walcott and Michael S. Harper: The Muse of History"; "Jean Garrigue" (review of *Studies for an Actress*); "James Wright" (review of *Two Citizens*); "W. S. Merwin: The Church of Ash"; "Mark Strand" (review of *Reasons for Moving*); "A. R. Ammons" (review of *Briefings*); "William Stafford and Frederick Morgan: The Shocks of Normality"; untitled reviews of Richard Hugo, Stanley Kunitz, Josephine Miles, and Theodore Weiss

Special thanks to the UIUC Research Board and the Arnold Beckman Endowment for a fellowship that supported completion of the essays in this book.

Beyond the Muse of Memory

Introduction

This compilation of essays and reviews, written over a thirty-year period, makes no pretense to an overview of contemporary American poetry; rather, it highlights my own experience as a reader and interpreter. The essayists I most emulate in my criticism are those informal critics whose writings often tend to be personal and instinctively charged. I take James Dickey's review-essays in *Babel to Byzantium* as one prototype for my approach to contemporary writers. Other exemplars might be Blackmur's articles on poetry, Lawrence's *Classical Studies in American Literature,* or Robert Penn Warren's marvelous introduction to Conrad's *Nostromo.* These essays may seem rather fragmentary and unfinished, rough-hewn if you will, but the electric pulse that is nakedly alive in such work is what I aspire to in my critical writings.

In recent years, I have turned my hand more and more to devising a mode of essay that focuses on one poem by a major author; in the process of illuminating that central opus, I strive to reveal abiding patterns in the poet's lifework. The long article on John Ashbery's poem "Self-portrait in a Convex Mirror," the title essay of my previous book *Unassigned Frequencies,* was my first experiment with this essay genre. In the present collection, my pieces on Robert Penn Warren, Dickey, and Lowell continue to explore this new form of the essay. Three of the Lowell pieces appeared as a single unit in *American Poetry Review,* and they tackle related problems in the poems of Lowell's last period, a sector of his work that has been wrongly undervalued by many of his critics. Lowell broke through into a vital innovatory phase of his work at the last, and I hope to persuade readers to give those final works another serious look. My newest writings on James Dickey focus on a few strong poems of his middle period, "Madness," "Mercy," and "Blood," which have usually been neglected by critics. Stephen Berg, one of Lowell's best students, has produced remarkable work in a handful of books that have been mistakenly overlooked or underrated. My comprehensive essay on Berg would invite readers to reassess his œuvre.

The shorter works in this collection were written on assignment for various magazines in the 1960s and 1970s. In 1980 when Robert Penn Warren sent me the galleys for his book *Being Here,* my shaky resolve to not write any more book reviews was put to the severest test. A great sea change had taken place in Warren's work, I felt, since the release of his *third* volume of selected poems in 1976. At age seventy Warren had launched a decade of new poetry that would surpass any previous ten-year cycle of his voluminous career. Only Thomas Hardy before him had achieved such an amazing late-bloom resurgence of poetry in English, following a virtual abdication of several decades of distinguished work as a novelist. Indeed, Warren the self-critic spoke openly of suppressing the impulse to write more novels, for fear the craft of fiction would drain away precious energies from his prolific outpouring of new poems. Technically he seemed equally adept at writing both free-verse narratives and those over-the-top visionary meditations on nature and the life of the spirit in measured couplets and quatrains. Nearly a whole generation had slipped away since Ted Roethke had embarked on a similarly double-barreled enterprise, seesawing back and forth between elegantly honed stanzas in conventional meters and free-verse sequences, meditations anchored to the American landscape. But Roethke's career was cut short just as he entered this phase of seasoned mellowness, and Warren, I felt, was picking up that mantle where Roethke had dropped it. As never before, Warren had attained a knife-edge keenness of line and image that could instantly transcribe the fierce and primeval encounters of his nature hikes into wisdom of Being. Lyric epiphanies abounded in this work. It seemed as if the man Warren could step up to any rock, tree, cave, bird, or beast and perhaps scare up his mystical twin entity, and each such random colliding of kindred spirits might provide him with the exact metaphor needed to define the next milestone of his existential journey. "Globe of Gneiss" struck me as being a particularly luminous metaphor, because—more than any other—it seemed to embody Warren's unique moment in both human and geologic history. The persona in such poems is caught up in the adventure of *going beyond, going beyond* the accustomed human limits. More and more we come to feel that Warren's art in these late works is an art of hardihood, survivorship, and craggy, gnarled endurance. Cumulatively the new poems appear to enact a quest for supernal Being. Warren's spirit, at the last, has evolved from aspiring to indomitable.

My essay on Warren, then, was the first in my new cycle of longer pieces focusing on a single poem, while perhaps casting light on a major phase in the author's career evoked by the one work's brilliant metaphor. The next year when I came to review James Dickey's book *The Strength of Fields,* I found a stronger kinship than I'd noticed before between Dickey's vision and the newest mode of his fellow southerner's work. Both Dickey and Warren seemed committed, above all, to moving beyond the world of nature to grasp moments of utmost purity of Being. Many years later when I was invited to contribute a new essay on Dickey's work for an anthology of critical pieces honoring the poet's seventieth birthday, I found myself drawn back to the crucial transition stage of his career following the overwhelming success of *Poems 1957–1967*. A number of the best new poems of that middle period seemed masterfully bent on breaking new ground, and I settled on the one poem that had most haunted me over the years, "Madness." In writing the essay, I set out to teach myself to read the poem at a deeper level than ever before. I felt compelled to explain to myself the poem's uncanny hold over me, and in so doing I might hope to enlighten other readers as well. (The whole discussion grew out of my earlier struggle to come to terms with the poem in my introduction to Dickey's keynote poetry reading at the MLA Convention in Chicago in 1985.) Subsequently the ideas generated by that essay prompted me to write pieces on other important poems of this juncture, "Mercy" and "Blood," which I felt had been passed over, or wrongfully disesteemed, by even some of Dickey's more sympathetic critics. In retrospect I could see that Dickey had been forging in these fast-paced lyrics a lean, sparer style that would better suit his mature work in the novel, though each was a unique commanding performance in its own right. Indeed, the plainspoken, idiomatic vernacular that was nurtured in these poems has peaked, today, in the assured cadences of Dickey's most lyrically vocalized novel, *To the White Sea*. Taking a course opposite to Warren's, then, James Dickey deflected ever more of his most radical creative impulse from poetry to fiction in late career.

All my early attempts to write about Robert Lowell's work faltered, my would-be reviews of *Notebook, History,* and *The Dolphin* ending in fumbled tries. Often when I strove to review the most audacious books in the narrowly prescribed word limits assigned to me by magazine editors, not to mention the agonizing time squeeze, I threw up my hands in defeat. Many reviewers had grown weary of Lowell's seemingly endless published revisions of the same *sonnets* in volume after volume, but I mostly reveled in the alternate versions, sometimes preferring an earlier variant, though usually espousing the new-minted poem. Finally, I found the whole enterprise to be adventurous and exhilarating beyond measure. A few years before, I'd felt that Lowell had painted himself into a technical cul-de-sac in the rather tepid forms of much of the work in *Near the Ocean,* and the new unrhymed fourteen-liners of *Notebook* struck me at once as a major breakthrough. The diaristic pulse of the unwinding sequence was clearly a marvelous strategy for liberating otherwise intractable sectors of Lowell's full-blooded personality, much as Berryman's ever-pliant new form in the *Dream Songs* gave him an exquisite device for tapping into the widest range of private and public resources in his most capacious work. Perhaps Lowell had taken the cue from his friend, and he too would pursue a limitlessly expansive labor in the successive versions of *Notebook*. However, when he had all but exhausted the power of the sonnetesque form in *The Dolphin*, he returned to a free-verse mode outwardly resembling the open forms of *Life Studies* in the poems of his last book.

Slowly, after many readings, I grew to find in the rawboned meters of the work in *Day by Day* a subtler, quiet artifice. Lowell had achieved, at last, a new restrained power to speak with halting urgency and direct-ness about the major crises in his daily living: forebodings of a possible breakup in his third marriage, horrors of the modern hospital ward, fainting spells, and premonitions of his own early death. The greater simplicity of his last style was deceptive, since the vacillating contours of his verse measure could now, as rarely before, accommodate the most harrowing and poignant events in his domestic life with utmost deftness. His language was lean and supple and fiercely attuned to the moment-to-moment texture of life struggles yanking him in opposite directions simultaneously. Once again, I found myself caught up in writing whole essays about single poems, and each of the best final works led me to conclude that Lowell had secured a whole new *ars poetica* in his last phase. The liberating aftereffect of writing for years with his throttle open at full stretch in the meaty sonnet clusters of the *Notebook* volumes was that the grueling effort had predisposed Lowell for the unparalleled radiance of *Day by Day*.

Part I.
Robert Lowell

Corkscrews of the Eternal

THREE ESSAYS ON LOWELL'S
LATER POEMS

1. TWO MARRIAGE POEMS

A. Film Scenario

Down the mountain walls
From where Pan's cavern is
Intolerable music falls.
Foul goat-head, brutal arm appear,
Belly, shoulder, bum,
Flash fishlike; nymphs and satyrs
Copulate in the foam.

"News for the Delphic Oracle," W. B. Yeats

Scenario for a futuristic film.[1] Urban setting. Outskirts of the city. A crowded suburb. Midnight. Pan, god of Greek mythology—half man, half goat—presides over a sexual comedy of horrors. The characters are computerized robots—half auto, half cow—herds of them. They stampede for the gas pumps, get drunk on Gasahol ("killing / gas like alcohol"), and crash into each other, again and again. Their supple cowhides offer resilience, in place of mangled chrome or metal; their features grow more personal as they approach orgasm, though the exhaust fumes create so thick a mist (steams of sweat and sex) that they turn invisible for moments, buried in smoke. But a lurid bumper flashes here, a pair of curved bullhorns there! Then most of the herd fall exhausted in sleep, though one restless lover, the insomniac, lies awake all night, his snoring mate propped on his crossed hooves—anxious lest he not rise to heaven of the car beasts:

---

1. These three essays originally appeared in *The American Poetry Review* in November/December 1985.

> You lie in my insomniac arms,
> as if you drank sleep like alcohol.

By noon the next day, the cars, all looking alike, wander aimlessly in lost circles, dizzied by too much sun and a nasty dose of auto hangover. When Pan stopped blowing his breath of love-fumes upon them, they returned to their drab everyday-business robot lives:

> In noonday light,
> the cars are tin, stereotype and bright,
> a farce
> of their former selves at night—
> invisible as exhaust,
> personal as animals.

> Gone
> the sweet agitation of the breath of Pan.

If movies, today, were loosely transcribed from poems, as they are from novels and stories, such a film might be fashioned after Robert Lowell's most experimental last poem, "Suburban Surf." But I have taken inclement liberties with the original text (as did Lowell, so often, in *his* translations), since I have virtually banished the human protagonists— a married couple reunited after a separation—from the cast of players. However, though the encounter between humans is clearly the poem's true subject, most of the work's explicit imagery refers to animals or cars, and my overelaborate paraphrase confines itself to the literal images, though I have freely added details, whereas the Lowell poem is brilliantly terse and suggestive. The drama of the cows and cars operates as an extended analogy to the engagement between the man and woman, who, through exhaustion, effects of alcohol, and dizzying trials of long separation followed by shocks of sudden reunion, greet each other nonverbally, "No conversation." Their mood is one of distractedness, irreality, each at a remove from what occurs between them; they seem, oddly, both inside and outside of their bodies, their actions, so it seems credible to a reader for the movements of their lovemaking to be projected as a surreal masquerade of images of auto sex, animal sex. In the movie version, the two dramas might be merged, persuasively, with superimposed layers of montage, the lilliputian autos and cows in the screen foreground, say, with stark clear outlines, while the human giants flutter in the backdrop, their silhouettes blurred, their torsos appearing to contain the frenzied fleet of animals and machines. Although we see the figures of the man and woman just once, concretely, at the poem's outset, we sense their disembodied ghostly presence, indeed their hallucinatory sex, throughout the carnival of auto-beast images.

But I haven't yet begun to take account of the poem's remarkably hybrid terrain, which converts the marital bedroom into an inland ocean (to take a turn upon Lowell's phrase "oceanless inland" in another last poem). The story's setting, then, mixes seashore and household images, dynamically interweaving the opposed worlds, antinomies, of land and sea; aptly, the poem's treatment of locale duplicates the unusual blend of images—nature, technology, and humankind—that depicts the performers of the action. In the film version, perhaps high waves of "suburban surf" can be portrayed cresting and foaming upon the shores of bedsheets and roadway alike. . . .

Robert Lowell achieved numerous technical gains in the art of "Suburban Surf" that advanced him to a radical order of experimentation beyond any of his previous works. An astonishing new poesy is instantly noted in the concision and brevity of stanzas, all one-, two-, and three-line units (except for the longer penultimate stanza quoted above); as the abbreviated clauses of stanzaic shorthand proceed, a reader attunes his ear to the increasingly dynamic spaces between units. When the conventional sentence structure of the first and second stanzas gives way to the broken syntax of a loosely spliced chain of fragments, those spaces improvise a new consistent syntax of their own, a syntax that maintains utter lucidity of sentence logic and transparency of meaning, despite the abdication of normal grammar. Hypnotically, this taut linkage of fragments, which constitutes the middle two-thirds of the poem, creates the rhythmic illusion of a single endlessly capacious sentence—a verse perpetuum mobile, as if the very lives of the human protagonists are held in suspension, hovering, while their bodies slowly rise above the bed, then halt in a stupor of levitation, just under the ceiling:

> No conversation—
> then suddenly as always cars
> helter-skelter for feed like cows—
>
> suburban surf come alive,
>
> diamond-faceted like your eyes,
> glassy, staring lights
> lighting the way they cannot see—

friction, constriction etc.
the racket killing
gas like alcohol.

Long, unequal whooshing waves
break in volume,
always very loud enough to hear—

méchants, mechanical—

soothe, delay, divert
the crescendo always surprisingly attained
in a panic of breathlessness—

too much assertion and skipping
of the heart to greet the day . . .
the truce with uncertain heaven.

A false calm is the best calm.

Despite the avoidance of speech between the lovers, it seems as if the fate of their marriage may hang in the balance during these first hours, days, of reunion; hence, their encounter peaks "in a panic of breathlessness," followed by a "false calm" that is felt to be, at best, a "truce with uncertain heaven." If the spaces between those middle stanzas suggest, finally, pauses of heavy breathing between spurts of sexual activity, the prolonged sentence itself, spread over many stanzas, rhythmically mimics a human feat of extended breathholding, both mates fearing asphyxiation perhaps ("too much assertion and skipping / of the heart"), which momentary dread of dying of heart failure during sex carries beyond this instant of passion to a commensurate dread that their marriage, itself, may be approaching suffocation.

After the two opening stanzas, which quietly delineate the bedroom scene for a normal narrative, the open-ended, spiraling long sentence is launched by the phrase "No conversation," and thereafter, the progressive elisions and ellipses of style suavely evoke the stages of protracted nonverbal encounter between the man and woman, as well as extemporizing a novel syntax that metrically imitates the hit-and-run, hit-or-miss headlong charge of their sex:

You lie in my insomniac arms,
as if you drank sleep like coffee.

Then,
like a bear tipping a hive for honey,
you shake the pillow for French cigarettes.

No conversation—
then suddenly as always cars
helter-skelter for feed like cows—

The abrupt shift in midstanza, here, from low-keyed domestic painting
of the human scene to manic auto-beast phantasmagoria, coincides with
the pivotal moment of slide from grammatical sentences to linked clauses.
Both swerves of the poem's technical means signal the sudden onset of
lovemaking. Lowell's familiar device of new-minting verbs from nouns,
or other unlikely parts of speech ("helter-skelter for feed"), is another
tipoff. The moment of yielding to impulse has arrived.

I note a more pervasive—if subtler—progression in the poem's tac-
tic of correspondences, slowly evolving from casual similes, expanded
metaphor, to a complex many-layered allegory. To begin, Caroline is
jokingly likened to "a bear tipping a hive for honey," and at the fin-
ish, conversely, the cars openly represent humans ("the cars are tin,
stereotype and bright, / a farce / of their former selves at night"), drunks
recovering from hangovers the day after, a brilliantly pungent and comic
metaphor. The two manifestly humorous moments in "Suburban Surf"
are these passages near the start and finish. So, despite the work's central
focus on marital strife and painful conflict, the main body of the piece is
framed by lighthearted tropes, providing some welcome comic relief, an
austere gaiety balancing the dominant mood of dread. In their virtuosity
of tone shifts, the succinct stanzas modulate swiftly across a wide emo-
tional spectrum from sensuous vivacity to anxious bewilderment and
insomniac stupor. The impressively broad antinomies of temperament
resolved in a final vision of becalmed self-restoration suggests that this
poem earns a claim, finally, to the very special genre of tragicomedy.
The imagery of grotesque frenzy is purged, and the vision breaks free
into a transcendent plane, a healing mixture of reverie and fantasy, yet
on a much smaller scale, certainly, than Shakespeare's *Winter's Tale* or
other permanent masterworks of this mode. Vastly disparate emotional
poles have been adroitly navigated with grace and matchless economy of
means, which may earn "Suburban Surf" a place in that special pantheon.

Another progression in the poem's imagery is its alluring sweeps from
one sensory threshold to another, tracing a course from basic eye images,
establishing the setting for readers and relaxed, strainless contact between

the mates; to ear images and tactile embossments (you can nearly feel them lift in raised relief from the printed page); to pulmonary, aortic, and ventricular incidents: the last, a most original and unforgettable way to transcribe and evoke the final moments of lovemaking, a culmination localized, if you will, not in the gonads but in measurable lung spasms and heart palpitations:

> . . . the crescendo always surprisingly attained
> in a panic of breathlessness—
>
> too much assertion and skipping
> of the heart.

Too clinical readers, I suppose, will simply dismiss these images as a confession of premature climax or partial impotence and thereby fail to take note of the far more intimate revelation of momentary slips of tenderness, fine shades of imperfect timing, vague errors of fumbled tempo that, to be sure, can make all the difference between success and failure. But the exquisite power of these lines is that with so few words the most delicate of sexual caprices and eccentricities are enveloped with a language that rings perfectly true to an experience for which no vocabulary is generally held credible, much less palpable, except the alphabets of touch.

By gradual tunings of the poem's key, or pitch, its style proceeds through gradations of simile to metaphor and dazzlingly luminous allegory, sight and sound impressions displaced, finally, by a whole-body imagery, a total stylistic sensorium—hence, the radical shift from the skin base, the organs of tactility, to the internal organs. Similarly, the poem's dominant vocabulary alters from sensory words to verbs, as description is absorbed into a prevailing tide—"unequal whooshing waves"—of action. The central metaphor of a single irresistible wave motion—which builds swiftly from an invisible ground swell into a towering wave crest that carries everything before it, assuming the form of the poem's long central sentence—is initiated by the explosive one-line unit, "suburban surf come alive," which repeats and heightens the poem's title.

The gluttonous, bawdy cows and cars of the preceding stanza are swept up into the one wave's advance like so much flotsam ("then suddenly as always cars / helter-skelter for feed like cows"), since it's the wave of human sex that has now erupted; from this moment forward, the machine and animal images, if alluring in themselves, are subsumed by the human drama, so many parts fitted into a stylized incandescent mosaic that expresses the more surreal elements of sex between the man and the woman, as in the brilliant *headlights* image of the following stanza:

> . . . diamond-faceted like your eyes,
> glassy, staring lights
> lighting the way they cannot see.

Lowell, to be sure, is himself a veteran jewelsmith, the sharp edges of image-diamond he molds, here, cutting many ways at once. Matters of interpretation aside, I am bent on exploring, purely, many literal entities in the two scenes of the montage—both the bedroom perspective and the auto-traffic vista superimposed thereon—that are masterfully interrelated by these few lines. To begin, consider the carryover of literal data from the preceding three lines:

> . . . then suddenly as always cars
> helter-skelter for feed like cows—
>
> suburban surf come alive.

Whether viewed from above, or a little distance to one side, aerial or lateral glimpse, the lineups of cars approaching service stations for fuel at night, converging from several highway angles at once, say, generate a whirling array of sparkles with their headlamps (brights and dims and yellow fog lights), which may resemble the effervescent glitter of starlight and moonlight reflected in surf of night waves rolling ashore. These equivalences, then, were securely established by the pivotal one-line stanza, "suburban surf come alive."

"Diamond-faceted," in the following stanza, is the key nexus word, linking the human world to the auto-traffic and seashore imagery alike, since the woman's eyes aglitter in bedroom dark are likened both to moonlit foam of the surf (a warm romantic association) and to the swarm of auto headlights (an icy mechanical semblance), which deflates the aura of romance, nullifying the conventional glamor one associates with images of lovers' eyes in traditional poems of the genre, a low-tech updating of Shakespeare's playing havoc with the clichés of romantic sentiment in "My Mistress' Eyes Are Nothing Like the Sun." Yet the following couplet—more explicitly likening the woman's eyes to car lights—skillfully blends the bitter associations with the sweet,

> glassy, staring lights
> lighting the way they cannot see—

the first line evoking the woman's dazed vacant stare, her lack of true involvement perhaps, while the second line implies her inner radiance of spirit, her eyes aglow with a healing light that may revive their languishing marriage, despite the room's blackout. In the same lines, Lowell successfully plays upon a half-forgotten enigma of modern technology, to which we've grown numb from habit. Cars can't see in the dark, *or* light, yet auto headlamps function like animals' eyes that can see in total dark for thousands of hours, across thousands of miles. These lines restore us to that cryptic lost fact of our everyday reality, a miracle of sightless synthetic vision we take for granted.

The next stanza, exploring painful imagery of body discomfiture, shrinks to three shortest lines, the moment of sexual constraint matched by the line squeeze:

> . . . friction, constriction etc.
> the racket killing
> gas like alcohol.

The poem's style now advances to a new threshold of compactness, so many motifs condensed in the few hyperactive words, the lines aquiver like a contracted muscle. The shift from visual to aural figuration is subtly enhanced by the half-hidden ear rhyme of "etc." (sounded as four syllables: et-ce-te-ra) with "they cannot see" of the line preceding. We hear, but don't see, this slant-rhyme, the abbreviated word "etc." illustrating, then, both the poem's shift in music from eye to ear and the contraction of Lowell's line rhythms.

The language of constraint is now displaced by an active language of fluency, while the line movement shifts back from rigid contraction to a wavelike alternation of long and short lines; also, the wave image, latent in the title metaphor, becomes explicit and overt in the next few lines:

> Long, unequal whooshing waves
> break in volume,
> always very loud enough to hear.

The analogy between human sex and gas hoses loading car tanks with fuel is maintained throughout this passage and the succeeding stanzas, but these parallels fade away in the complex motifs of the prevailing bedroom drama:

> soothe, delay, divert
> the crescendo always surprisingly attained
> in a panic of breathlessness.

The utter turnabout in the verse's delivery, from description to accelerated movement, from skin images to whole-body articulations, is enacted by even the smallest minutiae of style, as in the surprise mutation in Lowell's accustomed device of filling a single key line with a trio of adjectives, here altered to a trio of verbs ("soothe, delay, divert"). This line achieves a most apt innovation, since the three verbs function as adverbs, or modifiers, in delineating precise shades and tempos of rhythm, charting the last phase of lovemaking prior to "crescendo."

Much has been made of Lowell's debt to John Berryman's *Dream Songs*, but only this poem, in its explosive interruptions of normal syntax and its devising of novel sentence norms, approaches Berryman's acrobatics of sentence abbreviation; these three stanzas, in particular, create a Berrymanesque humor from technical ellipses, as well as their drawing zany parallels between controlled human hysterias and today's urban mechanistics. The deliberate clogging of one line with same-sounding internal rhymes, "friction, constriction etc.," shrewdly expresses psychic impasse or actual physical blockage, if momentary, between the inebriated lovers. Whatever sounds escape them, totally nonverbal perhaps, are reduced to the one word "racket," which, in Berrymanese, is noise filtered through ears numbed and distanced by alcohol. The last of five similes, one per stanza, underscores the poem's single pervasive analogy, "gas like alcohol." Much of the latent humor of this equation springs from the picture, a few lines back, of cars crowding the gas pumps, then likened to cows, greedy rivals for "feed," now implicitly equated to humans jamming a barroom. This line, roughly midway in the poem ("gas like alcohol"), sets off a chain of reverberations, moving backward and forward, most poignantly anticipating the final long stanza, in which the gas-booze-guzzler cars of the night before are transformed into the diminished hungover drunks of the day after.

"Suburban Surf" is the one poem in Lowell's very ambitious cycle of late works grappling with the painful complexities of marriage and divorce that restricts itself entirely to portrayal of images and events. Grand interrogations—which are formulated into proverbial couplets, rhetorical queries, and the like, in most other poems of the series—must be embodied, purely, in the language of action and description. In "Suburban Surf," Lowell has written about a prolonged speechless moment of reunion with his wife. The many strands of conflict and crisis in their relationship are held in abeyance, suppressed, during their nonverbal encounter, while the surreal elements in their sex are exacerbated by weariness and alcohol consumption. In the struggle to extend the usual limits of his art medium, Lowell finds he must rely on purely graphic and scenic resources to convey the perplexing multiple levels—between fits of waking and sleeping, dream and reality—of the troubled lovers in a night of half-failed sex and insomnia. Somehow, Lowell the artist knew that he could hope to harness this momentous experience more accurately and credibly in a structure that wholly dispensed with his reliable and dependable genius for aphoristic sententia. The unique commingling of images drawn from modern technology and animal husbandry must be employed to carry the broadest scope of intellectual burden if the poem's architectonics is to project its full quotient of mixed happiness, pain, terror, and even a resolution in calm ("A false calm is the best calm") on the verse cinematographer's screen. Indeed, "Suburban Surf" achieves a nearer approach to cinematic art than any other work of Lowell's I can recall—hence, my fantasia of the film scenario for this poem at the outset.

B. Corkscrews of the Eternal

Like the married lovers in "Last Walk?" who supposed they had just embarked on a midlife plateau, a securer peace and happiness than they'd ever known before ("We could even imagine / we enjoyed our life's great change then— / hand in hand with balmy smiles"), a reader, too, can be fooled by this poem's casual tone and graceful spiralings of the stanzas, long sentences weaving hypnotically across many lines, varying from long to short and back in a lulling motion like "corkscrews of the eternal / whirling snow," the ghostly image that both opens and closes the poem's discourse. The mood, to begin, is all insouciance, lightheaded dallying, that swiftly facilitates the power of the scene to cast a spell of enchantment on the carefree mates, as on the reader, alike. Not until repeated excursions through the poem's elegantly woven passages does a reader come to recognize that the master conjuror has provided ample early hints—subtly veiled behind a deceptive surface nonchalance—of the impending spiritual upheaval that causes a rift between the lovers, and finally, the breakup of the marriage.

This work's ambitious quest and risk is to recapture a particularly unique and haunted moment in the history of Lowell's failed marriage, and to somehow accurately transcribe that most remarkable and inexplicable event. Just one protracted instant before the marital collapse, the couple were entranced by the chance variables of weather and landscape, by a fortuitous blend of ingredients of scene and seasons that duped them into believing their marriage was most blessed, and thus, they were witnessing the advent of their lives' happiest hours. But the poem's enigmatic twist of fate seems to suggest that diabolical spirits lurking in nature, forces that won over their trust and unguarded faith in the beauty and harmony of nature's design, have played a horrible trick on them, their blind faith betrayed, their marriage poisoned. They might well find themselves to blame for having misconstrued the *language* of nature ("At first we mistook the pond for a lull in the river"), but then, shall they have been punished by an avenging angel for their openheartedness, for the healthy optimism of imagining that beneficent forces in the terrain might nourish or fortify their happy being?

> That unhoped-for Irish sunspoiled April day
> heralded the day before
> by corkscrews of the eternal
> whirling snow that melts and dies
> and leaves the painted green pasture marsh—
> and the same green . . . We could even imagine
> we enjoyed our life's great change then—
> hand in hand with balmy smiles
> graciously belittling our headlong reverse.
>
> We walked to an artificial pond
> dammed at both ends to reflect the Castle—
> a natural composition for the faded colorist
> on calm bright days or brighter nights.
> At first we mistook the pond for a lull in the river—
> the Liffey, torrential, wild,
> accelerated to murder,
> wider here than twenty miles downhill to Dublin—
> black, rock-kneed, crashing on crags—
> by excessive courage married to the ocean.

The quality of writing in "Last Walk?" may be immediately discerned as Lowell's art operating at full stretch. His technical resources have never been more fully mobilized to grapple with the most difficult crises of his manhood, the complexities of marriage and divorce, and the approach of old age and death. The play upon color images in the poem's opening lines establishes, at once, the painterly mode that comes to dominate this work's canvas ("leaves the *painted* [italics mine] green pasture marsh"), as if nature can best be apprehended via the mediation of a landscape painter's brush and pigments, though water colors, strictly speaking, are the undoubted medium of our "faded colorist," a vehicle that most truly articulates the fragility and inconstancy of this poem's tableaux.

To surmise that Nature, herself, is a painting ("a natural composition for the faded colorist / on calm bright days or brighter nights") is perhaps to treat life, the world, as subservient to the painter's art—Nature's colors, details, images tameable by his highly skilled handicraft. All depictions of Nature, then, must be refracted through the colorist's prism before the enchanted tenants of this landscape behold them. But to ascribe such tameness to a natural setting is to invite disaster, very likely the retributive justice that is meted out to the lovers in "Last Walk?," a rebuke, if you will, to any art that would attempt a facile chastening, or overrefinement, of the dangerous *actual* locales. Not until after several rereadings of the poem do we fully recognize the taint and nuance of tentativeness in the phrase "We could even imagine": at first, these words seem to imply a harmless posture of wishful thinking, but the apparent passivity and innocence of the fancied optimism coarsens, in the reader's ear, to accents of aggressiveness:

> We could even imagine
> we enjoyed our life's great change then—
> hand in hand with balmy smiles
> graciously belittling our headlong reverse.

Conditioned, in part, by the poem's bleak outcome, we seem to catch overtones of the speaker's duplicity and unconscious self-deception. Perhaps he has tried, falsely, to impose a willed calm and wished-for bliss, by manipulation, upon an intractable and unconsenting partner. Nature! Although guileless, has he fatally misread Nature's book?

In the original and innovatory final stanza, the author breaks into the poem's trance, decisively interrupting its absorptive reverie, to address the reader forthrightly:

> I meant to write about our last walk.
> We had nothing to do but gaze—

seven years, now nothing but a diverting smile,
dalliance by a river, a speeding swan . . .
the misleading promise
to last with joy as long as our bodies,
nostalgia pulverized by thought,
nomadic as yesterday's whirling snow,
all whiteness splotched.

Although much in keeping with the impromptu flavor of the work's de-livery throughout, the pivotal remark carries a ring of genuine artlessness and naïveté, "I meant to write about our last walk." It is the *author*'s voice we hear, and not the protagonist's, at this juncture—the two strands of the same voice are dissevered, irrevocably. Clearly, the artist's invention was derailed. The poem swerved off the tracks, plunging headlong in a dangerous orbit he couldn't have anticipated. His voice shudders with the pain and shock. His humble aim, he tells us, was simply to report a pure reminiscence, a true-to-life story about "our last walk." It was to have been a lightweight and lighthearted exercise in nostalgia, no more. But the power of this latest phase of Lowell's artistry is such that his vowed intent to hold his weight of intellect in check, and idly activate his free-floating memory to recall his last meeting with his wife prior to the rupture, is to invite the full-scale theater of his narrative genius to spring, unbridled, upon the poem's stage.

Lowell's program note for the small-scale poem he had hoped to write, divulged here ("I meant to . . ."), reveals that the story broke away from his controlling reins, exploded with a dormant passion he wasn't prepared for, "nostalgia pulverized by thought"; this unexpected burden of insight, cognition, triggered unstoppably by the poem's denouement, is a painful wisdom of horror and self-discovery. Truly, he had believed in the permanence of his marriage with all his soul, and it was shattered in a single moment. A soap bubble pinpricked. Yet the immense prevailing strength of Lowell's faith in a permanence of love in marriage is attested by the pained self-effacing eloquence of the couplet confessing his shock of disillusionment:

the misleading promise
to last with joy as long as our bodies.

The key to Lowell's surpassing artistry in "Last Walk?" is rendered explicit by the unusual disclosures of this final stanza. His intention to suspend all judgment, withhold all accustomed effort of his reflective intelligence, and carry on an exercise in pure nostalgia, sentimental remembering, clearly predisposed his tableaux for an emblematic and pictorial virtuosity, whereby the chief entities in nature—pasture, river, pond, male and female swans, massive swan's nest—are rendered plainly and accurately and incarnated with the heightened suggestive contours of symbols, or emblems:

> "Those swans," you said, "if one loses its mate,
> the other dies. This spring a Persian exile
> killed one cruelly, and its mate
> refused to be fed—
> It roused an explosion of xenophobia
> when it died."
> Explosion is growing common here;
> yet everything about the royal swan
> is silly, overstated, a luxury toy
> beyond the fortunate child's allowance.
>
> We sat and watched a mother swan
> enthroned like a colossal head of Pharaoh
> on her messy double goose-egg nest of sticks.
> The male swan had escaped
> their safe, stagnant, matriarchal pond
> and gallanted down the stout-enriched rapids to Dublin,
> smirking drunkenly, racing bumping,
> as if to show a king had a right to be too happy.

These, then, are *speaking pictures* of a very high order, and their amazing evocativeness as symbols is the result of their creator's fidelity to clean unadorned photography in words, his refined language of authentic description, exact and luminous at once in its visual lifelikeness, its verisimilitude. By a paradox of technical elegance, the more painstakingly Lowell toils to make his style modestly serve his subjects in nature, letting their actual physical attributes shine forth without ornamental excess or distortion, the more river, snow, castle, and swans are able to mirror, obliquely, the most complex and ambiguous and maddening questions about marital crisis that the poet—in his pledge to be a faithful naturalist ("weary of self-torture")—had chosen to evade. But to elude such questions with the will, even the spiritual intellect, is not necessarily to escape them. They may return in another form. The deep struggle to cope with these human conflicts—though submerged by the artist's commitment to sensory images, a painterly

tactile language—resurfaces, ineffably contained in the natural phe-
nomena themselves, their meanings doubled, or greatly enhanced, as
in the contrasted anecdotes of the royal swans, wherein these motifs
implicitly play themselves out, build toward a crux of revelation, then
fall away, exhausted. By a ghostly immanence in nature, the human
themes are embodied, brilliantly aflicker, in the painted surfaces of
forms.

"Last Walk?" commences with the jaunty stride of a relaxed stroll, but
the anxiety lurking beneath the happy spirits of the hand-holding couple
works its way, gradually, to the foreground. Unobtrusively, the artist's
palette darkens from carefree gaiety to somber gravity by infinitesimal
shifts in tone, a painter in words altering his hues and shades from light to
dark by adding sprinkles of gray pigment. Once the reader has traversed
the full gamut of the poem's color spectrum, from the pure white of
the snow image that begins the poem and the whiteness of the pure-
hearted, ever-faithful royal swan who starves herself to death for grief
over the death of her mate, to the tainted white of the philanderer-
drunk runaway male swan of the second pair of mates, and at last, the
besmirched "nomadic" snow of the poem's final couplet,

> nomadic as yesterday's whirling snow,
> all whiteness splotched—

swan's white, snow's white, both defiled, forevermore; he rereads the
whole poem with a fresh eye and ear, newly receptive to all early
hints of the deeply troubled—not to say haunted—inner lives of the
characters. And one by one, every image in the scenic nature tableau
is felt to be emblematic, indeed symptomatic, of the impending crisis
and rupture between the humans who float across this tragic landscape,
lulled in a miasma of false bliss. While they hide their terror from
each other, and from themselves, the interior odyssey of their spirits'
journeying into chaos and divorce proceeds by laws of its own, like fate,
in a dimension outside the bounds of their consciousness. The landscape
they pass through seems to enact the step-by-step process of their love's
dissolution; or rather, for moments, the landscape seems, eerily, to inhabit
them and to navigate through their minds, while they hover immobilized,
transfixed. The scene and events in nature foretell dooms that await them,
just after they turn the next corner in their lives. How punishingly ironic,
on repeated readings, the author's summarizing of that day's events in
the final stanza:

> We had nothing to do but gaze—
> seven years, now nothing but a diverting smile,
> dalliance by a river, a speeding swan . . .

Indeed, they "had nothing to do" but stand by, idly, while the horrible truth of their collapse was acted out before their eyes, as in a film in which the performers, disguised as royal swans, pond, and river, were really themselves. The theater of their inner lives, hidden from their minds, is mirrored by the whole panorama spread before them; they do nothing but watch, while all the worst is done to them, everything is taken from them, the rock on which they'd founded their happiness ("hand in hand with balmy smiles") is swept away by torrential waves they cannot see. In their blindness to their "life's great change," they are paralyzed, helpless to alter the course of their tragedy.

The more we reread the poem, the more astonished we become by the pervasiveness of dark omens. Clues of imminent tragedy signaled by nature, hints of approaching disaster, are everywhere, everywhere, and we come to see that the poem's total panoramic sweep is a projection of the state of the lovers' psyches, superimposed upon the landscape. The author has succeeded, mercilessly, in fashioning a total natural cosmos sculpted—indeed, architected—in the exact likeness of the condemned souls of those mortals who heedlessly saunter through its ostensibly idyllic havens. Warning signals are missed, or ignored, because, in their blindness to the true state of their own psyches, they prove equivalently blind to the many diverse reflections of their foretold collapse scattered about the setting.

The reader, by slow initiation into the otherworldly dread of this poem's ambiance ("yesterday's whirling snow, / all whiteness splotched"), grows to feel as if he inhabits an eerie universe like the great supernatural purply interior of an El Greco painting, in which every aspect of razor-sharp wave crests, scrolled clouds, and jaggedly storm-lit sky quavers with a single pervasive overriding mind frequency, or temperament. The very mists of the starlit air shimmer with that one haunted effluence. A single irreducible mood, psychic state, or emotion rules the broadest or loftiest expanse of canvas: that one passion—grief, pain, ecstasy, mania, dejection, laughter—governs the texture and design of this spiritually monochromatic netherworld. The people appear outstretched, their faces elongated; the trees loom tall and thin; the night mountains sprout peaks like Matterhorns. . . . Nature, rendered with a stark, if mannered, realism, simultaneously evokes and magnetically expresses the one integral psychic climate, as if no other mood could possibly share the canvas, or coexist, with the reigning mentality—an obsession that shuts out, or shrouds, all that is not itself. The vast land, sea, and skyscapes, rolling pasture or windswept plains, all terrestrial *and* divine settings are modulated to serve, and to perpetuate, the one abiding, visionary trance. All figures in the painting—human, saint, demon, animal, or demigod—are modeled after that *constant* of mood or feeling. The one tone or shade is the norm that acts as unchallenged imperator of the painting's stellar and celestial cosmos.

Lowell, too, has achieved in a few of these final canvases—illumined by the tonal sweep of high allegory—that grand encompassment. In "Last Walk?" landscape and weather and creatures alike are interlocked in one controlling design; taken together, they are a mirror and metaphor that reflects the exact particularities of the central human dilemma and crisis, such that unfolding details of the animal fables involving the two pairs of mated swans work, by indirection, to unravel and resolve the complexities in the lives of the man and woman.

Nostalgia pulverized by thought. The pure white snow "sunspoiled," density, lushness, saturation; this poem's style, more so than any other in Lowell's last book, is a glut of sensuous portraiture! Clusters of images resemble a handkerchief that has wiped a sweat-sopped brow too many times, or a sponge that has soaked up its fill and then some. A few single lines, such as the first ("That unhoped-for Irish sunspoiled April day"), are drenched to saturation after the manner of compulsive nostalgias, the mind's obsession to retrieve lost aromas of a recent past, the craving to recapture piquant flavors and fragrances while they're still fresh enough in memory to be revivified. Style becomes a medium for retrieval and storage of the lost efflorescences, the few most redolent lines like old auto batteries charged and recharged, until you wonder how much wattage of sensuous reek, teeming impression, they can hold without overspilling.

Each of the stanzas comprises a long sentence or two that winds around the alternately long and short lines like spirals of a corkscrew, while the longest lines—those most rife with sensuosity—begin and end stanza coils, or bisect a stanza in the midsection. The poem ends with the shortest line ("all whiteness splotched"), bottommost curlicue, or retracted curl at the point of the corkscrew. It bites. . . .

After the fashion of many of Lowell's earlier free-verse poems, in *Life Studies,* most lines do rhyme, but the rhymes avoid brusque end-stopping, barely perceptible slant-rhymes scattered at uncertain intervals. Rhymed couplets are the exception, the norm being lines that rhyme with diversely separated mates, two to five lines removed. Irregularity and impromptu waveriness are the modi operandi of rhyme patterns and variations in line length, as well.

The lines most thickset with density tend to be pentameters, five-stressed lines with extra accented syllables layered into spondees or hyphenated new word coinages, such as "unhoped-for" and "sunspoiled" of the first line, or "double goose-egg nest of sticks" and "gallanted down the stout-enriched rapids" in other most fecund, sonorous lines. These lines epitomize the poem's essential device and pervasive ritual of ransacking memory's grab bag, culling a number of pointed sensations and condensing them in a single line or chain of phrases. Language, packaging the rescued treasury of flavors and impressions in nuggets, enshrines them, the poem's style forging an impregnable armor to shield and insulate the most prized moments of recollection against time's dilution. Tarnish. Fading. Corrosion. But the enemy that cannot be walled out, finally, by however many coats of imagistic shellacs, expressionistic stains and varnishes, is thoughts of failure. Pangs of disillusionment. However much the reflective intellect and will to self-judgment, "self-torture," is held at bay, the pain of loss in the present ultimately shatters the glamorous jewelwork of revivified past beauties, past capsules of intensest joys.

All of the poem's blessed nostalgias are, as the final lines disclose, "pulverized by thought," and though this shocking revelation is withheld until the finish, from the very first stanza the reader has sensed that the poem's trance is beleaguered by pulls in opposite directions. In a number of single lines even, the battling between rival forces of idle reverie and self-reproach, between joy in cherished residues and agony of bereavement, between the fruits of nostalgia and self-inflicted wounds of reflection, makes the line vibrate fiercely, and the reader is held spellbound by the power of one line to contain such warring contrarieties—without fracture! One end of a line seems to contravene both the rhythm and the logic of the other end. Yet the new meters devised to accommodate and harness these warring factions, which cohabit in the one integral linear unit of verse measure, may well be a species of line pulsation that we have not witnessed before in Lowell's poetic art, or in anyone's:

> That unhoped-for Irish sunspoiled April day
> heralded the day before
> by corkscrews of the eternal
> whirling snow that melts and dies
> and leaves the painted green pasture marsh—

and the same green . . . We could even imagine
we enjoyed our life's great change then—
hand in hand with balmy smiles
graciously belittling our headlong reverse.

The last line, here, is both a key example of the internal strife be-
tween antipodes locked into one metrical unit (the second half recoiling
upon the first), and a thematic prototype for all such self-capitulating
passages in the poem. Images keep toppling forward, or backward, in
time, falling into their mirror opposites, inimical alter egos. The wonderful
phrase "headlong reverse" suggests, to my ear, something like a gymnast's
backward somersault. A variety of strategies achieve basically the same
function as this familiar two-word device of oxymoron, instant paradox,
self-contradiction. In every nuance of style and technique, this poem is
perhaps struggling to unlock the riddle that is at its fulcrum, the enigma
so well rendered explicit by this double-barreled line. Just one prolonged
moment before the marriage went to pieces, the lovers had seemed to
be in perfect harmony. That metaphysical backflip, or volte-face, was a
lie and betrayal so cruel, so confounding to the sensibility of the man in
the artist, Lowell finds that he must locate and sift the offshoots of his
life's peril in the vast panorama of nature, in the landscape and in the
seasons. Thus, for the poem to mirror, truly, this illness that appears to
have blighted the bottommost roots of the Creation, like a disease bacillus
that has spread to the whole organic Tree of Life as by an omnivorous
epidemic, the work's technical means would reverberate—in countless
hues, shades, nuances—with the poison of betrayal that has struck at the
very heart of things!

So it is that *surprise reversals* are the norm, the one given, the very key to
the riddle of existence in this cosmos of self-mockery. So it is that the first
line of the poem looks back over its shoulder to line two, which occurred
"the day before," proclaiming false promises that are promptly negated by
today. So it is that the fates reveal themselves in the downward spiralings
of a corkscrew, and each progressive unwinding of the spirals purloins,
today, the false gifts of yesterday, the source of all misery and tragedy to
be found, then, by taking just one backward step. *The Day Before.*

Languor, a phlegmatic temperament, is firmly evoked by top-heavy
words in the poem's first lines, the heavily accented first syllables in
"unhoped-for" and "sunspoiled," the lumbering weight of these words
accentuated still more by the internal rhyme of "un" and "sun." The
man and woman set out to take a relaxed, slow walk, and, as the poem
unfolds, they linger ever more slowly, stop to gaze and commune

and idly converse. Finally, they "sat and watched." Every forward step the poem takes seems retarded, or offset, by two backsteps. The question mark following the title, "Last Walk?," is prototypic of the recurrent backsliding motif, the gesture of turnabout likely to occur at any shift of the metrical gears. The poem's rhythm is shrewdly unsettling: the line-weave, as I've said, does seem to take the corkscrew image as a model, and Lowell achieves a remarkable dizzying effect, a trance-like suspension and hover-pace, by shifting the heaviest locus in the line from ends to starts, even running an enjambment between two halves of a double-edged phrase, as in "eternal / whirling," such that the sudden weight-shift back to the head of the line undercuts, offsets, reverses—if you will—the impact of the previous line ending. Usually, as in this example, the rhythmic switchback coalesces with a thematic zigzag,

> . . . corkscrews of the eternal
> whirling snow that melts and dies.

Again and again, this poem has affirmed its author's undying wish for eternalities, his credo of the permanence of love and fidelity in marriage, despite any lapses or strayings from that ideal. But as early in the poem as these lines, we can *hear,* incontrovertibly, that he fights a losing battle for any claim on lastingness. All four words that undulate the muscular second line, here—adjective, noun, two verbs—attest to the indomitable force of transience. Each word, independently, counteracts the thrust of "eternal," and the line as a whole is, in itself, a horizontal, linear corkscrew twisting and twisting against the feeble wish for forever.

The camera-eye of the poem is prescient, ill omens lurking everywhere, but the protagonists are blind to them. Prescience might be too late to save anything, too late to avert the fall. Until the finish, prescience is conquered by the nostalgic pleasure of reliving past moments now, an exulting in the joy of the poem's present moment. This work's special power and beauty spring from its luxuriating in indolence, its emotional force a strength of inertia, but inertia of a positive, heart-lifting poise and vivacity, anything *but* apathy or boredom. The dynamic inertia of heady spiritual energies held in restraint, savored, a lethargic dragging-of-heels counterforce, is the poem's characteristic rhythm and timbre, all forward momentum checked by halting devices. (Indeed, a power to foretell the future, if unleashed, would smother all joys in the moment that fueled the luxuriant nostalgias, as swiftly as the snows of "the day before" were melted by the "sunspoiled April day." We readers must be grateful that

Lowell's power of nostalgia held prescience in check until the last stanza, or we'd have lost a marvelous poem. . . . We would have no poem.)

Perhaps uniquely in the art of "Last Walk?" Lowell's abrupt shifts in rhythm from one line extremity to the other creates a seesawing movement that ineffably builds into a mood of vertigo, the ultimate psychic state of the speaker, whose vertigo turns to nausea when, in a moment of uncontrollable revulsion from the story's painful revelation, he interrupts the narrative in the final stanza and explosively brings down the curtain on the unfinished drama—cut off, inexplicably, in the midst of high action, high romance, echoing the crushing blow that severed the lovers' marriage ties.

2. Dark Smiles of the Terminal Ward

> Bred to a harder thing
> Than Triumph, turn away
> And like a laughing string
> Whereon mad fingers play
> Amid a place of stone,
> Be secret and exult,
> Because of all things known
> That is most difficult.
>> "To a Friend Whose Work
>> Has Come to Nothing," W. B. Yeats

> Somewhere your spirit
> led the highest life;
> all places matched
> with that place
> come to nothing.
>> "In the Ward," Robert Lowell

Robert Lowell traces the stages of a noble spirit's swift decline into terminal illness. Swift! This is not a slow dying:

> Ten years older in an hour.

"In the Ward" is one of a handful of works that carries Lowell's most radically chiseled late poetics to an ultimacy of rawboned spareness. None of his earlier modes could have matched this poem's harrowing depiction of body ravaged, wasting away to nothing, and dragging exalted mind down with it to vacuity, to emptiness. By a fine-tuned reciprocity of means and ends, Lowell's keenly honed cutting edge is coupled with those few excruciating subjects in his life that can best refine and ennoble the scrupulous austerities of his most advanced technique of prosody. The instrument is so well attuned, calibrated with hairline-fine precisions, to the intensified pains of a hospital-ward torture chamber, it is difficult for a reader to say whether the poem's style has—by luck or instinct—chosen exactly the subjects needed to carry Lowell's craft to its most exacting *borderlines,* or if the life situation has found its ideal language and form in this author. It may seem a perfunctory exercise, at best, to try to disentangle form from content when the two have been so masterfully wedded—suffice it to note, here, that in the course of the poem's dour litany of deprivations, as each next layer of bedrock humanity is carved by disease from the victim, as each lower threshold of body's and mind's struggle to cling to bare minimal tag ends of the human collapses into the next bottommost limit, the work's artistry evolves through congruent dismantlings of its most evident virtues of musical resonance, suavity, charm. As if style and content were beleaguered mates, the one following the other into slow demise by poison, style—with the highest fidelity to each shade and nuance of diminishing life force and mind force in the human protagonist—takes the utmost pains to match its tempos and measure of privations to those of the languishing victim.

Lowell's passion for authenticity, his stubborn will to rid his art of any niceties that may belie the horror of his subject (his personal witnessing of the powerlessness of a great mind to resist its collapse, when ravages of body have proceeded uncurbed), leads him from extremity of revulsion in the hospital ward to an equivalent response of aversion from the tools of his craft—a withdrawal that spreads, at last, to the very words and pages of poems, to his "vocation" as author. His poetic instrument is battered and shaken, accordingly, and there are moments near the poem's finish that strike a note of terror on behalf of the art of poetry itself! We overhear the artist's cry of anguish, his indomitable rage against his hand-scripted page of verse, an art medium that proves itself to be helpless, finally, either to assuage the human tragedy he beholds or to achieve any healing vision adequate to his own consequent plunge into unrelieved despondency:

> It's an illusion death or technique
> can wring the truth from us like water.
>
> What helpless paperishness,
> if vocation
> is only shouting what we will.

That incredible phrase, "helpless paperishness," stings like a whip lashing the very printed page it fills, venting Lowell's fury at the limits of his own art, and by extension, all poetic art; but as we shall observe, his kicking at the traces ultimately stretches those limits, and the confessed defaults of this passage are revealed to be, at last, *advances* in "the ever retreating borderlines" of technique.

"In the Ward" is fittingly scaled in Lowell's leanest stripped-down prosody, lines shortening, thin stanza columns narrowing, as the poem's versification devolves. A cursory perusal of the work's wide range of free verse units reveals a few wavery norms. The two one-line units disclose bleakest facts of the victim's physical discomfort, the poem's first line, "ten years older in an hour," counterpointed by a single line midway in the dialectic, "your feet are wired above your head." Both lines infer fleeting glances at eye-searing realities, then a looking aside from these scorchers. Three formal couplets are scattered, at approximate intervals, in the poem's central matrix:

> Being old in good times is worse
> than being young in the worst.
>
> If you keep cutting your losses,
> you have no loss to cut.
>
> It's an illusion death or technique
> can wring the truth from us like water.

Each two-line stanza is a sententious capsule of thought, each a desperate mental lunge of the aghast onlooker, a failed effort to devise a condensed formula to explain away, and thereby contain, the horror. A cumulative aesthetic distress builds, from couplet to brilliant couplet: for all the achieved nuggets of wisdom, the human tragedy remains untouched, mind's and art's power—at full stretch—deflated, and this frustration culminates in the passage in which Lowell turns an avenging rage, momentarily, upon the accoutrements of his craft.

Consider the bold risk of jump-starting this poem with a line that, in itself, defies the accepted limits of body's aging process, "ten years older in an hour." Lowell begins with a cliché idea—mortifying illness makes a person *appear* to age very quickly, but the author gives the cliché new spark. By one clean stroke, a reader is swept into the final stages of a process of witnessing unbounded pain. No preliminaries! This art dispenses with any formalities of introduction, as if to say there is no way to prepare yourself for this horror, except head-on meeting it. The mind cannot cope with these actualities by any frugal economizing of resources or levelheaded previsions. The first moment of dumbfounded beholding shatters any poise or self-containment in the witness. The mind's accustomed supports are snatched away, and in a single moment of existential amnesia, blankbrained, the hospital visitor must begin again to invent a plausible grasp of our mortal life, and to reconceive an integral self.

From the opening lines, the poem's tone is one of restrained mockery, a muted sardonic humor:

> Ten years older in an hour—
>
> I see your face smile,
> your mouth is stepped on without bruising.
> You are very frightened by the ward,
> your companions are chosen for age;
> you are the youngest
> and sham-flirt with your nurse—
> your chief thought is scheming
> the elaborate surprise of your escape.
>
> Being old in good times is worse
> than being young in the worst.

The dying man's twisted "smile," like a face permanently tilted awry by stroke, establishes, at once, this poem's pervasive mood of grotesque parody. The most pungent agonies, mental or physical, often evoke a lip-biting laughter. Lowell's images suggest that the only way the sufferer can maintain a grip on his sanity, and prevail over the horror, is by performing a slapstick theater of the absurd, as does the victim here, who dissembles passes at his nurse and improvises plots to escape the hospital. Likewise, the poet-visitor to the ward must employ humor, at intervals, to keep his observer-eye from flinching, and indeed, to provide the reader with nominal flashes of comic relief to temper the tonality of sheer desolation. This poem's center of vision verges on cruel jokiness, since the abiding message, if you will, is that the effects of excruciating bodily pain on a human corpus, in terminal disease, outrageously resembles—and thereby mocks—the minimalist techniques of a number of "modernist" classic artists, such as the composer Arnold Schönberg. The symptoms of disease and approaching death, then, perversely seem to imitate, or parody, artistries that—like much of Lowell's own last work—are scrupulously committed to paring away excesses, to gauntness of measure, concision.

The pained comic nuances—dark smiles—that flicker, here and there, on one of Lowell's otherwise bleakest canvases, recall many of the distinct bittersweet comic flourishes in *King Lear,* a unique species of humor that Wilson Knight sapiently delineated in his remarkable essay that characterizes the play as being, in essence, a brilliant *comedy* of the grotesque, wearing the guise of tragedy. In his poem "For John Berryman," Lowell berates himself for having no gift for humor, Berryman's forte perhaps ("just the other day, / I discovered how we differ—humor. . . ."), but this infirmary poem exhibits frequent touches of a surreal loony comedy closely akin to Berryman's black humor of the hospital wards. The portrait of Israel Citkovitz as clown and prankster in the opening stanzas is, in fact, a creditable stepbrother to Henry of the *Dream Songs,* executing his repertoire of vaudeville routines, whether in emergency rooms or locked wards of the mental asylum. And both characters arguably may claim a kinship with the jester in *King Lear,* whose best-crafted lunacies parody his master to much the same effect as Henry's and Citkovitz's wise mischief, the jests a foil to the horribly painful moments or events they mock that, by a paradox not unlike this poem's central strategy, fortifies the mind's power to keep its beleaguered sanity intact, the grip on mind's health enhanced the more firmly in direct proportion to the extremity of bizarre and irrational elements in the burlesque. While these instances of humor may provide comic relief, easing the tension of tragic emotion, conversely, as in the cavils of Lear's jester, they may serve, rather, to intensify the pain and anguish of the principal actions derided; but in all such charades of mimicry, the preponderant effect is one of bolstering the mind's capacity to endure, and indeed, to surmount excruciating torture.

Terminal disease is dramatized as a sadist persona, hospital paraphernalia in place of medieval torture instruments. Since this allegorical Satan is also projected as a merciless parodist of modern art, his methods imitating and speciously denigrating the radical techniques of such distinguished artists as Arnold Schönberg and poet Lowell, it is fitting that this poem's style employs sardonic devices, both to mirror and hopefully, at last, to depose the vicious joke on humanity that is enthroned at the summit of the work's psyche:

> I see your face smile,
> your mouth is stepped on without bruising.

The comic undertones of this couplet are subtle and oblique, "stepped on" engraving in a reader's mind's eye the demonic image of a large invisible foot pushing on the mouth just hard enough to twist it permanently a little askew, but never quite using enough force to impart any telltale marks ("without bruising"), and thus, sinisterly concealing its act of slow sadism. Disease, of course, is the big-footed henchman, implicitly personified by this allegorical trope. Normally, Lowell's humor is much less overt than Berryman's, and his irony, like a slow-blowing fuse, releases its energy in stages, the comic discovery building slowly over a few stylistic intervals, as in the play upon words that denote contrarieties of youth and age in the opening stanzas:

> Ten years *older* in an hour—

> . . . your companions are chosen for *age;*
> you are the *youngest.*

> Being *old* in good times is worse
> than being *young* in the worst.

A recurrent motif in numerous last poems is Lowell's bewildered struggle to differentiate, and thereby render manageable, various discrete shades, or stages, of longevity:

> Age is another species,
> the nothing-voiced. The very old
> made grandfather look vulgarly young
> when he drove me to feed them at their home.
>> from "To Frank Parker"

> After fifty,
> the clock can't stop,
> each saving breath
> takes something. . . .
>> from "Our Afterlife I"

> The old boys drop like wasps
> from windowsill and pane.
>> from "Our Afterlife II"

I loathe age with terror.

from "Wellesley Free"

Lowell's playing off finer shades of age levels against each other, in the passage quoted from "In the Ward," is no less comic for articulating a nervous and fearful jocosity. To begin, the victim looks "ten years older," and that is horrifying in itself, since age is *loathsome* to Lowell. But Citkovitz, despite his vastly accelerated quantum leaps into senility, is yet noted as better off than his ward mates, somehow, since he is—in strict chronological terms—the "youngest" of the lot (though aging at the rate of a century every ten hours, the inner man has long since passed them all by decades); and taking a pixieish delight in being outwardly the most unaged man present, he fantasizes himself much younger, and feigns passes at his nurse. The imagination's only defense against the incomprehensible sudden age jumps is to magically reverse the equation, to become young—ever younger—in quantum backleaps. I'm reminded of James Dickey's poem, "The Cancer Match," in which the victim achieves a weird elation and transcendence over dying by staying home, no hospital wards for him, getting drunk on bourbon, awake all night, imagining cancer and bourbon are two punch-drunk fighters, evenly matched, squared off in their all-night battle. The Lowell victim's absurd mania and sexual chicanery is pathetic, to be sure, but it is the proof of mind's half-successful attempt to forestall death's utter debasement; and acts that, in a normal context, would seem to be certain evidence of hopeless senility do smack of bravery or heroism, of sorts, in the terminal ward. Thus, the comic undercurrents of the passage emit a mild optimism, a healing—if momentary—succor. It is, as I say, a saving humor, one that salvages meager time capsules of sanity, but frail hope is always on the verge of being punctured by the skepticism of a sententious Lowellian couplet:

Being old in good times is worse
than being young in the worst.

For all the deflation of gaiety, here, reversing any uplift of spirit, the comic momentum is carried forward, partly by the deft lightness of rhythm and partly by the canny stylistic good humor of rhyming "youngest" and "nurse" (a couplet half-hidden in the longer stanza) with "worse" and "worst." The proverb's arch mockery of the victim's faking youth is no less funny for the pain of the insight, and though the latter rhymes aptly undercut the logic of the victim's fantasy, their music also evokes an aesthetic chuckle that perhaps both dignifies and redeems the mind's health in its sexual impulse, bodily postmortems notwithstanding.

I cannot possibly overstate how much of the Lowell poem's *message* is conveyed by tones, subtones, and overtones generated by the interplay of syllables, whether scattered half-rhymes, or near-inaudible assonances. Lowell's drift of meaning in his art at its most refined and elegant, as here, is propelled more by these musical ingenuities and interstices than by sheer force of statement; and yet, alas, so many readers and commentators on Lowell's most complex late works are eluded by the many-layered laminations of sound play, as well as by the subtle findings, evocations, divulgings, awakenings of Lowell's inquiry into great *last questions* of mortal limits—in pain, hope, sustainment of love and the creative spirit—beyond collapse of body, the very enigmas to which the mind of "In the Ward" profoundly addresses itself. Many readers are perhaps too willing, not to say eager, to take at face value Lowell's explicit admission of his own failings, misgivings, when—in verse page after page after page—he has patently outdistanced his own declared shortcomings. Even as he, too willingly as well, *confesses* defeat, don't take him at his perfectionist overscrupulous word, say I. He, ever, compulsively his own hardest taskmaster! Reader, be on the watch, vigilantly, in these last innovatory, pioneering, extravisceral depth-probe works: these self-plumbing divinatory texts, for moments, passages, whole pages, in which the implicit breadth of revelation witheringly surpasses the avowed limits of guarded authorial expectation.

Consider the implicit metaphysics of the next stanza, for example, so much a measure of the indelible resonances of two pairs of palpable touch words—"grill"/"mattress" and "sickness"/"physical"—weighing upon the four immaterial, revered sacrament words, "wisdom," "piously," "memory," "future." Don't fail to observe how the purported indestructibles buckle under the strain and impact of collisions with *the fact*, the immitigable brute fact—if you will—of limitless physical agony, pain without letup, and one by one, we witness the collapse of sovereign word deities:

> Five days
> on this grill, this mattress
> over nothing—
> the wisdom of this sickness

is piously physical,
ripping up memory
to find your future—
old beauties, old masters
hoping to lose their minds before they lose their friends.

Reader, the shake-up in *our* metaphysics, here, is not small potatoes! This poem's very special time continuum was established at the outset, "ten years older in an hour." Why not take this formula of expanded time scale literally, and follow up its implications for the wisdom borne of bodily pain. Five days, by my reckoning, adds up to twelve hundred years of body's aging, a millennium and a fifth of skin-blood-and-bone smarts. The "grill" and "mattress over nothing" are the great classroom, pain the master teacher, in the world's record accelerated learning program; and what is taught is that such oldfangled concepts as religion ("piously"), history: private *or* public past ("ripping up memory"), and prophesy ("to find your future") are rendered obsolete, all record of their findings scraped away, the mind's ledger struck dumb. The mind, a pristine template, divested of all past teachings, is purified for the brand-mark of the one knowledge that obviates, precludes, and supersedes all others, replaces all predecessors. Pain the one great teacher. Body its obedient medium and perfect student, at once.

It is my claim, reader, that not without a few strokes of searingly cryptic humor these words carry the ring of authority and ultimacy of radical second sight, or existential reawakening, akin to Lord Hamlet sweeping the deck of his consciousness, scoured clean, freed of all alien concepts learned since birth, to make way for a single irreducible axiom and wisdom. Revenge! The filial passion of avenging his father's murder the one dictate, or precept, of that wisdom. Likewise, to witness ultimate bodily pain in a loved one without flinching, and to achieve in one's own spirit a permanent reservoir of compassion, is the one incontrovertible precept of wisdom in Lowell's "In the Ward." That, I adduce, is this work's hardbought, single-minded, guileless metaphysics. It is Kierkegaardian, as well as Hamletesque. *Purity of heart is to will one thing.* Lowell, in his relentless pursuit of his heart's truth, like other noble metaphysicians before him, won his gateway to that truth, even as he despaired of ever securing his high aspiration and goal. Lowell, at each new phase of his art, was faithful to the ever-changing burdens of keeping his style alive and true to the feel of his pulse, though his will and intellect openly confessed failure, confessed in this poem that his faith in technique—the honestly wielded tools of his craft—to "wring the truth from us" was, at bottom, "an illusion." But his passional being, implicit in this work's final soft-voiced catharsis, has embodied that truth, and had Lowell but lived for a while longer, his artist-censor, the severest taskmaster of our day, might have recognized that his grace of technique at full stretch and its power to embody the truth had caught up, at last, with his manly power of beholding and witnessing. Yeats, in *his* final phase, declared—toward the finish of his prose work *On the Boiler*—"You can embody the truth, but you cannot know it." Perhaps it is the final saving grace, a last blessing, that Lowell did not come *to know* the permanent truths his last work demonstrably incarnates for us all.

The truth that abides in the vision of "In the Ward" is contained in the shivering rivalries, internecine battles, between the *words* themselves, as if each were a warrior in the struggle-to-the-death, and valiant hero after hero is slain by the invincible pair of captains, "sickness" and "physical." Each of four opponents, "wisdom," "piously," "memory," "future," is vanquished, in turn, each falling before the sword of the conqueror's higher truth. The *sickness* makes mock of knowledge, mocks religion, mocks history, mocks hope for the future—*its* truth, then, the only truth left standing. I have carried Lowell's personification and allegory not one step beyond his own explicit rendering, "sickness" given a will and intelligence, and still more remarkably, endowed with hands! Its power is "piously physical," oxymoronic, but we know the fate of that apparent self-contradiction, since body's pain must easily defeat body's piety, and the bodied "sickness" takes violent hands to "ripping up memory." Implicitly, then, each word is an allegorical personation in its own right.

Most precise data of ward life, disclosed in these early stanzas, seems to infer an ongoing exchange of talk between patient and speaker, which peaks in the following lines, perhaps the nearest approach of any passage in the poem to the candid familiarity of direct quotation:

> The wisdom of this sickness
> is piously physical,
> ripping up memory
> to find your future—
> old beauties, old masters
> hoping to lose their minds before they lose their friends.

Knowing the author's predilection for searching out noted historic figures as exemplars of one ideality or another, a reader may safely surmise that the two men collaborated, verbally, in ransacking history for heroines and heroes ("old beauties, old masters"), whether actresses, opera divas, or artists, who, dying of a terminal illness, chose one faith or another to face the future. But so little hope is generated by this futile exercise that the patient finds himself presuming they, like himself, were all reduced to opting for insanity before death, "hoping to lose their minds before they lose their friends." This last line, evoking a characteristic Lowellian wail of self-torture, cuts two ways. Either they felt terror lest their friends should desert *them*, abandoned in their worst pain of final days of illness; or terror of losing their friends to terminal disease, themselves abandoned to the living: twin horrors, both counseling madness over sanity.

Ironically, the speaker does appear to desist from the conversation at this moment (how can he tolerate more of this prattle of pleading for insanity?), and in a fashion, he forsakes his friend; although he stays in the ward, he apparently withdraws from open communion and broods on the scene, relating to it from an emotional remove, in the succeeding stanzas:

> Your days are dark,
> your nights imaginary—
> the child says,
> *heaven is a big house*
> *with lots of water and flowers—*
> *you go in in a trunk.*
>
> Your feet are wired above your head.

Whereas the fright and anxiety of the poem's start were ascribed, solely, to the patient, the visitor to the ward adopting the role of his dying friend's supportive confidante— now the sufferer appears to have drifted off into delirium, losing touch, and the horror has been transferred to the appalled witness. Indeed, it is the buried child in Robert Lowell himself that ruminates over half-forgotten picture book versions of Heaven, and those secretly cherished idyllic scenes revive, suddenly, in a moment of idle reverie. Horrific the impact of collision between the residual child's-view of Heaven *("heaven is a big house / with lots of water and flowers")* and the hallucinatory prevision of his friend's interment in a coffin *("you go in in a trunk")*, shattering, irrecoverably, any last vestiges of Lowell's naïve subliminal yearnings—shared by the child in all of us, to a degree— for a paradisiacal afterlife. The latter line pulsates with a tone redolent of Hamlet's words despatching Polonius's just-slain corpse, "lug the guts into the neighbor room," and it evokes a kindred demystification, a purging of any false niceties of reverence for defunct bodies, or their quasi-blissful destinations in the beyond. Much of the spell-breaking power of Lowell's single line is generated by the halting retrograde syntax of the paired "in," the doubled preposition recoiling upon itself, as does the deflated idylls of Heaven in the preceding italicized lines.

Further, it is simply awesome to speculate upon the amazing force of context, in the opening lines here, to transform the normal meaning and connotations of the word "imaginary" to signify hellish disorientation, and even psychotic irreality:

> Your days are dark,
> your nights imaginary—

a harrowing dislocation of the senses and rational consciousness that is, in fact, a pastiche of Hell, matching the child's pastiche of Heaven that fills out the stanza. This nighttime imagination *is* Hell (the equation conveyed by the line "your nights imaginary"), for all the healing balm such insomniac ravings of nocturnal sleeplessness may afford the tortured victim, a true bankruptcy of the faculty of imagining. This passage anticipates Lowell's agonized ruing of a surmised bankruptcy in his poetic instrument itself, abhorred in the poem's later stanzas. More immediately, the depiction of Hell is rounded out by Lowell's one-line condensed tableau:

> Your feet are wired above your head,

an updated caricature of the crucifixion, complete with wires in place of nails, hospital traction poles and pulleys sufficing for a cross, this last image as devastating to any illusions in the reader of a savioresque nobility in martyrdom as the preceding lines' abrogation of fatuous illusions of Heaven.

The following pair of stanzas, roughly the work's midsection, shifts focus to Citkovitz's lifelong ardor for classical music. The second passage, much the longer of the two, is a reminiscence in the form of an extended anecdote, the poem's single backward look at past events. The first unit, a bridge between the grim hospital-ward setting and the flashback scene in a "coldwater flat," is a dirge for those lost joys of music:

> If you could hear the glaring lightbulb
> sing

your old modernist classics—
they are for a lost audience.

In the world of music, youth and age, the old and the new, yesterday and today, are merged, happily, in one timeless continuum, which is suavely envisaged by the phrase "your old modernist classics"; and there is a mildly whimsical humor in the double oxymoron of "old modernist" and "modernist classics" that contrasts, ironically, with the pathos of the swiftly aging old man of the first stanzas, who mimes the gestures of youth. These three words, then, exquisitely condense the power of art to transcend *age,* a distressing foil to the humans on the ward, whose last hours of life are breathlessly flitting past.

If there is a surrogate deity in the hospital ward, it is surely the one bare lightbulb, which hauntingly arrests and freezes the transfixed victim's blank stare of a devotee in a later stanza:

Nothing you see now
can mean anything;
your will is fixed on the lightbulb,
its blinding impassivity
withholding disquiet,
the art of the possible
that art abhors.

But in the earlier lines, the bulb horribly usurps the sovereignty of music ("If you could hear the glaring lightbulb / sing"), and by extension, all of the arts. One who has heard lightbulbs in antique buildings maddeningly buzz or sizzle can doubly respond to Lowell's ascribing a voice to the bulb over their heads. Surely it is no accident of style that the sole one-word lines in this poem are "sing" in this short stanza, "Music" (note capitalization) in the next, since the victim's great passion for music has been reduced to a grotesque joke, the fantasized song of the lightbulb. We are reminded that the patient's delirium and distancing has steadily widened, "they are for a lost audience" ("lost" both to Music and to the visitor), and this line, which ends the stanza, marks a deft transition to the anecdotal flashback that follows:

Last year
in buoyant unrest,
you gathered two or three young friends
in the *champagne room*

>of your coldwater flat,
>to explore the precision
>and daimonic lawlessness
>of Arnold Schönberg born
>when music was still imperfect science—
>Music,
>its ever retreating borderlines of being,
>as treacherous, perhaps, to systems,
>to fecundity,
>as to silence.

This remarkable vignette, without for a moment detracting from its full credibility and ring of truth to the reported episode in the life of the protagonist, operates, simultaneously, as a vehicle that advances a more revealing blend than I have witnessed in any of Lowell's other late writings of its author's own music criticism alloyed with his most current private aesthetics of poetry-writing, and thereby, the dialectic rehearsed here prepares the reader for the traumatic crisis in the author's faith in his chosen vocation that erupts, and is luminously resolved, in the poem's final passage. Note the polarization of the words "Music" and "science" at opposite line extremities, and again, the final rhyme of "silence" with "science." Music exists halfway between the two, as does all art, and to survive in freedom, it must oppose both—warring against rigidly exact "science" at one pole, "silence" at the other.

There is more than a hint that early symptoms, as yet unrecognized, of the illness that would subsequently menace Citkovitz's life, had already been manifested the year before, "Last year / in buoyant unrest. . . ." At that time, his manic interlude—if exhausting—appears to have stimulated his capacity for sociability and intellectual pursuits. Lowell, himself, might easily identify with sudden mood swings, or radical shifts in metabolic energy levels. It is clear, both from Citkovitz's installation in a populous terminal ward and his dwelling in a "coldwater flat," that the persona is a man of limited means. It is clear, too, that there are *no* limits to Lowell's adulation for this man (Caroline Blackwell's ex-husband!), who is most himself when generously whiling away a whole afternoon in the company of a few young protégés eager to share his erudition of the "modernist classics," and to be enlightened:

>. . . you gathered two or three young friends
>in the *champagne room*
>of your coldwater flat,

to explore the precision
and daimonic lawlessness
of Arnold Schönberg born
when music was still imperfect science. . . .

The yoking of apparently incongruous tenets of art theory might apply equally well to Lowell's current free-verse practice and Schönberg's music, since, for all the poet's "daimonic" compulsion to transcend formal rules, laws, strictures ("lawlessness"), in devising novel patterns of line weave and stanza flux, his language rarely strays from its highest standards of "precision"; and he is painstakingly exact in the perfecting of his verse rhythms, or prosodic meters, alike. To suggest that "music was still imperfect science" before Schönberg is both a tacit rebuke to the postmodernist composers of today (who, unlike Schönberg, compose atonal music while adhering to Schönberg's tenets, as if *they* are now—at last—dogmas of an exact science), and a high tribute to this matchless composer for being such a true empiricist of the tools and medium of his art as to resemble a pioneer in science: one who is skeptical of all laws that are, for most people, accepted givens or norms, and devoted to testing all institutionalized strategies afresh, subjecting them to his own private canons, before striking out for *new thresholds, new anatomies.*[2]

Robert Lowell's characterization of Hart Crane's pioneering ventures in poetry suggests, I feel, that Lowell may have linked Crane with Schönberg as kindred innovators in "modernist" verse and music composition, since his vocabulary for coming to terms with apparent dichotomies in Crane's life and art, in another poem of this period, so closely resembles his abbreviated précis of Schönberg's salient art tenets:

Where is Hart Crane,
the disinherited, the fly by night,
who gave
the drunken Dionysus firmer feet?

from "Seventh Year"

Is this not a rough paraphrase of "precision" and "daimonic lawlessness"? The uncanny matchup between Lowell's grasp of the essential art identity

---

2. *New Thresholds, New Anatomies* is the title of R. P. Blackmur's essay on Hart Crane's poetry.

of Schönberg's music and Crane's poetry, revealed here, strikes me as indicative—a reliable index, perhaps—of Lowell's aspiration for wedding apparent incongruities in his own art. The minicritique on Crane can be viewed as a mediating aesthetic, a middle ground so to say, bridging the gap between Lowell's view of Schönberg's and his own artistries in the passage before us; and clearly, the two art credos must grow ever more intertwined in the mind of this poem as it evolves, given the swerve in the final stanzas to a radical grilling and revaluation of Robert Lowell's own art's underpinnings.

All passages in the main body of "In the Ward," roughly three-fourths of the poem's length, converge and gravitate toward the pivotal couplet that articulates the work's most punishing insight:

> It's an illusion death or technique
> can wring the truth from us like water.

The litany of corporeal agonies, which builds intensity as the story unfolds, peaks here—exploding into a vast spiritual anguish and consequent aesthetic impasse. Religion would have us believe that martyrdom of dying in horrible pain will "wring the truth from us," much as Art dictates that painful deprivations of a relentlessly perfectionist technique will secure a catharsis, a breakthrough into lasting and permanent truths. Whereas Lowell—witnessing his friend's devastation by disease—has absolutely no choice but to repudiate the first maxim as illusory and false, likewise, he feels he must disclaim, or renounce, the second axiom as well, since the poem's full import, prior to this couplet, is the agonizing conviction that death proceeds by the same ghastly rules as those Lowell has espoused in his current *ars poetica.* Though secretly the poet still hopes that death may be proven a fraud in its parody, and hence grotesque mock-imitation, of a more exalted art, at this moment in the work's dialectic, he finds he must undergo the aesthetic outrage and catharsis of the penultimate stanza, before a resolution in earned quietude can be wrought:

> What helpless paperishness,
> if vocation
> is only shouting what we will.

Lowell's fury of disappointment in the very medium of written alphabets, here, reaches such a pitch, we fear the poem can never recover from the shock, can never survive its creator's assault upon the sinews of its integument—and beyond this poem, the craft of poetry itself may be pulverized irreparably, shattered beyond repair. But we discover, the next moment, that it is only one step from the refusal of the man Lowell to shy away from his friend's debasement by pain and disease to the refusal of the artist Lowell to abandon, or desert, his crippled poetic instrument. He is saved, then, by his heroic will to continue to serve his craft despite untold amputations that, paradoxically, infuse the art with a survival power, a durability, he could never have foreseen. He carries forward to the poem's finish *by virtue of the absurd,* having no hope whatsoever that his "vocation" may yet be saved. But he must see the utterance through to the finish, viable poem or no poem, to pay his friend the high tribute that only Lowell's voice raised to such a pitch as this poem has rendered possible may afford, and such is the grandeur and majesty of homage evoked by the plain bare lines that end the poem:

> Somewhere your spirit
> led the highest life;
> all places matched
> with that place
> come to nothing.

One step, just one step was to be taken, from Lowell's victory over his horror of the dying man's utter ruin to a careless triumph over repulsion from the flawed tools of his profession, and that step is the quietly passive transition between the last two stanzas. It is a triumph of passivity, not unlike Lowell's strength of passion held in reserve, fortitude masked by restraint—that worldly discipline he had learned two decades earlier, when he served one year in jail for being a conscientious objector.

"In the Ward," among the most re-readable of Lowell's last poems, is a strenuous exercise in demystifications. The wounded intellect of the speaker, like a cornered bobcat, springs with spread talons at all of his cherished aesthetic ideals—he holds up each naïve half-lie to ridicule. One by one, the proud intellect's fondest pretensions are deflated, torn away from the dwindling bastion of defenses against utmost body debilities, the mind of the poem reaching out, desperately grasping for supports. How difficult it is for him to part with his most prized illusion! The creed that high-mindedness, in art or religion, can sustain itself in a lofty sphere that cannot be touched, much less corroded, by body's pain, nor punctured by mere speeded-up geriatrics of aging in the hospital ward. But no false hopes can be indulged. The integrity of this vision will make do with less and less:

> If you keep cutting your losses,
> you have no loss to cut.

What, if anything, is left upon which to found a continued faith in the human spirit's power to endure, and indeed—as in Faulkner's code— to prevail? Last questions must be broached, at whatever cost, after the mode of Yeats's self-interrogations in "The Man and the Echo." In that last extremity of body and spirit stripped naked, that last haunted solitude of staring Death in the eye, it is the Spiritual Intellect—in Yeats's phrase—that may quietly exult, winning its way back through dense thickets of memory, clogged like old arteries, to those places wherein "your spirit / led the highest life." The exultation of those moments, salvaged by memory, survives all horrors of pain, disease, aging; and the highest task of the poem's vision is to retrieve from countless layers of sleep and recollection that preserved—that permanent—sanctuary.

3. Inextinguishable Roots

"Grass Fires," the best of a cycle of Robert Lowell's last poems that recaptures the authentic flavor and essence of childhood events, is prototypic of Lowell's most advanced mode of austerely disciplined reminiscence. His fidelity to plain literal facts, anecdotal, diaristic, dredged up by his "realistic memory's" foragings, makes rigorous demands on his craft. In his last book especially, memory seems to function like an athlete's superior muscle, always in training, never satisfied with finite gains, stretching and stretching to exceed its limits, to widen its breadth and extend its grasp. His style divests itself of many accustomed graces in an effort to recover the authentic bare minimum details of dramas of his juvenility, and then, to pictorialize graphically—for a reader—crucial moments of boyhood and adolescence that may have shaped his adult sensibility, or which may offer a key to unlock painful enigmas in his manhood:

> In the realistic memory
> the memorable must be forgone;
> it never matters
> except in front of our eyes.

In these opening lines, Lowell vows to forego a storyteller's normal leaning and license, the propensity to select colorful or melodramatic details that can be guaranteed to rivet a reader's attention. Lowell is committed, as never before, to recapturing the very ambience of the actual lived events. The opening stanzas, in the manner of a prologue to the poem's visionary anecdote, are a litany of restraints and denials—the artist refuses to follow any practiced familiar routes in his craft. He will settle for nothing less than a wholly new raid on the most poignant days of his growing up, and all virtuosities of his verse technique are to be harnessed in the service of a nearer and nearer approach to the saliencies of childhood moments. He will settle for nothing short of truth of experience, an ever more palpitant retrieval of the real happenings of his formative days.

At face value it would seem that a work recounting episodes of boy-hood crisis that restricts itself—by authorial edict—to skirting around the most *memorable* facts, images, occurrences, shall perhaps be foredoomed to dullness. It would appear that the author's prescription may have stymied, in advance, all best options for passionate revelation or utter-ance. But "the memorable," here, implies overtly spectacular details of a narration, lurid or garish motifs of a story's plot, say, of a kind that maintain suspense in a popular novel or television drama. As Lowell explains his new poesies in the poem "Epilogue," this art aspires to a condition both "heightened from life" *and* "paralyzed by fact," and, in these paradigmatic poems of youthful reminiscence, he seems, more than ever, willing to subjugate his passional scale of voice to the low-keyed undertones of mundane quotidian fact, divesting his accustomed devices of heightening, thinning out nearly all bold colors from his painterly palette. He would shift the balance of artistic priorities more and more toward reportage of lean, taut notation of events. Twenty years before, he had been guided by William Carlos Williams's example to cultivate a style that lent itself to bare journalistic reporting, as in the poems of *Life Studies;* now he carries much further his penchant for getting his technique in step with the frayed, intensified edges of things.

Lowell's aspiration in these poems of his boyhood is not merely to tell the true stories of the child whose voice was once his voice, whose face his face, but to resuscitate that child's spirit and breath and being in the poem's entrancement of reverie:

> it never matters,
> except in front of our eyes.

Lowell's aesthetic, then, is a desensationalizing of style. At times, his language, as in the first stanza, approaches a deadpan tonality. The events reenvisioned by the work's transport must be sighted, again, through the child's own eyes, since only *that* child's psyche, revivified, can invest those occasions with the consequentiality—both the sting and the radiance—they would imbue into the entire sweep of Lowell's future manhood:

> I made it a warning,
> a cure, that stabilized nothing.
> We cannot recast the faulty drama,
> play the child,
> unable to align
> his toppling, elephantine script,
> the hieroglyphic letters
> he sent home.

We are given a rare insider's view of the hesitations and doubts, the ambivalences, of the author's workshop here, as we observe Lowell struggling to find a grip on the fragile untested materials of "the faulty drama"—the painful collision between the child and his revered grandfather that constitutes the poem's essential plot. Luckily, for readers, the artist chose to include in the body of the published work this record of the stages of disbelief, which he haltingly surmounted in his preliminary sketches for this successful exercise in remembered self-portraiture. These moments of acknowledged backsliding ("the memorable must be forgone," "we cannot recast the faulty drama") may be viewed here in the context and perspective of the remarkable story that follows, as the artist's trial-and-error gambits, primings of his deep wellsprings of vision, prior to the poem's inspired forays of childhood reenactments.

It would appear that in preparation to write "Grass Fires" Lowell studied the surviving letters he wrote to his parents as a child, in which he helplessly tried to explain his misdemeanor, no doubt to defend himself against his grandfather's (or the public fire marshall's) accusations of deliberate arson. I fancy the poet tremulously poring over the yellowed pages of his old missives, much as a scholar scrutinizing the text, or transcripts, of private journals, diaries, while he sought to decipher the "toppling, elephantine script" of his own child-psyche's struggle to verbally articulate and come to terms with the traumatic events of the awesome day of the fires. That adventure must have been terrifying and exhilarating at once, a precursor, clearly, to the grown man's impulsivity to court danger—or figuratively speaking, his playing with fire:

> I made it a warning,
> a cure, that stabilized nothing.

Although these lines foreshadow the accents of helpless, astonished resignation of the poem's final moment—"I cannot blow out a match" (not to mention their divinations, early youthful signals, of the onset of Lowell's incurable mental illness, which could be "stabilized," at best, intermittently by medication)—at this point in the work's prologue, he apparently refers to such vows, or promises, as the child must have made to his parents in the "letters / he sent home," not to set fires, or perpetrate other equivalent forms of mischief.

We can only surmise the exact terms that the child's hand-scripted oath may have taken, but the adult poet, today, brooding over the clumsily "toppling" alphabets penned by his own child hand, assays the first seeds of his pristine male intellect employing words as tools to grapple with a worldly crisis, and indeed, to define an integral self. His mustering of a *worded identity,* even then, for all his ungainliness in penmanship, suffices to carry the child's spirit through the family upheaval intact, and as we come to see, not only does that child's brave spirit survive, unbroken, but also it prevails—late in the poem's dramatic enactment—by a high-minded elation that transcends the conflict. But at this early juncture in Lowell's creative process of perusing the child's "hieroglyphic letters," the poet is befuddled. He finds the uninitiated young mind's rationale to be inscrutable. He can't quite synchronize the pungent events with the child's self-admonitions, a formulized code of magic preventatives for the future—"a warning, / a cure, that stabilized nothing." However, the author continues to sift through the letters with horrified fascination, ostensibly convinced that he is powerless to efficaciously translate the child's perceptions into a logic that can be apprehended by his adult mind-set:

> We cannot recast the faulty drama,
> play the child. . . .

Even as he confesses failure, his restraint in the quest achieves—as if by accident—a magical reentry into the child's psychic cosmos. Despite the defeat of his conscious will in its repeated attempts to decipher the child's totemic or mythic reasoning ("elephantine script, / the hieroglyphic"), the process of communing with the letters does, indeed, induce a trance that triggers the poem's marvelous central episode. For all the denials uttered by the author's intellect, his passional being—released by a ritual not unlike self-hypnosis—initiates a wholly credible replaying of the mysterious childhood tale, a ghostly scene in the poet's past that had haunted his dream life and waking consciousness alike for perhaps four decades. Intuitively, he must have known that to resurrect the full ongoing scene and the child's dynamic perspective within it, via the poem's clairvoyant luminous historical present,

> I hold big kitchen matches to flaps of frozen grass
> to smoke a rabbit from its hole—
> then the wind bites them, then they catch,
> the grass catches, fire everywhere,
> everywhere,

the Past alive and revitalized in its original cast of features, pulsing forward with original momentum, the full-scale drama itself must be the only way to launch a possible confrontation, or communion, between the two Lowells, child and adult. Thereby the art's vision may generate wisdom of wounds in the self, aching and unhealed, first laid bare at that early age, then masked by frail layers of ego insulation, irrevocably shorn away by the poem's denouement. The grown man's soul might now be freed of its false self-protective shrouds.

A reader may easily trace the suave transitions that carry the persona's voice from the void of negations, the pose of technical bankruptcy at the poem's start, to the buoyant, unstoppable onrush of the living protagonists on center stage in the third stanza. The process by which the mood swings from one pole to the other suggests that the artist-creator's will has been submerged by his imagination, or, in emotional terms, it may be perceived as the conquest of his skepticism by a spontaneous eruption of passional reserves.

Like the child Lowell who snatches a snapping turtle's foreleg, mistaking it for the tail, in another poem of this period, "Turtle," the child hunter pursuing a rabbit in "Grass Fires" doesn't have the remotest inkling of the lofty scale of danger he invokes with his "big kitchen matches." Much in keeping with the familiar perils of adolescence, the child's accident-prone mental enclave is besieged by traumas, shocks, on a grand scale. It appears as if he inhabits a special rarefied landscape in which his innocent playful impulse is fated to catalyze supernatural disasters that lurk even in the grass roots and earth clods. The hell-fire conflagration sparked by his lit match spreads demoniacally—as if by a will of its own—to all grasses that surround the child like a sea of fire. And finally, the fires threaten his grandfather's tall shade tree:

> I hold big kitchen matches to flaps of frozen grass
> to smoke a rabbit from its hole—
> then the wind bites them, then they catch,
> the grass catches, fire everywhere,
> everywhere
> inextinguishable roots,
> the tree grandfather planted for his shade,
> combusting, towering
> over the house he anachronized with stone.

With sweeping fluidity of rhythm and luxuriance of tone, Lowell here instills the atmosphere of a half-hidden malevolence, a secret will to mischief, that coexists in nature and the child's subconscious mind. The one is so closely linked to the other that when the fire spreads—accidentally and swiftly—from the few "flaps of frozen grass" near the rabbit hole to all grasses in sight, it seems as if the wind that "bites them" is propelled by a human volition, the fires having erupted from the child's psyche—overspilling, inundating the acres of family yard. Some obscure part of his being seems to know this, and to exult in the mysterious inner powers he has unleashed, albeit inadvertently:

> I can't tell you how much larger
> and more important it was than I,
> how many summers before conscience
> I enjoyed it.

Thus, the author, addressing the reader directly, *confesses*—with casual nonchalance—that he took a secret delight and pride in the events, both at the time they occurred and for "many summers" thereafter, the forbidden gambit harbored and relished in his evolving adolescent memory.

In the preceding stanza, we were already struck by the child's evident mixture of fear and exhilaration, guilt and ardor, as revealed by the nuances and overtones of the passage reenacting the apocalyptic onset of the blaze ("the grass catches, fire everywhere, / everywhere / inextinguishable roots"). Lowell's style again achieves an amazing panache in combining virtues of palpableness and elasticity, since the story is told with utter naturalness and verisimilitude, while the images both condense the child's broad range of emotions and project the illusion of an omnipresent spiritual *inscape* that merges the child's psyche with the hidden spirit in the grass. Hence, the oracular twice-repeated phrase, "inextinguishable roots," reverberates with a mystical kinship, or identification, between the grass fires and "the infernal fires" in the soul of the poet, child and adult alike. We are persuaded that such images have the potency and rigor needed to reintegrate the child Lowell's soul with the man's in the luminous final stanza, that—for all its pallor of helplessness and resignation—solidifies utmost integrity of person in the confessed failure, author Robert Lowell. Such are the unforetold gains of *an aesthetic of self-forgiveness* that holds to openly—and, indeed, unflaggingly—admitting the worsts:

> My grandfather towered above me,
> "You damned little fool,"
> nothing to quote, but for him original.
> The fire-engines deployed with stage bravado,
> yet it was I put out the fire,
> who slapped it to death with my scarred leather jacket.
> I snuffed out the inextinguishable root,
> I—
> really I can do little,
> as little now as then,
> about the infernal fires—
> I cannot blow out a match.

"Grass Fires" is distinctive among Lowell's poems of childhood in its power to hold up a mirror to the man-sized passions surging, precociously, in the half-formed gangling boy. The most sustained and compelling motif, unprecedented in Lowell's earlier work, is this poem's rendering lucid the child's struggle to contain the dangerously outsize compulsions that were tearing him apart—colossal appetites, emotional and spiritual, warring in his immature physique. Evidently, the episode of the fires, in and of itself, loomed in the child's memory for many years as a grand symbol for his own deep inner, unrequited passions. Even at the time of the conflagration, the child felt—perhaps unknowingly—the megalomaniacal lordly power of a God, as if the limitless destructive blaze were a projection of his own inner nature, and consequently, a disenburdenment of his unwieldy passions.

The perplexing disjunction in the child between massive heady impulses and his frail self-definition goes straight to the focal center of this poem's style and vision, such that the embattled factions in the child's sensibility are reflected in a remarkably hybrid mix of plain and fastidious language, as in the recurrent phrase, "inextinguishable roots": like the cumbersome body of the pubescent boy struggling to cope with his inflated glandular discharges, the six-syllable word, "inextinguishable," is enacting a contest to constrain the monosyllabic "roots," and by extension, to stifle the fires. Or the polysyllabic words are an exhalation of the plain words, in their momentary fits of insurgence—teutonic flarings of those bare spoken idioms that are the poem's chief vocabulary, a natural vocal language of the common storyteller's art:

> We cannot recast the faulty drama,
> play the child,
> unable to align
> his toppling, elephantine script,
> the hieroglyphic letters
> he sent home.

Much of the poem is cast in Lowell's plainest low-keyed language and conversational idiom, approaching an unobtrusive fluency and relaxed precision best suited to its documentary subject matter—a heightened journalese. This lowbrow style accommodates itself, at one extreme, to the author's professedly off-the-record asides, taking the reader into his confidence, a language that partakes of both the familiar essay and personal letters ("I can't tell you how much larger and more important it was than I . . ."); at another pole, the style befits the deadpan, faceless speech of a character whose manner utterly lacks any grace or personal flavor, the child's grandfather:

> My grandfather towered above me,
> "You damned little fool,"
> nothing to quote, but for him original.

Notice how aptly and consistently the negative timbre of the phrase, "nothing to quote," fits into a patterned cycle of such depreciatory asides that have appeared—at intervals of roughly one instance per stanza—throughout the poem and culminating, astonishingly, in the work's last lines:

(1) "It never matters . . ."
(2) "We cannot recast the faulty drama . . ."
(3) "I can't tell you how much larger . . ."
(4) "Nothing to quote . . ."
(5) "I cannot blow out a match."

To begin, I noted that this device of refusals, proclaiming the limits of imagination or art, functioned as a priming tool, a tactic for inducing the poem's genuinely clairvoyant trance. If instances of negative disclosure in later stanzas operate differently, all bespeak an avowed preference for the unglamorous detail, the overtly unspectacular event, the nonexplicit assertion of message ("I can't tell you . . ."), the least vivid or vital aspect of character ("nothing to quote,"), and finally, the author-persona's least-engaging human profile. Most profound, truly, is Lowell's windup of the work with this cameo portrait of himself in the guise of one intellectually and spiritually enervated:

> I—
> really I can do little,
> as little now as then,
> about the infernal fires—
> I cannot blow out a match.

Lowell's genius at the finish of "Grass Fires" is most evident in his strategy of making the poem's voyage of accurate reminiscence, the recital of viscerally tangible childhood events, *swerve*—by shrewd deft turnings in the self's inner-city map—from yesterday to today: "I can do little, / as little now as then." Today! *The grown man.* Lowell's very age in years, months, weeks, days, grasped and identified, seized and tagged, by this poem's mercilessly exact and precise calipers of self-measurement.

Beyond the Muse of Memory

Robert Lowell's Last Face

Roughly midway through Robert Lowell's poem "Turtle," the narrator interrupts an introductory prelude (two stanzas of meditation and prayer, one stanza of nostalgic childhood reminiscence) and launches into the story of a slugabed day in the author's life.[1] Moving swiftly from a wintry morn's sunny waking to his sunset dying, a day in the life is translated, if you will, to *the day of* his life, the poem's finale an awesome premonition of death by drowning and underwater—indeed, *underworld*—dismemberment by a giant killer turtle. So much more body: so much ampler girth, breadth of substance, than the modest prayer—apostrophe or invocation to the Muse—had bargained for in the first stanza:

> I pray for memory—
> an old turtle,
> absentminded, inelastic,
> kept afloat by losing touch . . .
> no longer able to hiss or lift
> a useless shield against the killer.

In later career, Lowell had learned, increasingly, to ground his aesthetic trust in the limitless resources of the Muse of Memory; little might he have supposed that his plainspoken wish for memory to toss up a few near-forgotten tidbits of childhood reminiscence would plunge him into a psychic eruption and visitation of such proportions as are unleashed by this poem's raids upon Lowell's subconscious; nor might he have anticipated that the turtle casually likened to memory in the poem's relaxed opening metaphor would be transfigured—by a succession of magical alchemies, dizzying enchantments—into the final monster sprung from the abyss of racial/mythic preconscious that, Frankensteinlike, strangles and devours its creator. Such, then, is the unforeseeable risk of invoking

---

1. This essay originally appeared in *The Southwest Review* in winter 1986.

racial memory—confrontation with such explosive images as may be summoned forth from those depths of mind.

Condensed in its terse fifty-three lines, then, is one of its author's most pungent verse autobiographies. The work's range is astonishing. Its vision mediates with masterful deftness and economy between anecdotal childhood flashbacks and several end-of-life flashaheads: revivifying familiar nightmare mirages; life's-end hallucinations common to old age; brink-of-the-grave visions of ghosts of old friends (deformed, disguised as hybrid beast-humans) returned from death, sojourns from the other world, paying brief visits to the living; followed by premonitions of the author's early death.

Both the haunted portraits of Lowell's old friends and the scenic enactment of a preordained death at the poem's finish are projected with supernatural clarity and starkness of detail. Those pictures, in their graphic realism, seem, chillingly, more *lifelike* than portraits of the living child and turtle in the first half of the poem. Indeed, the poem's vision persuades a reader that, as death approaches even a totally clearheaded and alert person of advanced years, reembodied spirits of old friends crossing over into life for a brief interval may be infused with a heightened vividness, a cast of features and figure, that makes them appear more real, more alive to the captivated witness, than his actual flesh-and-blood companions. They bristle with a pained ghastly humor, a perverse extrahuman jokiness, as if the old stick-in-the-mud relic who has overstayed his welcome among the living may now be laughingly coddled, with who can say what bloodcurdling enticements, into hurrying his last laps to the grave:

> They are stale and panting;
> what is dead in me wakes their appetite.
> When they breathe, they seem to crack apart,
> crouched motionless on tiptoe
> with crooked smiles
> and high-school nicknames on their tongues,
> as if they wished to relive
> the rawness that let us meet as animals.

Of course, the persona's psychic comportment is that of one who tries to resist their beckoning gestures, their cunning allurements, in vain. We sense, implicitly, his helpless, complete ravishment by these apparitions, even before he plummets to death by drowning in the claws of the depth-diving killer turtle of the finale.

To my mind, this poem is supreme among Lowell's numerous late works that incorporate into their structural format adroit fluctuations between finely terraced mental levels of waking and sleeping, worldly and unworldly seeing, touchable and impalpable images, materiality vying with immateriality. In its climactic passages, this lyrical phantasmagoria is perhaps unique among Lowell's works for its sustained posture of hanging between the two opposed worlds: a controlled dialectic, double-voiced; a two-barreled utterance, a speaking from both sides of the verse mouth at once, lipside and skullside, facetongue and ghoultongue. Who can tell them apart? Who can say which is which, those ghostly antinomies, when Lowell's most light-stepping metrical feet dance across the ineffable threshold between the alive and the dead, dream and reality, his lines fluttering—in poised balance—on the sill that divides full, conscious awakeness from subliminal life. Perhaps he advances, at last, to a midway zone in which subconscious glimmerings are so seamlessly appropriated into mind's flux of consciousness, that dream images and world images (eye's glimpsed *snapshots* of reality) can no longer be differentiated. They grow to look more and more alike. One moment we find ourselves mistaking one for the other; the next moment we *know* there's no mistake. They are identical. In some lines, they do combat with each other, rivals for a commanding vantage in Lowell's voice cosmos. Appearance and reality, waking and sleeping, mirror each other again and again until the pattern of recurrence builds into surprise *coincidence!* The one dimension coincides with the other, and no matter which side seems to absorb— or swallow—its mate, once they have merged, they inhabit one integral skin of languaged images. In *this* higher awareness, the woke-up person sees through the sleeper's eyes: dreaming becomes just another way of extending awakeness.

But how did Lowell's art advance itself, finally, to this ultraviolet or infrared plateau of clear-sighted seeing within the forbidden blind alleys and dead zones of the dream? As Lowell took utmost pains to clarify in repeated afterwords to successive versions of his major sonnet-sequence-opus *Notebook* ("accident threw up subjects, and the plot swallowed them—famished for human chances"), his *ars poetica* prescribed that he "plot" with the literal diaristic happenstance facts of each day's life; but he would be alert for intuitive opportunities for surreal turns of phrase, or surreal bends of mind. And indeed, he wrote a slightly altered credo for this artistic programme in his late poem "Epilogue":

> But sometimes everything I write
> with the threadbare art of my eye

seems a snapshot,
lurid, rapid, garish, grouped,
heightened from life,
yet paralyzed by fact.

His raw materials are to be, still, the "poor passing facts" of his *day by day* mundane routines of living, an art that aspires to be "heightened from life" at one extreme, but "paralyzed by fact," perhaps depreciatively, at the other. Yet while these modest goals and avowed limits are claimed as an explicit aesthetic, the implicit art theory I find to be earned, and fully realized, in a handful of the most accomplished last works dazzlingly outstrips those proposed boundaries. It is entirely fitting that an artist striking out for new frontiers in his craft should find himself having to improvise new-minted rules to accommodate a radically new order of experience and its attendant welter of unfamiliar feelings asserting a will of their own, devised step-by-step, extemporaneously. The self-critic in the poet can forbear, fall into abeyance, gladly relinquishing the task of explanation for what is, inspiritedly, beyond explanation as it unfolds. He can hope to catch up later, decades later maybe (as in the case of Henry James's *Prefaces*), if time permits. If not, not. Today's show goes on. . . .

Perhaps the chief access to new technical strategies, coupled with unaccustomed new strengths of vision, in Robert Lowell's handsomest late performances may be ascribed to his impetus to dispense with most forms of explicit *sententia*. The new intellectual restraint leads to a consequent shift in the fullest burden of message, or revelation, having to be carried—and if possible, evoked—by strict dramatic portrayal and episodic juxtaposing of scenes and events. In "Turtle," by a subtle progression, the pictures transcribed from life with the "threadbare art of my eye"—whether remembered slide show of past events or ongoing action in the historical present—are slowly displaced, and finally superseded, by hypnotic dream choreographs. The dancelike scenarios gain intensity, from stanza to stanza, peaking in the apparition of three old men returned from the grave and disguised as turtles ("crouched motionless on tiptoe"), Lowell's aged high-school cronies of the first dream tableau, followed by the monstrous giant snapping turtle and his victim: a shrunken doll-sized effigy, totemlike, of the adult Lowell himself in the last dream tableau, in which the nightmare presentiments of the author's own impending death shatteringly end the poem. The grotesque figures in the dreamscapes are all conceived in dance poses, postures of dream puppetry; their feeblest moves, even grimaces of their mouths, tongue waggings, heavy breath pantings, appear to be performing a ceremonial dance, such a dance as

Diaghilev might have choreographed for the youthful Stravinsky. Yet the unlikely vitality and magnetic élan of the cast of dream marionettes, for all their grimness, generates more life-affirming energy and brio into the poem's foreground than the live protagonists, child or adult, who commenced the work's drama. So it would appear that the spectral figures of the dream sequences, though "heightened from life," usurp the poem stage's center of attention, wrested away from the real-life performers.

What we are witnessing, then, is a major shift in priorities in Lowell's aesthetic of the balance between everyday journalistic elements and their surreal afterimages. If the latter were formerly held in reserve, then daubed on the canvas, at intervals, employed sparingly for cosmetic purposes like dashes of eye shadow and penciled eyebrow liner in a barely perceptible face makeup, now a markedly distorted mask covers the whole face; soon the face shall absorb, and indeed, be transformed into the mask. Surreal quantities, the dream tableaux, rival the life stories they mirror, and by a dynamic juxtaposition or interrelation of snapshots from life, past or present, with dream parodies, the one version of our human cosmos is engaged in a fierce competition with the other: the banal notation of tallied moments in a day's domestic routines, say, must battle the illimitable scope of the dream life, measureless imagination, each making its rival claim upon our sanity. As we shall observe, here, the proportionate ratio of real-life to surreal elements in "Turtle" swings, incontrovertibly, in favor of the dance cosmos of the dream.

"Turtle" 's concisely honed structure moves with unwavering inevitability, from first stanza to last, toward a final resolution of the poem's action in which *all* the characters—turtles: old, young, and middle-aged, floaters and submergers, tame and snappers; humans: child, adult, dead friends returned from the grave—are revealed to have been projected fragments of the author's sole irreducible self. Thus, a reader is persuaded that the speaker may feel, paradoxically, equal identification with the genial, sickly, aged turtle who commences the poem and the merciless killer turtle who slowly dismembers the protagonist at the finish, and eats him alive.

By a simple equation, the old turtle of the prayerful first stanza is likened to the aging poet's memory:

> I pray for memory—
> an old turtle,
> absentminded, inelastic,
> kept afloat by losing touch . . .

> no longer able to hiss or lift
> a useless shield against the killer.

"Losing touch," for memory, is a way of survival by escaping pain—too much pain can make the brain crack and drown. But the brave poet-persona of "Turtle" and several other last poems of Lowell's final volume, *Day by Day*, will risk himself, again and again, by disciplining memory like a muscle, training memory to uproot many painful areas buried in the psyche, enabling the mind, at last, to cope with the worst terrors hidden in the past, and to exorcise demons embedded in the self by the poem's catharsis of action and interplay of images.

In stanzas two and three, the overt analogy to humans is, in itself, *submerged*, now symbolic or implicit, no longer metaphoric, *afloat*, as in stanza one:

> Turtles age, but wade out amorously,
> half-frozen fossils, yet knight-errant
> in a foolsdream of armor.
> The smaller ones climb rocks to broil in comfort.
>
> Snapping turtles only submerge.
> They have survived . . . not by man's philanthropy.

How pragmatic, to begin, for Lowell to differentiate float-turtles of the surface from diver-turtles of the depths, thereby doubling the rigor of the animals' capacity to dramatize the poem's many-layered complex of human themes with a minimum of overt explanation. Lowell's art in this book is usually firmest, most condensed and sinewy, when picture and image express a maximum of thought, as in this passage, whereby the author ridicules his own recklessness in marrying a woman much younger than himself ("Turtles age, but wade out amorously, / half-frozen fossils, yet knight-errant / in a foolsdream of armor"). Old males are quixotic, suicidal, if they wade into deep waters of romance, courting young women. Lacking adequate shields, they are too vulnerable, but lost "in a foolsdream of armor," they cannot admit their fragility.

The political overtones of the following couplet, evoking man's history of indiscriminate turtle slaughter, sets the stage for the avenging turtle to punish the persona at the poem's finish ("They have survived . . . not by man's philanthropy"). In retaliation for the animal genocide practiced by humans, the brutal merciless tonality of the poem's final lines comes to feel like a slow methodical execution, a racial vengeance of turtle against man transmitted through the collective subconscious of one man's dream, and hence, the bitter irony of the word "philanthropy" in this early passage.

Stanza four, a self-contained vignette of childhood reminiscence, is the poem's longest verse unit. Little does the child Lowell guess, while hunting turtles, that his terror is chiefly a subconscious fear of castration:

> I hunted them in school vacations.
> I trampled an acre of driftstraw
> floating off the muskrats' loose nests.
> Here and there, a solitary turtle
> craned its brown Franciscan cowl
> from one of twenty waterholes.
> In that brew, I stepped
> on a turtle's smooth, invisible back.
> It was like escaping quicksand.
> I drew it in my arms by what I thought was tail—
> a tail? I held a foreleg.
> I could have lost a finger.

By a slow unfolding of guises and disguises, the male child becomes initiated into this turtle purgatorio, a prevision of the underwater hell that shall emerge in the poem's denouement. Like layers of camouflage, disgorgings of the muskrats' nests hide the submerged turtles, one animal helping to shroud others. Now the reclusive turtles appear, disguised as hermit clergymen withdrawn into cave sanctuaries, their monk's-hood cowls peeping from several of the "twenty waterholes." Prefigured, here, are the undead spirits of old friends inhabiting the depth-diver turtles' bodies, cunningly returned from the grave: so does this passage of the masked and hooded turtle heads anticipate the adult's dream sequence in which a puppy nuzzling bedclothes metamorphoses into three snapping turtles, who transform, yet again, into Lowell's three old school chums, known by the poet to have preceded him in death.

At last, the child steps on "a turtle's smooth, invisible back," the turtle donning its cloak of invisibility, partly to protect itself from the hunter, partly to entrap the unsuspecting child male victim in an encounter with overtones of homosexual terror, as well as fear of castration: the creature's "foreleg" (*foreplay, foreskin*), mistaken for a tail, instills ambiguities akin to a woman's genitalia mistaken for a man's, or vice versa, and this translates swiftly into the child's horror of losing a finger that masks, or disguises, his deep-seated fear of castration. "It was like escaping quicksand," still another of the turtle's disguises, foretells the final drowning sequence, since the child feels he is being sucked downward, but he fearlessly continues his pursuit of the phantom turtle, a mythic creature that adopts numerous masks and faces. D. H. Lawrence's snake, "king of the underworld," is a clear-cut precursor, or ancestor, of Robert Lowell's turtle, though Lawrence's enthralled witness knows enough to keep his distance, finally, from the otherworldly being, lest he be vanquished by its indomitable spirit. The subsequent lines carry unmistakable overtones of a lover's embrace ("I drew it in my arms by what I thought was tail . . ."), innocent love-fondling, unguarded and defenseless. Once again, we feel a suggestion that the turtle enchantress, hidden behind alluring veils, becomes invisible to entice and inveigle the male-child hunter, who has already become *the hunted* by a sudden trick role switch that anticipates the adult's being cannibalized in the Armageddon battle that ends the poem.

Both the child protagonist of this anecdote and the old man mirrored in stanza two are ill-equipped for the sexual encounters they recklessly pursue; for both, a psychic or fleshly catastrophe is hinted as the probable outcome. Neither is armed with the necessary weaponry to defend himself "against the killer." In the erotic cosmos of Lowell's last poems, the odds against surviving full-scale sexual adventures intact, uncrippled, are, at best, poor, even for a male adult in his prime. Against that backdrop of everyday sexual hazard, consider the magnified incest terror of a male *only child* with an overpossessive mother, or that of an ailing man of sixty mated with a voluptuous woman twenty years his junior. Those actual dramas in the theater of Lowell's domestic milieu (recollected combats with his mother during adolescence, the upheaval of his current marriage to Caroline Blackwell) infuse a fierce propulsion into autobiographical poems, such as "Turtle," that grapple with these crises of the author's life obliquely via the childhood anecdote and dream sequences that comprise this story poem's narrative line.

The work's shift from the childhood flashback of stanza four to the story taking place today in stanza five, a radical shunt from past to historical present, precipitates the chain of pictures that, like a succession of frames in a movie, enacts a dynamic interplay between real images and dream images, hallucinatory states and sleep states, that is perhaps the most remarkable hallmark of "Turtle"'s uniquely condensed structure:

> This morning when
> the double-brightness of the winter sun
> wakes me from the film of dreaming,

> my bedroom is unfamiliar. I see
> three snapping turtles squatted on my drifting clothes—
> two rough black logs . . . the third is a nuzzler
> dressed in see-through yellow tortoiseshell,
> a puppy squeaking and tweaking
> my empty shirt for milk.

Lowell's large debt to the sister arts of photography and film, implicit in the design of "Turtle" and many other late works, aptly emerges into the poem's foreground, here, an explicit metaphor that carries through to the final stanza ("Too many pictures / have screamed from the reel . . . in the rerun, / the snapper holds on . . ."). The most powerful films, whether lifelike to the point of documentary or bizarrely surrealistic, may have the same radical—if momentary—impact on the viewer's psyche as any deeply unsettling dream, or nightmare, such that the moviegoer, exiting the theater, finds the everyday world strangely transformed, the very look of common things rendered foreign and unfamiliar; likewise, the sleeper-protagonist, here, awakens from his "film of dreaming" to find "my bedroom is unfamiliar." As in many another of Lowell's art-life equations, the film-dream metaphor works both ways, either dimension *illumining* the other. Indeed, it is the very special quality of light in the room that, like stage-set floodlighting, first mystifies the reader, drawing him into the charmed spell of the speaker who drifts to and fro between the twin realms of waking and sleeping for the balance of the poem:

> This morning when
> the double-brightness of the winter sun
> wakes me . . .

By these few shimmery details of the scene's queer radiance, we are already tipped off that this is to be no ordinary waking. This day in the life, again, will be amplified, in the few succeeding stanzas, to *the day of* its author's lifetime: "the winter sun" evokes both a time of year and a season in an aging man's full apportionment of years. "The double-brightness" portends both the fierce intensity of illumination of the vision to come in the poem's denouement, and the vulnerability of the maturing artist's eyes (or mind's eye) to such blinding flashes as may be visited upon a word conjuror who is willing to take the utmost risks of following out the pain of childhood memory's deft inroads to the subconscious to attain wisdom of the self, at whatever cost.

How does the sleeper know whether he wakes, or merely dreams that he has wakened, within the ongoing flux of his sleep, that hall of mirrors? How is the reader to distinguish between the real, the hallucinatory, and the dream images in the poem's vision, since the writer mediates with dazzling celerity between these three distinct levels of visual witnessing without providing conventional transitions? Ingeniously, Lowell perpetuates for the reader the protagonist's illusion that all three states, matched by three concomitant tiers of images, are part of a seamless continuum of visualizing in the poem's arrival, at last, in a psychic plateau that synchronizes and blends waking vision with the dream. To unravel this enigma, we may trace the many subtle links from one psychic level to another.

The speaker, convinced he has been wakened by the "winter sun," supposes that he actually observes three turtles on his bed:

> . . . I see
> three snapping turtles squatted on my drifting clothes—
> two rough black logs . . . the third is a nuzzler
> dressed in see-through yellow tortoiseshell,
> a puppy squeaking and tweaking
> my empty shirt for milk.
>
> They are stale and panting. . . .

This passage connects with my recent experience, I believe. A deep-seated problem struggles toward resolution in a series of dreams, interrupted by momentary fits of waking. We wake up, relieved by morning's light, feeling grateful, as if we've been saved from the infernal demons locked inside, only to drift back asleep; then the dream resumes in slightly altered form, inhabited by a similar—but revised—host of characters. Our waking self seems to voyage into the dream. We feel more alert, more *awakeness*, even, than conscious wake-up usually affords. The figures in the dream seem, for a time, more real, more true to life, than most people we encounter in the palpable world. Perhaps we coast in and out of sleep several times in just a few minutes, since our time scale seems vastly accelerated. Many years pass in a few seconds. Each reentry into the dream brings us closer to the showdown, the fulfillment, whether in joy or pain, toward which the cycle of fragmentary dramas was hurtling us. Often, we spring awake, wondering if we are still asleep, still locked in the dream; conversely, we insist, in the midst of a dream, that we are wide awake.

The second half of "Turtle" exquisitely dramatizes the stages of this process. The speaker truly has wakened, briefly, from a dream of turtles, and in his half-sleep state, he hallucinates turtles squatting on his bedclothes, which appear to alchemize suddenly into "two rough black logs," another hallucinatory image. He passes from a fantasy state of half-awakeness into full conscious alertness, then notes that the actual flesh-and-blood "puppy" on his bed is nuzzling his "empty shirt for milk." But before it registers upon his interpretative mentality that the dream, after its shrewd and heartless fashion, has twisted the innocent sounds and moves— "squeaking and tweaking"—of the real-life canine into "three snapping turtles" (each a dream-heir-descendent of the menacing snapper he'd confronted as a child), he has been sucked back down into a deeper sleep. The resumption of sleep is signaled by the stanza break immediately following the short-lived picture of the puppy, which the reader recognizes to be an actual live creature, however fleeting the persona's momentary glimpse of the dog, snatched in the interval between two sleep states:

> They are stale and panting;
> what is dead in me wakes their appetite.
> When they breathe, they seem to crack apart,
> crouched motionless on tiptoe
> with crooked smiles
> and high-school nicknames on their tongues,
> as if they wished to relive
> the rawness that let us meet as animals.
> Nothing has passed between us but time.

In this second sleep, the specters instantly become more aggressive toward the person of the dreamer, who is so much more than a detached onlooker now. Cleverly masquerading as turtles, they are soon discerned to be three of his high-school classmates reclaimed from the grave. Their surprise reunion with Cal Lowell seems to excite mixed passions in them, a desire to come back to life ("as if they wished to relive / the rawness that let us meet as animals") alternating with the gluttonous craving to wheedle him, prematurely, down into death, and to feed upon his corpse ("what is dead in me wakes their appetite"). The wish to cannibalize him does finally prevail in the third and last dream, augured, here, by their "panting," slavering like beasts of prey, while they stalk their victim ("when they breathe, they seem to crack apart"); for now they are perhaps content to socialize with him, resuming school-day dialectics:

Nothing has passed between us but time.

"You've wondered where we were these years?
Here are we."

But even this semblance of good fellowship is suspect, a mere hollow playing upon the late-middle-aged poet Lowell's predilection for mulling over great riddles, enigmas of geriatrics: pained time-shunts between one generation and the next, the fate of mortal souls in death and the afterlife, preponderant questions that are recurrent motifs in numerous major poems of Lowell's last phase. The cronies' false guise of chumminess is betrayed by their "crooked smiles" and their militant ominous preattack stance ("crouched motionless on tiptoe"), as if they cunningly try to win over the protagonist's confidence and disarm his defenses, just prior to the battle to the death of the final tableau.

I would love to have heard Robert Lowell read this death-beleaguered poem aloud, since I surmise he would deliver these three spooky time-haunted lines with gruff reticence and sardonic restraint. They must be read haltingly, especially the oddly reversed syntax of "Here are we," which recoils, falls back on itself, underscoring the negative rigor and lavish expressiveness of the blank spaces between Lowell's stanzas, negative energies swirling around the poem's only couplets. So often, as in this instance, Lowell employed bare, stark two-line units in the latest poems to condense a gasped shudder of thought, such that the forward momentum is retarded, decelerated to a near halt, and the disproportionately wide spaces around the stanza modulate a radical shift in tempo or pacing. The orchestration seems to take a couple of deep breaths, as if a spring has been compressed, held taut, just prior to its explosive release in a last flash of insight, pained trope, or incisively memorable tableau, as in this poem's sizzling finale:

They lie like luggage—
my old friend the turtle . . . Too many pictures
have screamed from the reel . . . in the rerun,
the snapper holds on till sunset—
in the awful instantness of retrospect,
its beak
works me underwater drowning by my neck,
as it claws away pieces of my flesh
to make me small enough to swallow.

Waking from the second dreamscape, the peripatetic sleeper, blurry-eyed, sees the creatures momentarily collapsed into harmless inert shapes:

> They lie like luggage—
> my old friend the turtle . . .

He takes cognizance of the source of his dream beasts in the rumpled bedclothes, and further, in the recollected snapping turtle he impulsively snatched from the swamp water hole as a child that, after four or five decades, elicits his fond nostalgia, here, restoring the turtle-friend equation of the poem's introductory passage. Whereas in the cosmos of the dream, the turtles resemble, and indeed reincarnate, three of his high-school chums known to be dead, now, in his relaxed serenity of a wakened man, rescued from his dream's terror by bursting out of sleep, he can bask in the safety of the calculable memory-turtle, perceived to be "my old friend," to whom he'd addressed the poem's opening invocation and prayer.

But the solace of these lines, alas, is short-lived, fleeting. This waking is a mere momentary respite, or false reprieve, from the doom that was foretold by the earlier tableaux of this consecutive and cumulative vision, which rolls forward—following the protracted moment of peace—with a terrible inevitability like fate:

> . . . Too many pictures
> have screamed from the reel . . . in the rerun,
> the snapper holds on till sunset—

The prior claim of the dream upon the victim's soul is stubbornly unrelenting, and its sentence cannot be forestalled by his mere temporary wake-up. As in Marlowe's *Doctor Faustus,* he'd sold his soul to the demons of the dream life, and though he should have taken heed and been forewarned by his childhood sojourn in turtle purgatory, he chose to ignore the early warnings. Now he has no choice but to submit to the descent into turtle Hades. He must pay the fee in full. He'd prayed to the Muse of Memory ("my old friend"), investing his life's contract in the rights to "the film of dreaming," and much the greater share of his best human energies were contracted to the dream pictures, frames of the film so to say, than to his conscious worldly life—"Too many pictures / have screamed from the reel." The accumulated debt and account of his career earnings, as might be owed to a tax collector, Lowell had divulged in another last poem:

> . . . This is riches:
> the eminence not to be envied,
> the account
> accumulating layer and angle,
> face and profile,
> 50 years of snapshots,
> the ladder of ripening likeness.
>
> We are things thrown in the air
> alive in flight . . .
> our rust the color of the chameleon.
>
> from "Our Afterlife I"

Too many pictures. 50 years of snapshots. His dreams, like the poems that embodied them, made the strongest claim, and though some dream pictures betrayed their promise of joy, affording instead a vision of pain and horror (hence, they've "screamed from the reel"), nevertheless, the movie projector must spit its preordained succession of frames to the bitter end:

> . . . in the rerun,
> the snapper holds on till sunset—
> in the awful instantness of retrospect . . .

The "rerun" is the recurrent nightmare. The protagonist, like the film addict or film buff, is helplessly sucked down into the bog of this last showing of the film, anticipated by the child's vertigo when he stepped onto the "escaping quicksand" of the turtle's back. In this final tableau, the pictures recall highlights of the childhood tableau, but it is no ordinary *rerun,* since the characters have evolved into new forms, aging versions of the originals, the innocent boy hunter now a late-middle-aged artist pathfinder, a life-risking huntsman of the dream wilds; the normal-sized turtle now a giant antediluvian monster that attacks its prey like a killer whale. Indeed, a recurrent nightmare resembles a movie remake, or sequel, more than a rerun, though in either case the dreamer knows he has entered the antechamber of this dream's room before, many times perhaps. Despite the fragrance of the familiar, wafted like an incense through the sleeper's dreamscape, the keynote of the repeating dream is the new casting of performers, the novel choreographies and stage sets, the new twists on old plots.

However, we do know that the fourth tableau in the cycle is to be the last, since the one central character who appears in all the replays, the poet-dreamer-protagonist, dies, unmistakably and irrevocably. It's a psychic dogma—if you die in your dream, you stay dead. Stone dead.

The artist has arrived at this final dream, evolved from a long consecutive chain of linked pictures ("50 years of snapshots"), and there is no turning back, no turning away from the climactic dream of the series, despite the vision of a painful death. The recurrent dream keeps evolving and reshaping itself in its passion to work through the conflicts in the soul that it must, compulsively, resolve, whether in pain, joy, or a mixture of the two, in whatever proportions. The dreamer-poet, too, has no choice but to see the film vision through to the finish. How can the artist turn his back on the culmination of a lifetime's dream portraits? He must settle for his vision's arrival, finally, even though, as Lowell disclosed in his poem "The Withdrawal," he'd built a life and career upon the habit of chronically sidestepping necessities of "arrival," rotating from home to home, from marriage to marriage, resisting lockup in permanent residency, permanent love unions:

> When I look back, I see a collapsing
> accordion of my receding houses,
> and myself receding
> to a boy of twenty-five or thirty,
> too shopworn for less, too impressionable for more—
> blackmaned, illmade
> in a washed blue workshirt and coalblack trousers,
> moving from house to house,
> still seeking a boy's license
> to see the countryside without arrival.
>
> Hell?
>
> Darling,
> terror in happiness may not cure the hungry future . . .

Lowell foresaw, then, that arrival was to be a one-way ticket to hell, and "the hungry future" could only be postponed for a limited interlude by the love alliance with his "darling" ("terror in happiness"), before tomorrow, that glutton, would eat him alive, as does the killer turtle in a passage augured, perhaps, by the finish of "The Withdrawal":

Darling,
terror in happiness may not cure the hungry future,
the time when any illness is chronic,
and the years of discretion are spent on complaint—

until the wristwatch is taken from the wrist.

In sum, midway through the poem "Turtle," the marvelous unin-
terrupted cycle of light sleeps, wakings and dozings, commences with
the glare of winter sunrise, and the last dream tableau finalizes with a
sunset dying; thus, the single calendar day spanned by Lowell's dream
of this poem is translated into the day of his whole life, this poem more
than any other in its author's oeuvre, perhaps, comprising a complete
verse autobiography, its horrifying conclusion a true precognition of his
impending early death:

> . . . in the rerun,
the snapper holds on till sunset—
in the awful instantness of retrospect,
its beak
works me underwater drowning by my neck,
as it claws away pieces of my flesh
to make me small enough to swallow.

The unearthly tone of this denouement leaves a reader stunned, haunting
overtones of clairvoyance, foreknowledge, flooding the vacancy in its
wake. As so often in the last poems, the author had struck a bargain
with his muse at the outset ("I pray for memory—an old turtle"), and
his wish has been lavishly, indeed munificently, granted. Once again, he
appears to have won a heftier gift of vision than he bargained for, and
consequently, he would have to pay a higher price.

The Muse of Memory holds a lofty place of honor in the pantheon
of Lowell's saints of poetic art, in the last poems particularly; tirelessly,
in verse after verse, he sings the praises of memory for coming to
his rescue in times of creative drought or exhaustion. But his inspi-
rational dependency on memory's bonuses and rewards in this poem
traverses an emotional gamut ranging from reverence in the poem's
opening lines to horror in the final stanza, while the metaphoric turtle
of memory undergoes gradual transfiguration from the benign senile
creature of the opening stanzas to the brutal man-eating giant tur-
tle at the finish. So it is perhaps not surprising that memory, Low-
ell's adored patron saint, is characterized more pejoratively in the last

stanza of "Turtle" than in any other late poem as "the awful instant-
ness of retrospect," though we'd learned in "Last Walk?" that flights
of nostalgia, begun in heart's gladness, might end in bitter disillusion-
ment,

> nostalgia pulverized by thought,
> nomadic as yesterday's whirling snow,
> all whiteness splotched.
>
> from "Last Walk?"

In a final coming to terms with memory in the poem "Shifting Colors,"
Lowell had grown to regard the exercise of his retrospective faculty as
being hazardous to his physical well-being, often dragging him down to
a pit of hopeless enervation. In pursuit of a new self-protective creed,
a healing balm, he found he must abandon his powers of memory
altogether; henceforth, he would cultivate a poetics of plain description:

> I seek leave unimpassioned by my body,
> I am too weak to strain to remember, or give
> recollection the eye of a microscope. I see
> horse and meadow, duck and pond,
> universal consolatory
> description without significance,
> transcribed verbatim by my eye.

I take this aesthetic to be the stage of his evolving art theory immediately
following the Apocalypse that ends "Turtle," wherein the credo of exploit-
ing memory was felt to have reached a cul-de-sac, if not a dead end. So the
depreciatory phrase "awful instantness of retrospect" may be discerned
to complement and resonate with passages in a number of other last
works that register, as here, Lowell's growing disenchantment with rem-
iniscence as his primary wellspring of poetic raw materials. I apprehend
this passage in "Shifting Colors" to be indicative of his latest emerging *ars
poetica,* an austere passion for dwelling on *the present* (a turning away from
the past, the hopelessness of "backlooks"), a pure descriptive aesthetic of
the photographer of snapshots, the portrait painter, the watercolorist of
nature, and finally, as in "Turtle," a dreamer of films.

Part II.

James Dickey and

Robert Penn Warren

James Dickey

The Worldly Mystic

The persona in James Dickey's new poems, those that appear in the final section, "Falling," of his book *Poems: 1957–1967,* is a unique human personality.[1] He is a worldly mystic. On the one hand, a joyous, expansive personality—all candor, laughter, and charm—in love with his fully conscious gestures, the grace and surety of moves of his body. An outgoing man. An extrovert. On the other hand, a chosen man. A man who has been picked by some mysterious, intelligent agent in the universe to act out a secret destiny:

> . . . something was given a life-
> mission to say to me hungrily over
>
> And over and over   *your moves are exactly right*
> *For a few things in this world: we know you*
> *When you come, Green Eyes, Green Eyes.*
>
> from "Encounter in the Cage Country"

How does a man reconnect with common, unchosen humanity when he has just returned from the abyss of nonhuman, chosen otherness? That is the chief problem to which the final volume addresses itself. How to be a man who feels perfectly at home, and at his ease, in both worlds—inner and outer. A man who can make of himself and his art a medium, a perfect conductor, through which the opposed worlds—both charged with intensity—can meet and connect, flow into each other. The worldly mystic. It is the vision of a man who for years has been just as committed to developing his potential for creative existence as for creative art. All discoveries and earnings, spiritual or worldly, must carry over from one universe to the other.

---

1. This review of *Poems: 1957–1967,* (Wesleyan University Press, 1967), originally appeared in *The Hudson Review* in 1967.

In the best poems of the previous volume, *Buckdancer's Choice*, the self is frustrated, paralyzed, helplessly unable to establish liberating connections with the world. The chief obstacle to self-liberation is a sense of moral guilt. In "The Firebombing," "The Fiend," and "Slave Quarters," the self is pitilessly subjected to encounters with life that induce feelings of criminality. Clearly, the writer has deliberately trapped the persona in predicaments of contemporary American life that automatically create an aura of grave moral jeopardy. In all three poems, the conflict between the worldly-mindedness of modern life and the inner life of the spirit is dramatized. Materialism of a kind that blocks the persona in its struggle to connect with the world is embodied in the indulgences of suburban middle-class home life of "The Firebombing"; in the businesslike exterior of "The Fiend," his guise of normalcy and ordinariness; and in the catalog of inferior occupational stereotypes, earmarked for African Americans by our society, in "Slave Quarters."

Wherever being is trapped in oneself or in others, the existential self must work, either through art or directly in life, to make lifesaving connections—all those connections that create the free interchange of spirit between being and being. The word *connect* is the central one in Dickey's new poetry. His spirit must connect with the world, with "all worlds the growing encounters." In the best poems, all the connections are good. "I am a man who turns on," and when he turns on, all worlds he connects with turn on, since wherever he connects, he creates personal intimacy, injects intensity: "People are calling each other   weeping with a hundred thousand / Volts."

The one poem that perfectly reconciles the contradictions between worldliness and the inner life of the spirit is "Power and Light." The happiness of power and light heals all broken connections, "even the one / With my wife." For the artist, the hardest connections to "turn good" may be the home connections, the ones thorny with daily ritual and sameness: "Thorns! Thorns! I am bursting / Into the kitchen, into the sad way station / Of my home. . . ." But if the connections are good, all worlds flow into each other, the good healing, cleansing the bad. There is woe in the worldly side of marriage, but it is good in its spiritual and sexual dimensions, in the "deep sway of underground."

"Power and Light" dramatizes the secret life of a pole climber, a technician who works for the power company. Through the disguise of the persona, Dickey explores symbolically the ideal relationship between the artist and his audience, the poet and his readers:

> . . . I feel the wires running
> Like the life-force along the limed rafters   and all connections
> With poles   with the tarred naked belly-buckled black
> Trees I hook to my heels   with the shrill phone calls leaping
> Long distance   long distances through my hands   all connections
>
> Even the one
> With my wife, turn good . . . Never think I don't know my
>   profession
> Will lift me: why, all over hell the lights burn in your eyes,
> People are calling each other   weeping with a hundred thousand
> Volts   making deals   pleading   laughing like fate,
> Far off, invulnerable   or with the right word pierced
> To the heart
> By wires I held, shooting off their ghosty mouths,
> In my gloves.

The pole climber's spirit raises the spirits of the dead and damned from Hell—marriage, too, being a kind of hell. The "ghostly mouths" of the spirits can all reconnect through the power lines—lines of the poem—and save themselves. The poet is blessed with such an access, a surplus, of lifesaving joy, that he can afford to let it—the flood of power and light—overflow into the grave, into Hell. He doesn't so much give life to the damned as open them up to hidden resources of life, newly accessible in themselves, by making connections. "Long distance," an eerie experience to begin with, becomes more haunting still when Dickey extends it to include connections between living and dead spirits.

Dickey proceeds in his vision to a point "far under the grass of my grave." No matter how deep he travels, even to Hell, in the fuller mastery of his art he is confident that "my profession / Will lift me," and in lifting him, it will lift thousands of others from Hell, his readers all over the world, symbolically making long-distance phone calls all night, connecting, all the connections good. He feels the same power, whether in the basement of his home, "or flung up on towers walking / Over mountains   my charged hair standing on end." The spirit that pervades and dominates this poem, finally, can be identified as the spirit of laughter, a laughter closely akin to that of Malachi the stilt jack in Yeats's "High Talk," or the mad dancer of "A Drunken Man's Praise of Sobriety." Like these poems, "Power and Light" verges on self-parody in its hyperbolic imagery and rhetoric: "And I laugh / Like my own fate watching over me night and day."

The comic spirit of "Power and Light" recovers the ground lost by the tragic spirit in the moral dilemmas of "The Firebombing" and "Slave Quarters." If modern man feels helpless before the massive political nightmare of his time, he finds he can retreat into "pure fires of the Self" for spiritual sustenance. This is the artist's escape and salvation. If he can't connect with the tragic people of this world's hell in daylight, by direct political action, he must reach them in "the dark, / deep sway of underground." The artist's night is the "night before Resurrection Day." He will resurrect the imagination, the spiritual life, of his age. He performs these wonders, ironically, drunk in his suburban basement. A general in disguise. An unacknowledged legislator of the world. Regrettably, the philosophy *if I turn on everyone turns on with me* may offer small comfort in the political world.

If the worldly mystic spends a good portion of his day-to-day existence reconnecting with the world, at other times we find him searching for the pure moment in solitude, waiting to receive messages from the unseen beyond and to answer the call. If he is receptive enough, he may pick up clues to learning his being from a wide range of sources: a rattlesnake, a blind old woman, a caged leopard. In all such poems Dickey himself would seem to be the protagonist, the poem being a kind of reportage of an event from the author's life, in contrast with poems such as "Power and Light" and "Falling," in which the persona and the author are completely separate, on the surface level.

"The Flash" is a weak poem, hardly more than a fragment of verse, but it gives the key to understanding the revelatory moments in the other poems in the group:

> Something far off   buried deep and free
> In the country   can always strike you dead
> Center of the brain. There is never anything
> It could be   but you go dazzled . . .

You can't explain the flash logically, or fasten hold of it with your senses, but what is felt when "you go dazzled" is instantly recognizable, and can be distinguished, unerringly, from other events of the spirit. The flash is a spiritual fact that registers in the poet's intelligence with the same cold, tough certainty as a snakebite. It is a guarantee of the inner life, but also insists on the inner life of the Other, of others "far off   buried deep and free."

In "Snakebite," the encounter with the Other seems fated. "The one chosen" finds "there is no way not / To be me." There is no way out, or through the experience, except saving oneself:

> . . . It is the role
> I have been cast in;
>
> It calls for blood.
>
> Act it out before the wind
> Blows: unspilt blood
>
> Will kill you. Open
> The new-footed tingling. Cut.
> Cut deep, as a brother would.
> Cut to save it. Me.

One must act out the roles that are thrust upon one by the Other, inescapably, as by the rattlesnake's poison. Art must invade those moments in life when failure to perform the correct self-saving gesture is to die. Art is a strange kind of intimacy, a blood brotherhood, between the artist and himself. The poem must be an act of bloodletting. In saving the poem, as in saving one's life from snakebite, a man must be his own brother. No one else can help.

Midway through the action, the speaker shifts from the mortal necessity of lancing the wound to a moment of comic staging. At this point in Dickey's art, it seems appropriate and convincing for the comic spirit to interrupt the most serious human act of self-preservation. The laughter of self-dramatization parallels similar moments in "Encounter in the Cage Country," in which comic relief enhances the seriousness of the exchange between man and leopard:

> . . . at one brilliant move
>
> I made as though drawing a gun from my hip-
> bone, the bite-sized children broke
> Up   changing their concept of laughter,
>
> But none of this changed his eyes, or changed
> My green glasses. Alert, attentive,
> He waited for what I could give him;

My moves   my throat   my wildest love,
The eyes behind my eyes.

In "False Youth II," the blind grandmother's message, like the word of an oracle, is delivered with absolute certitude: "You must laugh a lot / Or be in the sun." Her advice strikes a reader as being a deeply personal and literal truth in the author's life at the time he wrote the poem, and this hunch is borne out by the relevance her words have to many of the best poems of the new volume. A comic spirit pervades poems such as "Power and Light," "Encounter in the Cage Country," and "Sun" that one had not met or foreseen in Dickey's earlier work.

Dickey presents an experience from life in "False Youth II" that taught him to see deeply into the shifting sands of his own personality as he slid, imperceptibly, from youth into middle age. Youth is a "lifetime search" for the human role, or roles, that, when acted out, will serve as a spiritual passport of entry into middle age. The necessary role may take the form of a physical gesture that perfectly corresponds to deep moves of the spirit: "My face froze . . . in a smile / That has never left me since my thirty-eighth year."

The old blind woman unknowingly assumes the role of a fortune-teller. She has developed a superhumanly receptive sense of touch. Her life is contracted intensely into her hands, her fingertips having grown fantastically sensitive and alive. As she runs her fingers over his eyes and forehead, the poetic images envision a scientific and quasi-scientific composite of data linking electromagnetism, finger painting, astronomy, genetics, and fortune-telling:

> . . . I closed my eyes as she put her fingertips lightly
> On them   and saw, behind sight   something in me   fire
> Swirl in a great shape like a fingerprint   like none other
> In the history of the earth   looping   holding its wild lines
> Of human force. Her forefinger   then her keen nail
> Went all the way along the deep middle line of my brow
> Not guessing but knowing   quivering   deepening
> Whatever I showed by it.

The wisdom of the old woman has a primeval quality about it. Her acutely sharpened instincts and sense of touch precede the scientific age and surpass recorded modern science in a revelation of human personality that draws on the learning of many sciences, but goes beyond each in its ability to *connect* them all, which is not to say this literally happens in life. It happens, rather, in the images of the poem's vision.

She leads him to discover that he has come to a crossroads in his life and art. He must learn his life, as his art, and each stage of existence—in both worlds—concludes with a search for the blueprint to the next stage. The blueprint cannot simply be willed into existence. It is contained as a deeply true, hidden map of possibility within his developing self. If there are alternative paths latent and waiting to be journeyed in the self at any particular spiritual crossroads (as in Frost's poem "The Road Not Taken"), there is one best route available at each crucial juncture. It is discoverable, and, once discovered, it has an unmistakable ring of truth: "Not guessing but knowing   quivering   deepening." Although the answer waits inside him to be released, he cannot find his way to it by himself. He arrives in himself through a deep conjunction with another being, in faith, "some kind of song may have passed / Between our closed mouths as I headed   into the ice." There must be communion with the Other. Connection.

If one of the major new themes in Dickey's fifth volume is comic dramatization of his own personality, another is sexual realism. In both, he parallels the later Yeats. If we compare the vision in "The Fiend" with that in "Falling" and "The Sheep Child," we can get an idea of how far Dickey's art has traveled between the first major poem dealing with the theme of sexual realism and the last. In "The Fiend," the free-flowing form and the split line are fully exploited. This technique is well suited to sustained psychological realism. Also, the fiend is a thoroughly convincing persona. The encounter between him and life experience, though voyeuristic and "abnormal," is presented as final, incisive, fulfilling.

But somehow, the center of the poem's vision is too far from tragedy and believable danger: the poem lacks risk, the emotional pitch of a cosmos of love/beauty stretching to contain and transform a brutal agony of being. The sexual transcendence the persona unknowingly achieves is almost too evident, preordained. Equipoise is not felt to be the outcome of a fierce yoking together of oppositely charged beings, as in the act of coitus between the farm boy and the mother ewe of "The Sheep Child":

> *. . . It was something like love*
> *From another world that seized her*
> *From behind, and she gave, not lifting her head*
> *Out of dew, without ever looking, her best*
> *Self to that great need. . . .*

The stench of evil in "The Fiend" is smothered under the catalogs of domestic inanities. There is no trace of the searing terror of "The Sheep Child," the terror of our settled scheme of things being ripped apart. It is too easy to dismiss the fiend as a genial saint—spiritually, if not bodily, harmless. "The Sheep Child" and "Falling" threaten us with glimpses into a world of becoming that is grimly near to us, a mere hand's reach away from those extensions of being into the beyond that we all easily attain in moments of emotional intensity. And yet, that farther reach somehow eludes us, staying just out of our ken. The secret of uncompromised being is just a spiritual stone's throw away, but we are cut off. These poems soar into that further beyond with a sense of effortlessness and inevitability.

"The Fiend" was a breakthrough into the hinterland of sexual transcendence, but what begins as a reader's sympathetic identification ends as a comfortably removed appreciation of the poem's novelties. "The Sheep Child" and "Falling" trap the reader in a haunting, if inexpressible, certainty that a much larger, grander, demonic world—compounded of Heaven and Hell—lies just the other side of the limits of his known, calculable existence. And it waits, like the dead, for him to step inside:

> *I woke, dying,*

> *In the summer sun of the hillside, with my eyes*
> *Far more than human. I saw for a blazing moment*
> *The great grassy world from both sides,*
> *Man and beast in the round of their need,*
> *And the hill wind stirred in my wool,*
> *My hoof and my hand clasped each other,*
> *I ate my one meal*
> *Of milk, and died*
> *Staring . . .*

The reader must be willing to drown, fly, burn with a flame that sets all dreams on fire, and be the fire.

From "The Fiend" to "Falling," Dickey has been trying to find a medium that would enable him to *use* the maximum of his creative intelligence in poetry. To this end, he has chosen in "Falling" exactly the right subject and form. Both are moving toward a rhythm of experience that can sweep away all obstacles to realizing the fullest human potential: *"One cannot just fall   just tumble screaming all that time   one must use / It."*

When a woman's life space has suddenly contracted into a few seconds, the necessity to conquer mental waste, to salvage every hidden but discoverable shred of mental possibility, becomes absolute.

The opening sections of the poem stress the extent to which the girl's will, intention, participates in her experience. Her body and mind are both forced initially into reactions of powerful self-protective resistance, a mere reflex response to shock. But her will and creative imagination take on a larger and larger quotient of control. The female style of control is mixed with passivity, but the dynamic passivity of girding the body, sensually, as she "waits for something great to take / Control of her." The beauty of healthy, fulfilled physical life is Dickey's momentary stay against the chaos of the poem's life-crushing void. Within a moment of perfectly fulfilled physical being, her spirit lives an eternity.

The girl is strangely mated to air. The first half of her long, erotic air embrace is a turning inward. She is learning how to be, to be "in her / Self." She masters "one after another of all the positions for love / Making," and each position corresponds to a new tone or motion of being. The second half of her adventure is a going outward. She is no longer waiting to be taken hold of, but now *she* is the aggressor, who "must take up her body / And fly." The shifts in her body cycle—falling, floating, flying, falling—stand for consecutive stages in a being cycle, rising, as she falls to her death, to a pinnacle of total self-realization. It is a movement from extreme self-love to extreme beyond-self love, a movement from being to becoming, from becoming to going beyond. Although her fall concludes with an autoerotic orgasm, she connects, at the moment of climax, with the spirits of farm boys and girls below; there is a profound flow of being between them. This unobstructable river of feeling between the self and the world is the life process to which Dickey ascribes ultimacy in his vision.

If ideas of rebirth and reincarnation are among the most compelling and pervasive in Dickey's art, the idea of resurrection by air—not water, earth, or fire—is the one that rises, finally, into apocalypse. A cursory glance at Dickey's biography might well support my hypothesis that, since the gravest spiritual losses to his manhood were incurred in air—via the incineration of women and children in the napalm bombing of Japan— he could be expected to seek compensatory gains to redeem himself, paradoxically, through that medium. In fact, he does achieve his most sustaining spiritual and poetic gains through the vision of air genesis. It is my hope that in the years to come Dickey will return to the perplexing questions of war and race dealt with in "The Firebombing" and "Slave Quarters," and bring to his renewed treatment of those themes—surely the most troubling specters of our day—the larger generosity of spirit we find in the vision of "Falling" and "Power and Light." If there is a passion today that can counterbalance all the hell in us, it is the ardor that fills these poems.

Erotic Pantheism in
Dickey's "Madness"

I.

In "Madness," a work ostensibly pure animal fable, James Dickey has written one of his most personal—and indeed, personally revealing—poems.[1] Under guise of the astonishing story—immediately rising to the permanence of myth or legend—of the bizarre sexual encounter between the household dog and a "rabid female fox," Dickey has enacted his most powerful allegory for the terror of human sex. Sexual terror, the turmoil of even normal ordinary sex, is his true subject, disguise it as he will with the southern gothic tall tale. To be stricken by *illicit* sexual craving is equivalent to being infected with rabies. The only cure may be death by beheading: decapitation is synonymous with total loss of rational controls, a descent into sexual *madness*. Perhaps the only *help* for such an affliction, if you happen to be a poet of genius as well as a man-soul prey to strong sexual passions, is to write a work of utmost purgative release:

> . . . strangers
> Cut off the head and carried and held it
> Up, blazing with consequence   blazing
> With freedom saying   bringing
> Help   help   madness   help.

II.

At the outset, "Madness" achieves with flawless consistency of tone the illusion of a household pet's point of view. The voice of the speaker captures the total innocence and naïveté of the dog persona with a matchless command of nuance and an economy of style that recalls Faulkner's orchestration of the idiot Benjy in *The Sound and the Fury:*

1. This essay originally appeared in *The South Carolina Review* in spring 1994.

> Lay in the house mostly living
> With children when they called   mostly
> Under the table begging for scraps lay with the head
> On a family foot
> Or stretched out on a side,
> Firesided. Had no running
> Running, ever.
> Would lie relaxed, eyes dim
>
> With appreciation, licking the pure contentment
> Of long   long notched
> Black lips. Would lap up milk like a cat and swim clear
> In brown grateful eyes. . . .

The keynote, here, is excessive comfort, too much soft effortless plea-
sure. To subject a wild animal—the wild animal locked in ourselves,
by inference—to a life of passivity and indulgence is unnatural, against
nature. It would be to invite the lawless Dionysian side of our species
to revolt, and to seek out the wild orgiastic counterpart of our neglected
hot-blooded being in the world at large:

> . . . it was best
> To get up and wander
> Out, out of sight. Help me was shouted
> To the world of females   anyone will do
> To the smoking leaves.
>
> Love could be smelt. All things burned deep
> in eyes that were dim from looking
> At the undersides of tables   patient with being the god
> Of small children.

Help me, the desperate plea for risk, for danger, is murmured by the soul
of one afflicted with a sickness unto death from inactivity, any wild fate
to be preferred to such enfeeblement.

The portrait of the female fox that follows is almost too transparently
humanized, but Dickey's comic wit and his command of southern ver-
nacular strikes the authentic ring to our ears. His zany caricature of "a
god's wild mistress" could take almost any form, creaturely or mythic:
centaur, mermaid, or minotaur (I am reminded of Yeats's poems about
sexual relations between divinities and humans, "Leda and the Swan" and

"News for the Delphic Oracle"—*Nymphs and satyrs copulate in the foam*), so why not a rabid lady fox?

> And there
> She lay, firesided, bushy-assed, her head
> On the ground wide open, slopping soap:
> Come   come close
> She said like a god's
> Wild mistress said come
> On boy, I'm what you come
>
> Out here in the bushes for. She burned alive
> In her smell and the eyes she looked at burned
> With gratitude, thrown a point-eared scrap
> Of the world's women, hot-tailed and hunted.

Like Dickey's "Sheep-Child," this fox partakes of the supernatural realm, part goddess, part human. Who among us could resist the allure of her ambrosial smell? Does she burn with earthly fires or fires of the demonic netherworld? Both, perhaps. No matter, the domestic pooch burns back, flame for flame, whatever the mystic consequences. The language of the encounter is so tactile and boldly rough-hewn, so vividly earth laden, a reader could easily overlook the gnostic, or spiritual, overtones:

> . . . she bit down
> Hard on a great yell
> To the house being eaten alive
> By April's leaves. Bawled; they came and found.

III.

A half-veiled erotic pantheism emerges here. The dog protagonist's plea, his cry for help, was "shouted" to "the world of females" *and* to "the smoking leaves," and both the fox and the leaves have answered—with a vengeance. He had been starved and hungered, equally, for sex and Nature: now both privations are resolved in the one fierce bite the fox takes into his snout.

As the drama unfolds, *firesided* evolves a startling double meaning. To begin, it suggests the light and warmth cast by the safe domestic fireplace upon the exposed sidehair of the dog lying by the hearth. Cuddled and pampered by the children, he has been *firesided* into a defenseless stupor.

The word, then, evokes all domestic security and placidity. But the fox lying in ambush, "firesided, bushy-assed," is on fire with her own heat, "burned alive in her smell." Now the word's overtones elicit danger, lethal risk. All the vocabulary of heat, of burning, has shifted from domestic safety, household comforts, to sexual incinerations, sexual flamings: "She burned alive / In her smell," while, in response, his eyes "burned / With gratitude," and finally, he is "being eaten alive / By April's leaves."

Somehow, the leaves of spring are in complicity with the rabid fox. Her rabies, not an isolated private affliction, runs rampant through Nature, and this erotic spirit is the secret pantheistic deity of this poem's cosmos. The leaves, then, by their multiplicity, are the aptest medium for this pervasive spirit. The dog shouted his yearning to the leaves, quite as intensely as to "the world of females," and hence, the leaves partake of his ravishment by the fox. This rabies can spread like *wildfire,* since the leaves themselves are secret carriers of the bacilli. At first reading, the rabid fox, alone, strikes us as being the demon who spreads the infection. But we come to know, tipped off by the luminous chain of images, that Nature hiddenly collaborates with the sex-crazed fox. In his mania, his feverish delirium, the stricken dog may dream that all the leaves are pecking at his flesh ("being eaten alive / By April's leaves"). Ultimately, they may appear to become as rapacious and all-eating as Hitchcock's *Birds.*

The children and "friends and family," hurrying to rescue the wounded pet, seem totally oblivious to signs of the tragedy that is impending. Their casual aplomb intensifies the ominous feel of secret terror building, the explosion that will devastate the placid domestic order and balance of the family household:

> The children cried
> Helping tote to the full moon
> Of the kitchen   "I carried the head"   O full of eyes
> Heads kept coming across, and friends and family
> Hurt   hurt
> The spirit of the household, on the kitchen
> Table being thick-sewed   they saying it was barbed
> Wire looked like
> It got him, and he had no business running
> Off like that. . . .

Do I detect a southern drawl in these minimal snippets of local speech? The few telling phrases of dialect seem to evoke the total verbal ambience that surrounds this scene. In their domestic malaise, the adults and kids alike deflate the dog's injury, putting it down to a mere run-in with barbed wire, little guessing that the tear in his muzzle will escalate to deep lacerations in the very fabric of their well-ordered social milieu. They suppose that the dog's wounds can be explained away as mild punishment for infraction of yard rules, "they saying it was barbed / Wire looked like / It got him, and he had no business running / Off like that. . . ."

But we, who have been briefed by the momentous overtones of charged language, know that a powerful demonic ritual has been set in motion, something like an ancient curse or plague upon the clan (a larger social unit comes into play here than a single family—the whole expanded familial community of this township), from the moment that great Nature herself commanded the dog to run astray,

> . . . and it was best
> To get up and wander
> Out, out of sight.

Now there would be no turning back, for even the "rain had sewn thick and gone / From the house where the living / Was done," and no amount of *"thick-sewing"* of the dog's rent lips with surgical black thread could undo the fateful scenario that has been decreed and initiated by the rain deity. Likewise, the reference to "the full moon of the kitchen" alerts us to the vampirism that has occurred, and the consequent transformation of the dog victim to werewolf that is quietly taking place below the kitchen table following the lip sutures, a mere cosmetic patch-up, hiding the deeper wound:

> Black lips curled as they bathed off
> Blood, bathed blood. Staggered up under
> The table making loud
> A low-born sound, and went feeling
>
> For the outer limits
> Of the woods   felt them break and take in
> The world. . . .

IV.

Although the drama in "Madness" is ascribed to a deep-South American setting, we now catch the expansive nuance of an international and timeless sweep of voice ("take in the world"). James Dickey, once again, starting from a narrowly localized episode, sets limitless vortices in motion. If we have moved beyond the "outer limits of the woods," we have been carried along by the synchronicities of the countless leaves acting in concert:

> Fireheaded   formed a thought
> Of Spring   of trees in wildfire
> Of the mind speeded up   and put all thirst
>
> Into the leaves. They grew
> Unlimited. Soap boiled
> Between black lips. . . .

A reader senses that all reckless, unbounded possibility looms here—the spirit of wild abandon is in the air. Like the marvelous psychic adventures, the out-of-body travels, of the stewardess in Dickey's poem "Falling," the dog's "mind speeded up" will crash through all barriers. We now perceive this to be a poem about mental capacities racing beyond the lawful, normal, domestic boundaries. The mentality is so radically new, it threatens to transform everything and everyone outside it into its own new reality. Hence, the terror of all other creatures that soon follows! Their very cosmos is intimidated by this totally unfamiliar alien force, which sends them all into panic, a community of repression. They, too, will rage "beyond their limits," mobilizing a power to match and contain the power of insurrection unleashed, as revealed by the rabid dog's scary "low-born sound":

> . . . the spirit ran
> Ran with house-hair
> Burr-picking madly   and after came
>
> Men   horses   spirits
> Of households leaping crazily beyond
> Their limits, dragging their bodies by the foaming throat through
>   grass
> And beggar-lice and by the red dust
> Road where men blazed and roared
> With their shoulders   blew it down and apart where it ran
> And lay down on the earth of God's
> One foot and the foot beneath the table kicked
> The white mouth shut: this was something

> In Spring in mild brown eyes   as strangers
>   Cut off the head and carried and held it
> Up, blazing with consequence   blazing
>   With freedom saying   bringing
>   Help   help   madness   help

Where does all the access of power and intensity spring from, we might ask? The emotional *seizure* that erupts, here, recalls the chaotic upheaval in the social order of a southern family triggered by incest in Faulkner's *The Sound and the Fury*. The violation of forbidden taboos, as in Dickey's poem "The Sheep-Child," unleashes a primitive brute energy. And there is no stopping this titanic flood of lawless passions until the violence and tragedy have run their course.

V.

I'm awed, afresh, by the celerity of syntax in "Madness." The speed of delivery in this poem, from first strophe to last, strikes me as unique in Dickey's entire oeuvre. The principle action could easily have sustained a poem two or three times this length. Merely to say that the work has pared away all excess is to miss the point. Dickey's technique advances to a bold thrust of delivery, a mastery of ellipses in grammar and syntax, a control of elisions that surpasses any of his previous works. His technique, as the poem unfolds, achieves progressively a tempo—a pacing, so to say—of *breathlessness*. This crescendo peaks in a passage near the finish in which the active verbs seem to multiply, incrementally, without strain or imbalance; there's so much raw, lively, intense happening, we don't think to question the quantitative proportions of style, parts of speech, or the like: "flaming . . . ran / Ran . . . burr-picking madly . . . leaping crazily . . . dragging . . . foaming . . . blazed and roared . . . blew it down and apart where it ran / And lay down . . ."

I include a few adverbs in my linkage, since they are so closely tied to the verbs they *amplify*—never merely modifiers—in these marvelously condensed lines just preceding the poem's final coda. The passage from which I extracted, above, is the closest approach to pure streamlined action I can recall in any contemporary poetry. This verse measure and medium is the Ferrari or Maserati speedster on the verse racetrack, the full velocity achieved—as in the case of the auto-Czars invoked—with no loss of elegance or classy verve of meters.

Then, I'm equivalently struck by the magical deft pullback of the denouement:

> . . . blew it down and apart where it ran
> And lay down on the earth of God's
> One foot and the foot beneath the table kicked
> The white mouth shut. . . .

Serenity, quiescence! Why aren't our hearts still pounding after the violent *effort*-ful gallop by all the players? How, indeed, does Dickey manage to scale down the feral syntactic hopscotch by so few jaunty shifts, all ease and lightness of modulation. I note that we have swung full circle in the color spectrum, as well, moving from "black lips curled as they bathed off / Blood, bathed blood," to "kicked / The white mouth shut." How do *black lips* come together in a *white mouth*? Is it simply the bloodless paleness of death? Or more soapy rabies foam bubbling out between the lips? So attentive Dickey is to the least detail of accurate anatomy, whatever the symbolic overtones to be sought, we feel that he must have witnessed a dying dog's black lips close on a final whiteness, whiteness blazing with all its inexplicable mystery. Plain, honest observation, rather than bold invention, seems to have been the guiding principle behind Dickey's imagery here. In any case, the sudden color reversion from black to white seems a perfectly apt visual counterpart to the abrupt deceleration of the action, the calming of tone and metrical pulse just prior to the poem's closing stanza.

The stanza form that Dickey has improvised for "Madness" resembles a gyroscope, a freely variable spinning top. Most stanzas whirl and interweave very long lines with short, the voice bridging the gap between one unit and another in midsentence, the spun top rarely falling to rest before the very last line, which is not a conventional line, after all, but four naked words waved like flags, or pennants, between blank spaces: "Help   help   madness   help." In midline, throughout the poem, spaces usually stand in for punctuation marks. Dickey gets more than the usual vigor of swerve or tilt from surprise line endings. Often, one-, two-, or three-word units take a measure or breath space to themselves. Several short units, in succession, as in the last line quoted above, may capture a rhythm all their own, which we can ponder as singular moments, fascinating entities of style, apart from their contexts.

VI.

The great pivot in "Madness," the irreversible shift in its scope from one family household to the full-blown pastoral community, is the moment when the now-rabid dog runs amok and bites "the youngest child":

> . . . the house
>
> Spirit jumped up beyond   began to run   shot
>
>   Through the yard and bit down
>
>   On the youngest child. And when it sprang down
>
> And out across the pasture, the grains of its footprints leapt
>
>   Free, where horses that shied from its low
>
>   New sound were gathered, and men swung themselves
>
>   Up to learn what Spring
>
>   Had a new way to tell, by bringing up
>
>   And out the speed of the fields. A long horn blew. . . .

Immediately, we know that this second bite down shall have far-reaching repercussions; it is more horrific than the first love bite, for it shall wreak havoc on all sectors of the rural society. Once the human child has been assaulted, the poem's equation tilts, inverts, all craziness redoubled, leaving no child, adult, dog, or horse untouched. One moment, the entire farm municipality lay dormant, unsuspecting, as the dog's rabies slowly incubated; the next, a "long horn blew," summoning all souls—humans and animals of the hunt, in tandem—to assemble into an army of resistance.

Simultaneously, too, warring factions in Nature—opposed divinities, say—may be perceived to choose up sides in the battle that follows. Pantheistic spirits may be at odds and come to blows, as enacted by the players they each inhabit in the drama. If the rabid dog and fox draw their superabundant energy from the leaves, from "trees in wildfire," and even wild burrs snatched from the weeds as the dog runs across the pasture ("house-hair / Burr-picking madly"), the men and horses draw their fiery power of the chase from the turf of pastureland itself ("to learn what Spring / Had a new way to tell by bringing up / And out the speed of the fields").

Their sole antagonist, the enemy that rouses them all to unified battle, is the dog's "mad head," which rages with a boundless supernatural force, a surge of erotic energy that we are reminded was conceived in one frenzied chomp of "the weather of love running wild":

>   . . . the mad head sang
>
>   Along the furrows   bouncing and echoing from earth
>
>   To earth through the body
>
>   Turning   doubling back
>
> Through the weather of love running wild and the horses full
>
>   Of strangers coming after. . . .

The head seems to have become an autonomous entity, whirling in its own orbit, self-hurtled, as if disengaged already from the dog's trunk, prophesying the actual decapitation soon to follow. This passage, more than any other perhaps, suggests that the infection in the dog's blood forms a tributary with the intense love currents rivering through Nature. The head sings in its passionate streaming, its juices reverberating with the "furrows" of just-tilled farmland, a life flow passing to-and-fro between the patches of earth it courses over; "doubling back," the head keeps drawing fire from the poison of the original love bite, and that fount is "running wild" through its blood vessels.

Finally, the currents surging through the dog and Nature seem to over-spill into an electromagnetic field, picked up by even the long segments of fence wire:

> Fence wire fell and rose
> Flaming with messages as the spirit ran
> Ran with house-hair
> Burr-picking madly . . .

Not the mistaken "barbed wire," this, which the deluded family had supposed gave the dog its slash. No, this "fence wire" seems to be everywhere continuous in the fields and, as such, it picks up the charge of the various creatures rocketing past. This mystic fence wire, like the wire in Dickey's early short poem named after it, serves as a secret conduit for fevers or passions coursing through the living creatures that grasp it or zoom near:

> . . . a man who holds
> His palm on the top tense strand
> With the whole farm feeding slowly
> And nervously into his hand.
>
> If the wire were cut anywhere
> All his blood would fall to the ground
> And leave him standing and staring
> With a face as white as a Hereford's.
>
> from "Fence Wire"

A force like lightning that can surge through animal flesh, metal fence wire, and tree trunks alike, this fierce charge of *rabies*—emanating from "the weather of love"—finally becomes a pervasive interconnecting effluence in the cosmology of "Madness." It is a wave pulse that easily leaps the usual genetic hurdles between animal species, or the atomic barriers between flesh and metal and wood and leaf cells. This effluence partakes of all beings and atomic structures in the cosmos of the fields. As the rabies of love grows ever stronger, it pulls more and more of the energies of the very atmosphere, earth and air and fire commingled, into its vortex.

In counterreaction, all humans and creatures in pursuit have been yanked into modes "beyond their limits," stretching their skins or hides to constrain the dog's dangerous new identity:

> And when it sprang down
> And out across the pasture, the grains of its footprints leapt
> Free, where horses that shied from its low
>
> New sound were gathered, and men swung themselves
> Up to learn what Spring
> Had a new way to tell, by bringing up
> And out the speed of the fields. A long horn blew. . . .
>
> Men   horses   spirits
> Of households leaping crazily beyond
> Their limits, dragging their bodies by the foaming throat through
>   grass
>   And beggar-lice and by the red dust
>   Road where men blazed and roared
> With their shoulders   blew it down and apart where it ran

The new reality, the revolutionary new element in this smug self-complacent backwoods culture, is heralded by the dog's "low new sound," which is scary and threatening. It is the voice of rebellion, the spirit of raw sexual freedom ("the weather of love running wild"). Even the horses *shied* away from it, at first. It is recognized to be a power so strong, it must either be vanquished and suppressed, or it may convert all things, all other beings and entities, into its radical new essence. By a stunning irony, implicit in the language and imagery of this passage, the various repressive agents mobilized and assembled to destroy the dog-carrier of this plague of love bacilli seem to be infected already by a rabieslike fever themselves, when they are just on the verge of catching up with the fugitive runaway hound and blowing him "down and apart" with their rifles: "leaping crazily beyond / Their limits, dragging their bodies by the foaming throat through grass . . ."

Their throats, too, are *foaming*, whether from rabies or some other equally abnormal fever and brain-twisting passion, the counterfever of resistance, say, putting down the erotic uprising. Such *madness*, it would seem, can only be countered and defused by an equal and opposing madness.

VII.

James Dickey's imagery in "Madness" compels the reader's ear to accept the amazing claim that inanimate things can become the vehicle and medium for ghostly spirits sweeping across the poem's landscape. Doubtless, this is a poem about the miracle world that lurks, always, within normal everyday happenings. It is the Other World of Holy Specters crying out for momentary rest stops in the world of matter, flesh or inanimate forms, interchangeably:

> Staggered up under
> The table making loud
> A low-born sound, and went feeling
>
> For the outer limits
> Of the woods   felt them break and take in
> The world   the frame turn loose and the house
> Not mean what it said it was. . . .

To state this unique mode of happening in the universe in terms of the house inscrutably hatching into a new form, an utterly novel identity: what a marvelous way to articulate the total annulment of domestic safety, all normal stability and expectation gone awry. A fantastic new species of event has taken over the scheme of things. The house itself speaks with a new voice; its speech, like the woods' speech, threatens to alter, permanently, the world around it.

The specter, the message-carrier, inhabits one host after another: the dog's larynx, the woods, the house frame, the leaves, the "grains" of the dog's "footprints," which "leapt free" of his doggy paws, the fence wire that "fell and rose / Flaming with messages." That disembodied spirit, perhaps, is the real persona in this enchanting fantasia which, like Shakespeare's *Ariel,* can inhabit a wide succession of beings and entities as it works its way across the poem's wildly expansive spiritual trajectory.

As I said at the outset, sexual terror is the central motif. The spirit of Eros lurks everywhere: it takes possession of the fox, passes to the domestic dog, and finally, is unleashed upon us all. The demonic possession becomes all-encompassing, and only an act of uttermost purgation, like the lancing of a great pus-swollen boil, can set things aright. Hence, the ritual beheading of the dog.

Polarities abound, everyplace, in the poem's imagery. Many key images, double-edged, cut two ways. Toward the last, two feet are mentioned, separately, in the same line:

> And lay down on the earth of God's
> One foot and the foot beneath the table kicked
> The white mouth shut.

"God's / One foot," the final resting place for the dog's head, is earth itself, while the "foot beneath the table" belongs to the master of the household, tapping the family dog's head for the last time. The dog, himself, was repeatedly designated the "god of small children," always printed with lower case "g", his head by the fireplace reclining on "God's foot," differentiated by capital "G". The "barbed wire," early on, signified a mundane boundary, lacking all resonance or overtones. It gives place to the "fence wire" that "fell and rose / Flaming with messages," a luminous conveyor of truth or vision. "The smoking leaves," lying dormant after the leaf bonfire by the yard, are supplanted by the leaves of "trees in wildfire" that "grew unlimited," these the direct recipient of the rabid waking dog's new expanded consciousness ("the mind speeded up"). The dog himself who, prior to the central action, "had no running / Running, ever," then compresses a whole lifetime's running into an unstoppable mad dash to his gun-down death.

Finally, the dog's *head,* forever lying by the fireside, or petted and tapped into lassitude under the kitchen table, by a single blast of lovesickness is sent into violent oscillations between furrows of farmland, "bouncing and echoing from earth to earth." Then, hacked from its body by the vigilantes, the head is held aloft for all to see in the passing procession of country folk, paraded as a trophy of the hunt, then foisted into the air as a warning to future transgressors of the civil order (not unlike the historic southern lynchings of African Americans accused of rape, burglary, or lesser offenses):

> . . . as strangers
> Cut off the head and carried and held it
> Up, blazing with consequence . . . .

VIII.

We are briefed, repeatedly, that Spring, "the weather of love," is the secret impresario, the mover and shaker behind the scenes of "Madness."

(1)   That was then, before the Spring
               Lay down and out
         Under a tree, not far but a little far and out
               Of sight of the house.

(2)   The head, lying on God's foot, firesided
                 Fireheaded   formed a thought
         Of Spring   of trees in wildfire
         Of the mind speeded up. . . .

(3)   . . . men swung themselves
               Up to learn what Spring
         Had a new way to tell. . . .

(4)   . . . this was something
         In Spring in mild brown eyes   as strangers
         Cut off the head and carried and held it
         Up, blazing with consequence   blazing
               With freedom saying   bringing
               Help   help   madness   help.

The last reference to Spring, which closes the poem, is the quietest. But it's the most spooky, premonitory, in its warning that even the least aggressive being in the safe domestic household can become, instantaneously and unwittingly, the agent of immense destructive passions. Do not be fooled by those "mild brown eyes"—they, too, can become limitlessly love-crazed.

The Long Cry

Dickey's ''Mercy''

In "Mercy," James Dickey's art is hell-bent on freeing itself from the bonds, the stylistic trappings, of literature.[1] The voice of his narrator approaches, more nearly than ever before, a primeval sigh of yearning— "this night mortality wails out." The one word title, as in "Blood" and "Madness," is the tip-off. These are poems of fierce singleness of message and intent. They bleed on the page. As in later Yeats of the *Crazy Jane* sequence and "The Spur," these poems scarcely hold in check a passion to condone unbridled sex:

<blockquote>

      Ah, this night   this night mortality wails out
Over Saint Joseph's   this night and every   over Mercy
    Mercy
        Mercy Manor. Who can be dressed right for the long cry
      Who can have his tie knotted to suit the cinder Doctors'
      Parking lot? O yes I'm walking   and we go   I go
          In   into a whorehouse
         And convent rolled
    Into something   into the slant streets of slum
        Atlanta. I've brought the house mother
         A bottle of gin. She goes for ice
      Rattling the kitchen somewhere over   under
         The long cry. Fay hasn't come in
            Yet; she's scrubbing
    For Doctor Evans. . . .

</blockquote>

Many lines and phrases veer off into lone orbits. They would function as separate free entities; the spaces around the clumps of words suggest that they flare out into openness, each a self-contained articulate *wail* that embodies the human essence, "the long cry." That marvelously hypnotic

---

1. This essay originally appeared in *The Texas Review* in fall/winter 1994.

phrase, a recurrent word chant, evokes, by turns, the prolonged moan of a sexual climax, or a hospital patient crying out in pain under the surgeon's knife.

The banal and purportedly barren setting of a brothel predisposes us for low comedy, so we are taken by surprise—late in the poem—when the moments of naked soul flights burst forth from the pedestrian template:

> O take me into
> Your black. Without caring, care
> For me. Hold my head in your wide scrubbed
> Hands bring up
> My lips. I wail like all
> Saint Joseph's   like mortality
> This night   and I nearly am dead
> In love   Collapsed on the street   struck down
> By my heart . . .
> She would bend
> Over me like this   sink down
> With me in her white dress
> Changing to black   we sink
> Down flickering
> Like television   like Arthur Godfrey's face
> Coming on   huge   happy
> About us   happy
> About everything   O bring up
> My lips   hold them down don't let them cry
> With the cry   close   closer   eyeball to eyeball
> In my arms, O queen of death
> Alive, and with me at the end.

It is a suavely purifying vision, for all the hopeless drab boredom of Arthur Godfrey's big face having its final blue-collar say-so, demystifying the lovers' last embrace as they leap into otherworldly trance.

The gabble of the *House Mother* in "Mercy" is a radical new push into bare, unadorned flatness of common speech. Dickey captures, perfectly, the feel of her sweet, clumsy, unaffected boorish chatter, a working widow reciting the unglamorous facts of her bio:

> The kids the Mother   the House
> Mother says, all act like babies these days. Some of them are, I say

                In a low scream. Not all, she says, not all.
                        You ever been a nurse?
          I ask. No, my husband was in wholesale furniture.
                    Passed away last year of a kidney
                Disease; they couldn't do anything for him
                    At all: he said you go and work
                  With those girls who've been so good
                      To me. And here I am, Good
                      Looking. Fay ought to be
              Here in a little while. . . .

So much human and artistic protocol is averted here by a few deft strokes.
The marriage was fine, hub went to whores, told his wife—his dying
wish, then, was for her to commandeer the women who had *cared for*
him. Whatever they gave, it wasn't just perfunctory or mechanical. He
might have *willed* them his estate, to spite an unforgiving wife. Instead,
he willed them his wife's caretaking. It's all in the family.

Dickey successfully thumbs his nose at social mores, literary conven-
tions, even his own more formal aesthetics, as once again, he's testing
the limits—ours and poetry's. How far can you go, in stripping away
any least veneer of civilized or cultured language and measure, how far
in transcribing an ordinary house *Madam's* speech, and still enjoy the
expressive power and intensity of lyric verse? The lilt of living speech
triumphs over the supposed literary apostasy, that apparent stylistic void.
Indeed, Dickey's style in "Mercy," as in Hemingway's best dialogue, wrests
from the most banal-seeming rudimentary speech a fiercely plain and
clean artistry.

How does the author mediate between levity and heart's true anguish?
How, in so short a space, to bridge the immense gaps between "low
scream" and "the long cry"? "Low scream" is amiable jokiness. "Long
cry" is both achingly sexual and otherworldly. Both of the body's passion
and of the soul's passion. The comic spirit in this poem, so earthy and
Rabelaisian, is deceptive. The lightheartedness, or lightness of touch,
inexplicably deepens the pained seriousness, even as it seems to soften or
shroud that pain: the sexual terror is real, it rings true in a new way, for
all the playfulness of tone, the genial good-hearted banter between the
persona and his interlocutress, "The House Mother of Mercy Manor."

House Mother suggests, alternatively, live-in chaperone of a sorority,
headmistress of a boarding school for girls, or chief nun of a convent: all,
to be sure, are nutty euphemisms, the last most outrageous and whimsical

and shameless, though it rings true in context ("I go / In   into a whore-
house / And convent rolled / Into something   into the slant streets of
slum / Atlanta"). The strength of the poem's humor, its resilience, effuses
from this character. All such roles are immanent in her brio of speech—
the voice can accommodate itself to the widest range of overtones.

"Mother of Mercy," set apart as a singular line centered on the axis,
most strongly connotes the role of spiritual mentor, or convent head. She
eludes, in all ways, the stereotype of a whorehouse madam, coming to her
new post from a purely respectable and wholesome past—housewife of
a businessman, a merchant "in wholesale furniture." Her career history,
if you will, is at the furthest remove from the cliché. No erstwhile—if
reformed—prostitute, herself, who has worked her way up the ranks
to the *headship* of her profession, she carries about her, rather, the am-
bience of a matronly volunteer for a social-service job, unremunerated
and selfless; the brothel itself might be a crisis nursery for orphans or
homeless waifs:

> The kids the Mother   the House
> Mother says, all act like babies these days. Some of them are, I say
> In a low scream. Not all, she says, not all. . . .

We may envisage, in her composite of the homely arts and brawny
physique, a figure akin to Chaucer's Wife of Bath. Indeed, by so few
snippets of her speech, Dickey has given us a portrayal of woman—
jovial and hammy and openhearted—as memorable in cameo as a fully
elaborated heroine of a novel.

One might well start with this poem, in launching a study of James
Dickey's women, both in poetry and in fiction. Already, in "Mercy,"
we can grasp the impressive range of his gallery of types. Consider the
contrast between the two central female prototypes, the *House Mother*—
who remains nameless—and Fay. If "Mother of Mercy" is a presiding
eminence who "bulks" like the omnipresent television set, looming large
by her extrovert pose from the instant the speaker arrives, Fay is an
elusive wraith, the lofty remote spirit of the household ("Fay hasn't come
in / Yet; she's scrubbing / For Doctor Evans"). Usually absent, employed
for long stretches as a nurse in the hospital next door, her popularity
with the clientele of Mercy Manor has endued her very name, Fay, with
a mythic status and aura.

So bodily preoccupied with keeping up the functions of the house,
the *House Mother* bustles from room to room. We hear her above ceilings,
below floors, through walls, mixing drinks and disposing refreshments

("she goes for ice / Rattling the kitchen somewhere over   under / The long cry"). Has she moved into the preexisting brothel, or transferred the whole gaggle of working ladies into her husband's house, following the funeral? It's ambiguous, either reading is plausible ("Turn out the light as you go up / To your husband's furniture"). Whichever, she comes across like a forward appendage, some human excrescence, of the house she so lustily oversees, her deportment a prow to the many-storied urban ship, whereas Fay, a sashaying legend, is the enchanted spirit of the household. She's a mermaid, of sorts, equally at home in her twin roles of nurse and whore. Yet we do perceive in her a Jekyll/Hyde turmoil as she molts from one skin into another:

> Is that some stranger's
> Blood on your thigh? O love I know you by the lysol smell you give
> Vaseline. Died   died
> On the table. . . .
> There must be some way she can strip
> Blood off   somebody's blood   strip and comb down and out
> That long dark hair. She's overhead
> Naked she's streaming
> In the long cry   she has her face in her hands
> In the shower, thinking of children
> Her children in and out
> Of Saint Joseph's   she is drying   my eyes burn
> Like a towel   and perfume and disinfectant battle
> In her armpits   she is stamping
> On the ceiling to get her shoes to fit: Lord, Lord, where are you,
> Fay? O yes, you big cow-bodied
> Love o yes you have changed
> To Black   you are in deep
> Dark and your pale face rages
> With fatigue. . . .

Perhaps Dickey conceives Fay as a self-embattled soul, struggling to merge the two socially antithetic roles that cohabit in her workdays ("you are in deep / Dark and your pale face rages / With fatigue"). Whatever pain, confusion, or ambivalence she may feel, she is redeemed by the honest passion and radiant being she brings to her work ethic, "you big / Bosomed hard handed hard / Working worker for Life, you." She appears to invest her *labors* with the same resilient skill and caring, whether "she's scrubbing / For Doctor Evans," or holding "my head in your wide scrubbed / Hands."

The poem marvelously enthralls the reader with Fay's mysteries of transformation. The juxtapositions of imagery of the hospital and brothel, operating room and bedroom, surgery and lovemaking, is totally credible and hypnotic. Dickey exquisitely plays upon our usually neglected sense of smell—the contrast of odors is most telling, since each switch in fragrance itself symbolizes, forcibly, her role reversals. Yet, for all the suggestive power of Fay's shower-taking, her washing and cleansing to rid herself of one identity before garbing herself in the other (black negligee replacing white uniform), the most gripping and revelatory images are those that suggest the two identities are seamlessly intertwined. There is no separating or disentangling them, finally: a mermaid, she is borne equally of land and sea, of medical ward and boudoir: "the lysol smell you give / Vaseline . . . perfume and disinfectant battle / In her armpits." The most abiding and incisively memorable images are these, which evoke her subconscious unity of being. She hangs together, we can whiff it, it's all one effulgence!

As the poem's action moves toward the arrival of Fay, whose impending appearance—though hinted, repeatedly—is delayed until halfway through the verses, Dickey's abiding tone and stylistic timbre slowly modulate from zany lowbrow comedy to high seriousness:

> The last door opens.
> It is Fay. This night mortality wails out. Who died,
> My love? Whom could you not do anything for? Is that some stranger's
> Blood on your thigh? O love I know you by the lysol smell you give
> Vaseline. Died   died
> On the table. . . .

Prior to this passage, the narrator struck the tone of a passive and slightly detached witness, one who enacts the camera eye and ear of an objective—if comic—reporter. But from the moment of Fay's entry on stage ("The last door opens. / It is Fay"), his voice quavers, it tilts into a surprising helplessness and tenderness. She sweeps him from poised remove to utmost vulnerability. He nearly swoons at her mixed scents.

This first glimpse of the speaker's raw passion gives over to an interlude of dialogue, the *House Mother* uttering a condensed bio of Fay's life, much as she had previously summed up in a nutshell her own marital history:

> She'll just be a minute. These are good girls, the Mother
> Says. Fay's a good girl. She's been married; her aunt's
> Keeping the kids. I reckon you know that, though. I do,
>   And I say outside
>   Of time, there must be some way she can strip
> Blood off   somebody's blood   strip and comb down and out
>   That long dark hair.

There's no turning back now. The male voice is pulled into irresistible trance; he is enraptured by anticipation of sex with Fay, but, simultaneously, his discourse is swirled into a zone "outside / Of time," a place of pure spirit where angels and demons hold court. We have moved from the temporal flux to the timeless *Other*, and James Dickey is at his most brilliant when he enters this supernatural dimension, still inextricably anchored to the flesh, the beautiful woman heard in the shower overhead taking him, audibly, into her privacies of body:

>   She's overhead
>   Naked she's streaming
> In the long cry   she has her face in her hands
>   In the shower, thinking of children
>   Her children in and out
> Of Saint Joseph's   she is drying   my eyes burn
>   Like a towel   and perfume and disinfectant battle
>   In her armpits   she is stamping
> On the ceiling to get her shoes to fit: Lord, Lord, where are you,
>   Fay? O yes, you big cow-bodied
>   Love o yes you have changed
>   To black   you are in deep
>   Dark and your pale face rages
>   With fatigue. . . .

When before, in Dickey's work, have we beheld the mysteriously shared communion of this passage? The woman in the shower *rages* to convert her very metabolism from nurse to paid lover, raging to overcome bodily exhaustion of her day shift in the hospital to renew her vigor for the night shift of amours, raging to give her best physical bounty, in equivalent drafts, to both livelihoods. This private ecstasy of *rage* in the shower, then, is tapped into by the protagonist, her secret sharer, the man one floor below who hears all, so feelingly, he might as well be present in the shower by her side. It is a quiet, tender voyage of empathy and vicarious participation that recalls the out-of-body transport and ecstacies, the dream flights, of Dickey's most legendary heroine—the stewardess in "Falling." As she slowly fell to her death, she underwent a series of miraculous rebirths and metamorphoses that fed our hopes for an immortal life, a survival beyond the grave, of the spirit of Eros that she gorgeously embodied and projected: "she still has time to die / *Beyond explanation*" (from "Falling"), "I say, *outside / Of time,* there must be some way she can strip / Blood off" (from "Mercy"); the italicized phrases are the male narrator's code words for grasping the woman's transcendent leaps beyond her body's peaks, her outer limits of fleshly experience.

Like the stewardess, Fay, unknowingly, travels on the wings of her physical beauty—via the male alter ego's witnessing—into a realm beyond time and space as we know it, "she's overhead / naked she's streaming / In the long cry." That ecstatic moaning, the prolonged sigh of the beloved, lifts us out of our accustomed limits, boundaries, and hurtles us into the life of the *Other.* In his exalted love state, his ardor, the male protagonist keenly *listens:* he garners prodigies in the voice of his beloved, and he reciprocates in kind:

> I'll give you something
> Good   something like a long cry
> Out over the ashes of cars   something like a scream through
> hundreds of bright
> Bolted-down windows. . . .

No matter how many "bolted-down windows," or how many floors and ceilings of a many-storied house, they cannot shut out or muffle that "scream"; it carries through all walls, over all obstacles. This outcry, starting in an ordinary person's larynx, attains supersonic levels that pass beyond the limits of normal hearing, but it is never lost on our bewitched persona's ears.

The listener in this poem, the ardent narrator, becomes elevated into his final love trance by gradual stages. Ever in the comic, lightweight opening passage of "Mercy," he is allured by the love cries that seem to be drifting up or down to him, through floors and ceilings of Mercy Manor:

> I've brought the House Mother
> A bottle of gin. She goes for ice

> Rattling the kitchen somewhere over   under
>   The long cry. Fay hasn't come in
>   Yet. . . .

Ice rattlings and sex cries are intermingled, randomly, in this pastiche of a domestic setting. But already, we find the otherworldly nuance in the cries coming at us from all directions of the house, above, below, to any side, as if the floors and walls, themselves, embody and articulate those wails, the whole house's integument a shell that bespeaks and echoes the voice box of lovemaking. *The long cry.*

Likewise, the "bright / Bolted-down windows" of the hospital next door cannot contain, or hold back, the screams and wails of sufferers. The windows, too, partake of the belted-out messages of love and pain that resound through them. In this sound-box cosmos, the floors and walls and windows magically inflate the dying wails and love cries of the inmates, rather than muting them. The edifice itself becomes an amplifier, a huge steel-and-concrete many-tiered equivalent to an electric sound box at a rock concert.

So much of the sexual undercurrent in "Mercy" accrues from a chain of such images. The craving for love builds, incrementally, as *the long cry* echoes and reechoes from floor to floor. Fay's unearthly sexual power in the poem is heralded both by the surreal mix of olfactory images ("perfume and disinfectant battle / In her armpits") and by the chorus of body rumblings and whistlings and tappings that come filtering down to the listener below floors, whose appetite for love-play is whetted by the many auditory enticements:

> She's overhead
> Naked she's streaming
> In the long cry   she has her face in her hands
> In the shower, thinking of children
> Her children in and out
> Of Saint Joseph's   she is drying   my eyes burn
> Like a towel   and perfume and disinfectant battle
> In her armpits   she is stamping
> On the ceiling to get her shoes to fit: Lord, Lord, where are you,
>   Fay?. . . .

The fury of erotic anticipation that has compounded in the course of these overheard body swishings is so potent, the love client who awaits Fay's amours can hardly contain himself: "Lord, Lord, where are you, Fay?"

If Fay survives intact on the page, an integral self despite her double life, it is perhaps owing to the vivacity with which her indissoluble portrait resonates with the poem's central dualism, as evoked by the cryptic frightful line that jump-starts the work, "this night mortality wails out." Those wails, we soon learn, are, interchangeably, love cries and death cries, wails of a lover in sexual bliss, wails of a patient dying "on the table." Fay amazingly personifies, by her twin careers, this mystic dichotomy at the heart of the poem's vision.

Does the narrator die of a heart attack in the poem's final passage, as a few of this work's commentators have suggested?

> . . . and I nearly am dead
> In love   Collapsed on the street   struck down
> By my heart, with the wail
> Coming to me, borne in ambulances   voice
> By voice   into Saint Joseph's   nearly dead
> On arrival   on the table beyond
> All help,

Or, as I surmise, has he been catapulted into a ghostly union with all mortally wounded, suffering, and deathbed humanity, the whole Global Family of anguish, *wails of mortality* circling the planet earth, "voice by voice," his community spirit fostered by his liaison, his sexual linkage, with Fay—the woman who perfectly embodies the dual essence of love and death, apropos her hybrid job shifts?

Such are the marvels spawned by transcendent love, a love that takes its mating couple into an otherworldly zone, "outside of time." Odd romanticism, this of Dickey's, which would ascribe to a man's infrequent couplings with a nurse/prostitute the power to conceive a vision of brotherhood and all-embracing community. Such I take to be the upshot of this work's denouement:

> She would bend
> Over me like this   sink down
> With me in her white dress
> Changing to black   we sink
> Down flickering
> Like television   like Arthur Godfrey's face
> Coming on   huge   happy
> About us   happy

> About everything   O bring up
> My lips   hold them down don't let them cry
> With the cry   close   closer   eyeball to eyeball
> In my arms, O queen of death
> Alive, and with me at the end.

Very chancy, indeed! Artistically, it's a perilous risk to attach to Arthur Godfrey's face on the perennially "flickering" television screen of the brothel a vision of all Americans, one nation of suffering couch potatoes, indivisible and allied in an odd faith in love with the talk-show host (yesterday's Letterman or Leno); but improbably enough, the serio-comic vision does come off. *A Blue Collar Apocalypse.*

False Murder

I don't know if I can put my finger on the secrets. All mystery, all limitless possibility, is lurking around the hard edges of these lines, the bare, pruned silhouettes of these haunted minimalist stanzas:

> In a cold night
> Of somebody. Is there other
> Breath? What did I say?
> Or do?
>
> Mercy.
> MERCY!
>
> There is nothing.
> But did I do it? I did something.
> Merciful, merciful
> O God, what? And
>
> Am I still drunk?
> Not enough O

The word blocks seem to dangle in space, *on* the page space, like floating cutouts hung from an invisible string, an axis cutting each line in half, strange four-sided parallelograms of words rotating in space like flat two-dimensional shapelets in a Calder mobile. Or perhaps they are glowing blood spots the narrator sees before his eyes, heavily blinking himself awake from a half-drunk stupor. Red and white neon-lit blobs hung in the pitch dark night of the strange motel room. The spots may flutter and sway as he blinks—hallucinatory. Are they real artifacts held suspended above his face, or mere eye blots he projects on the dark?

Each is a trembling spare message of syllables, a miniword packet, a blurted verbal sigh against the room's self-obliterating void:

108

Is there any light O where
Do you touch this room?
O father

Of Heaven my head cannot
Lift but my hand maybe—
Nobody is breathing   what weapon
Was it? Light smashes

Down there is nothing but
Blood blood all over

Me and blood. Her hair is smeared.
My God what has got loose
In here at last? Who is

This girl? . . .

All transpires in the few seconds before he reaches for the wall, desperate and helpless to find the overhead-light switch. The moment of turning on the light is dreadful ("Light smashes / Down"), brightness falling on the bloody bed like an avalanche of white falling on the red. When has the mere flicking of a light switch ever unleashed such frantic energy into a poem? To belabor the obvious, this *is* the dark night of the soul, all condensed in a single prolonged moment's middle-of-the-night wake-up in an unknown motel room.

The potential for scathing, merciless self-judgment, here, is unbounded. Do I awaken to find myself guilty of drunken rape, guilty of murder?

Mercy.
MERCY!

Whose forgiveness do I seek, but my own? Whose judgment do I most fear, but my own? Both an extension of God's wrath, or God's mercy.

The poem's genius is its power to isolate and illumine a mundane setting, an appointed time and place on the quotidian map, for the soul's unexpected excoriating cross-examination and purgation. It all happens so swiftly, but ends in such genial lightness of touch, such tender pathos of comic relief,

> She sighs she turns in the slaughtered sheets
>   To me in the blood of her children.
>   Where in what month?,

we can forget that—for a few agonized moments—the soul's fate hung in the balance, and the prognosis for reprieve was bleak.

Cross-examinations of the soul *in extremis*. As in Yeats's late master-work, "The Man and the Echo," the authentic timbre of voice leaves no question:

> All that I have said and done,
> Now that I am old and ill,
> Turns into a question till
> I lie awake night after night
> And never get the answers right.
> Did that play of mine send out
> Certain men the English shot?
> Did words of mine put too great strain
> On that woman's reeling brain?
> Could my spoken words have checked
> That whereby a house lay wrecked?
> And all seems evil until I
> Sleepless would lie down and die.

The experience recounted by both poems unmistakably rings true, friends, it's autobiography, it happened. The author goes back to this barely survived hiatus in his wholesome selfhood, his daily well-being. He's *been* there, and he takes us with him. Hence, we can judge Dickey on moral grounds—perhaps he was a habitual one-night stander. Or we can step back *with him* into a dimension beyond social mores to the gamble with eternity.

"Blood" is a brave, gutsy exercise in *True Confession* gone awry into transcendence. Revelation springs, as if by accident, from steady hard staring at the worsts, the self's darkest moments. O we all have them at the ready, deny them as we shall. This work is shot through with open admission of the ugly streaks in our spirit. Again, as in Yeats's "The Man and the Echo," no readers, or audience of listeners out there, makes any difference. This is cross-examination at the finish line, the only ump is the inner censor. All the safe trappings of conventional art, past successes in verse, are tossed on the dump:

Nobody is breathing   what weapon
  Was it? Light smashes

  Down there is nothing but
    Blood blood all over

Me and blood. Her hair is smeared.
  My God what has got loose
    In here at last? Who is

      This girl? She is
  Some other town some far
    From home: knife

Razor, fingernails O she has been opened
  Somewhere and yet . . .

"Got loose" refers, eerily, to the speaker's own body and psyche, as if loose nuts and bolts of the self are flying wild, flying apart; this breakdown, it seems, has been a long time coming on ("at last"). Such lines are hits to the author's solar plexus, nerve pinchings, wrenchings of the joints. The quiet syntactical swerves here are so abrupt that they may well take the writer himself by surprise. They have a chance improvisatory edge to them. They are, I feel, the verbal equivalent of acupuncture or chiropractic performed on the joints of the artist's musculoskeletal system. . . .

I'll try again. No other poetry of Dickey's, anybody's, quite prepares us for this abbreviated notation, perilous and grim in its self-accusatory lashings. Like Donne's *Holy Sonnets,* or Berryman's *Eleven Addresses to the Lord,* "Blood" is a prayer to the Holy Spirit in us all:

    In a cold night
Of somebody. Is there other
Breath? What did I say?
    Or do?

    Mercy.
    MERCY!

There is nothing.
But did I do it? I did something.
  Merciful, merciful

O God, what? . . .

There's so much space flying around the few words, we stand naked with him, admit all wrongs, but wait, none that we don't deserve. Own up to our worsts, but no more. "What did I say? / Or do?" Those two self-impugnings don't leave out much. Brutal self-examination, yes; but we've all been there, so it rings true.

Dickey's style is so thinned out, so lean and bare, why indeed should we call this poetry at all? Yeats wrote rhymed couplets in "The Man and the Echo." What trappings, what equipage of verse measure, still abides in "Blood"? Unfailingly, I feel, the measure captures the impulsive seizures of a spirit challenging itself, hurling spears of censure at the wrongdoer inside our skins. Style is a pure graph, or map, of sensibility at the dead ends. No frills, no literary ornaments, will be tolerated. This is total nondecorative art. The few chosen words will sink or save the artist's soul, artist's ass. No other words will be brooked:

> Nobody is breathing   what weapon
>   Was it? Light smashes
>
>   Down there is nothing but
>   Blood blood all over
>
> Me and blood. Her hair is smeared.
>   My God what has got loose
>   In here at last? . . .

Each line, each breath measure, is a raw instinct roaring out—erupting like animal squeals. Dickey's medium is more spare and austere than ever before. All his accustomed literary artifice has been scraped away, pared off. What remains is pure clean saying out. The urgency and terror of this voice, the voice of a naked soul trapped in its own private waking nightmare, must find a scale of language dry and plain enough to simulate that pure shock of rude wake-up in strange motel dark.

Each phrase is a keen-edged surprise, language working fiercely hard to erase itself, to push excess syllables off the page, words ridding themselves of the very pretense of conveying any but the most primitive and blunt particulars of this lived-through moment. The extended drawn-out few seconds have a magical ultimacy about them. The poem would take upon itself the absolute risk of uttering the charge that electrifies the speaker's intensely pained nervous system. The illusion bravely sought is for the poem to strike a reader's ear and eye as if those aches of first awakening—both sensory twinges and mental wails—have been translated, indeed transfigured, purely into these fewest words.

The art of "Blood" is stylistic pioneering, linear and stanzaic experimentalism, of the first order. And yet, the few sparse lines are so modest in their claim to space on the printed page, a fast reading could easily miss all of their terror of artistic brinkmanship, a terror that I feel transcends the living man's frightful wake-up in an unknown motel room with a stranger "in a cold night." The artist, then, in the half-drunk, half-hungover one-night stander, is embarked on a more dangerous pilgrimage of the spirit than the speaker's fear that he may have committed rape and murder, while drunk. The two terrors are juxtaposed in this singular voice, the one dread matching the other in intensity.

The Knife-edge of Supernal Being

James Dickey's *Deliverance* broke new ground in the art of fiction.[1] His first translations, which make up roughly a third of his remarkable new collection and are no less radical and innovatory, break new ground in the art of transcribing the poetry of foreign tongues ("un-English") into his native tongue. As Dickey moves across the sound barrier between the inscrutable *other* language and his own, we sense a wizardry of infinitesimal shifts and adjustments not unlike the atomic transmutations of one metal slowly alchemizing into another. Whatever the line and stanzaic pattern of the original poem, Dickey employs a characteristic spacing device to suggest the pauses of magical interlocking of two voices, two languages:

> The day works on
> works out its transparent body. With
> fire, the bodiless hammer.
> Light knocks me flat.
> Then lifts me. Hooked on-
> to the central flame-stone, I am nothing
> but a pause between
> Two vibrations
> of pressureless glow. . . .

Bewitched by the sorceries of dual authorship in "Mexican Valley," after Octavio Paz, a reader catches glimmerings of a profound cohabitation of two human spirits in the one verse-skin.

In other new modes of Dickey's ventriloquist art ("Exchanges," "Re-unioning Dialogue"), the author—via two alternating speakers—achieves the illusion that he *exchanges*, or barters, larynxes with a succession of kindred humans, as if organs of speech can be transplanted from one man's throat to another's. Dickey groans, sighs, "mumbles" lofty utterance with the vocal chords of "a dead poet" (Trumbull Stickney), the

---

1. This review of *The Strength of Fields*, (Garden City, N.Y.: Doubleday, 1980), originally appeared in *The Sewanee Review* in 1981.

newly inaugurated U.S. president (Jimmy Carter), a classic hall-of-fame football coach (Vince Lombardi), astronauts, New York City marathon runners, peacetime fighter pilots drugged in "flight-sleep," as well as the many supreme living poets of other languages, such as Paz, Montale, and Yevtushenko.

"The one authentic genius writing poetry in America today is James Dickey," chanted James Wright to a class of my creative-writing students some years ago. Now that Wright is dead, Dickey and Robert Penn Warren are among the handful of surviving visionaries of our language who belong to that elect few: master prosodists balancing on the knife-edge of supernal Being, whose genius for outstripping the supposed limits of available experience is wedded to matchless artistry.

The Glacier's Offspring

A Reading of
Robert Penn Warren's Poetry

"Yes, you are less strange to them than to yourself," Robert Penn Warren deduces at the open-ended finish of a luminous poem in his unique personal mode of free-verse couplets, "Dreaming in Daylight."[1] His breathless spatter of hurried short sentences—many are two- to four-word commands, exclamations, questions roared by the protagonist to none but his own ears—go spiraling around the edges of those two-line units as if they are so many hurdles to be leaped, or battered down, in an uphill race. The speaker *is,* in fact, scurrying uphill, and having to stop often to catch his breath, but never for long. He finds himself to be a man estranged, unwelcome in nature, enigmatic to the myriad "small eyes" of his fellow creatures who are "watching / your every move." He is a fugitive, in a panic to escape a phantom-pursuer, the swiftly rising tide, or flood, of "history":

> You clamber up rock, crash thicket, leap
> Brook, stop for breath—then standing still, quote
>
> A few lines of verse in the emptiness of silence. . . . Do you
> Know your own name? Do you feel that
>
> You barely escape the last flicker of foam
> Just behind, up the beach of
>
> History—indeed, that you are
> The last glint of consciousness before
>
> You are caught by the grind, bulge, and beat of
> *What has been?* Indeed, by

1. This review of *Being Here: Poetry 1977–1980,* (New York: Random House, 1980), originally appeared in *The American Poetry Review* in March/April 1981.

The heaving ocean of pastness? . . .

The climber, perceiving himself to be—in terror—"the last glint of consciousness," is chased by the voracious sea of the past, which seems hell-bent on snuffing him out. It would extinguish the Robert Penn Warren spark, as quickly as possible.

At seventy-five, Robert Penn Warren has lost none of his lifelong zest for strenuous nature hikes. In his book of poems, *Being Here,* Warren's many excursions through woods, up hillside, and across beach and rocky shoreline, run a gamut from sheer relish in the physical exertion—with lapses of muscle to explore a wealth of sensory perceptions—to profound meditations on the nature of Time and "Pure Being." By a succession of happy accidents, Warren's cross-country rambles lead him to encounters with living or nonliving *beings* that amazingly mirror a profile of the author himself. His incandescent moments of recognition of each of his secret kin in nature submerge him in trance ("I stopped . . . I stood . . . I stared," "I gazed"); the noise and bustle of nature are frozen, momentarily ("no leaf may stir, nor a single blade twitch," "no bird ever calls"); and his spirit soars into a dimension of pure silence and motionlessness, a haven outside time. He binds himself, steadfastly, to each of his accidental twins and lingers in this condition of "Platonic Drowse":

> I stare at the cloud, white, motionless. I cling
> To our single existence, timeless, twinned.

Each of these twinnings (with the "lonely . . . unmoving cloud"; an aged warbler with "beak, unmoving as death"; a drowned monkey, "wild-eyed" and "huddled by volcanic stone"; and a large boulder of gneiss perched on a cliff ledge) begins as a grateful identification with the other familial being, or entity. Then Warren enshrines the brief portraits in a reader's memory, lavishing his most tellingly precise description on the unique facets of each identity portrayed:

> Where are the warblers? Why, yes, there's one,
> Rain-colored like gunmetal now, rain-slick like old oil.
> It is motionless in the old stoicism of Nature.
>
> Yes, under a useless maple leaf,
> The tail with a fringe of drops, like old Tiffany crystal,
> And one drop, motionless, hung at beak-tip.

I see that beak, unmoving as death. . . .

Never do we sense that the other entity has been deprived of its own pristine native character, nor that Warren, with a cold eye of premeditation, has manipulated the living plasm *or stone* into literary images and symbols. But while the other being is cherished for its own novel particularity of traits, it undergoes slow transmutation into its role in the poem as emblem of a crucial phase in the journey of Warren's aspiring self in its many crossings-over of the "knife-edge frontier" into "Timelessness." To outwit Death, the cheat, he would sidestep Time.

Each episode in Warren's sequential cycle of Nature poems may be viewed, allegorically, as a milestone of existential discovery in the spirit's quest for truth about the nature of Time, Fate, God, Death, and Being. As in Yeats's "The Circus Animals' Desertion," the emblematic character of Warren's nature portrayals emerges as an accidental by-product, or "afterthought," following the spontaneous meeting between persona and alter ego in the unfolding of each poem's drama. Works that begin with raw physicality and joie de vivre end in parable and vision. The strainless ease with which Warren negotiates the gulf from naturalistic incident to complex allegory in the best poems marks out this author's matchless genius among contemporaries.

The one poem that I take to be most starkly prototypic of the strategy outlined above is "Globe of Gneiss." The poem's opening and closing lines are questions, the first capping the longest stanza, the last the shortest, a single-line stanza:

> (1) "How heavy is it? Fifteen tons? Thirty? More?"
> (2) "How much will I remember tonight?"

These two questions highlight the thematic antipodes, and to trace the many artful shifts in the poem's center of gravity from rock to human, from gneiss to Warren, is to take the measure of the distance traversed between story and parable in many of Warren's best poems.

In rhythm and meter, this poem begins with a swift-paced conversational thrust:

> How heavy is it? Fifteen tons? Thirty? More?—
> The great globe of gneiss, poised, it would seem, by
> A hair's weight, there on the granite ledge. Stop!

Don't go near! Or only on tiptoe. Don't,
For God's sake, be the fool I once was, who
Went up and pushed. Pushed with all strength,
Expecting the great globe to go
Hurtling like God's wrath to crush
Spruces and pines down the cliff, at least
Three hundred yards down to the black lake the last
Glacier to live in Vermont had left to await
Its monstrous plunge.

The opening lines, despite the staccato effect of blurted one-word enjamb-ments ("More?," "Stop!," "Don't"), follow a rough accentual tetrameter. The measure is a near approach to metrical regularity until, midway through the first stanza, the line wavers to trimeter, then to pentameter, and finally settles on a two-stress end line ("its monstrous plunge"), a pedestal of sorts, left to bulwark the weight and heft of the somewhat top-heavy verse unit.

This stanza is the only one in "Globe of Gneiss" that, in its reluctance to pull out all the stops and take the headlong plunge into nonmeasured verse, illustrates "meter-clash," an intriguing variant of prosody brilliantly defined by Peter Viereck in his essay tracing the development of a ten-dency with roots in the poetry of Shakespeare's plays and proliferating in the work of a handful of today's master prosodists, who work within *and* against traditional metrics by playing off a few out-of-measure lines against the many in a passage that does scan, regularly.[2] The offbeat lines seem to lean toward the regular stress count, then break away in one or more metrical feet, beguiling the ear of readers conditioned to fit near-regular lines comfortably into the prevailing pattern. Sparks fly, while readers try, unsuccessfully, to juggle the miscreant lines into fixed molds that they adamantly resist. For Viereck, I suppose, Shakespeare was having his little private joke of warring against the stolid iambic pentameter, while audiences kept hearing the accustomed fives. The modern poets, however, take some relish in challenging sophisticated readers, and hope to be found out by the more committed devotees. Not incidentally, Warren led Viereck's list as supreme experimenter among today's prosodists. Much in this book could be taken to enhance credibility for Viereck's theory.

---

2. Peter Viereck, "Strict Form in Poetry: Would Jacob Wrestle with a Flabby Angel," *Critical Inquiry* 5 (winter 1978): 203–22.

But for me, this poem—and other surpassingly crafted works in this assemblage—stands at the "knife-edge frontier" between traditional meter and free verse. A dominant passion shared by a great line of American prosodists ranging from technicians as diverse as William Carlos Williams and Robert Frost—at opposite ends of the continuum from open to closed forms—is the rage to design a meter and line configuration that is modeled after the timbre of the speaking voice and that appropriates the very accents and aural nuance of colloquial idiom into the measure. How lucky for readers today that the central craftsman in verse of our language brings to the aforesaid obsession the practical handicraft of fifty years of expertise in the art of the novel—a master of imaginative prose now diverting a far greater share of his chief energies than in the past from fiction to verse.

In acknowledgment of my debt to Viereck, then: he has presented as cogent and persuasive an explication as I have read of the special jarring and jangling effects in sound and scissoring of rhythm ("meter-clash") that Warren achieves in a number of his best poems in couplets, as well as in the first stanza of "Globe of Gneiss," by first teasing a reader's ear with the expectation of regular tetrameters or pentameters, give or take some metrical roughening around the edges in the shape of a poetic half-foot left dangling at the end of a line, now and again. The exceptional line abruptly diminished or inflated by a whole foot may be felt to reestablish the metrical norm by leaning away from a rhythm it inherently supports, as by a rule like syncopation in music.

Only a shoddy inattentive technician would switch from meter to free verse at whim; rather, the shifting *mean* of Warren's free verse alters by a consistent rationale, which derives from the changing contours of the poem's images and thematic substance. Perhaps the regular accentual line measure in much of the first stanza can be taken to articulate the unexpected fixity and immobility of the globe. Yet even in those opening lines the pattern of stresses in the line is offset by the nervous fragmentation of the spiel, the persona blurting a chain of warnings to himself ("Stop! / Don't go near! Or only on tiptoe. Don't, / For God's sake, be the fool I once was . . ."). But the speaker, ignoring his own insight and better judgment, cannot resist the temptation to try to push the globe off the ledge "with all strength." His confusion of motives—intuition at odds with physical impulse—may be mirrored by a line rhythm and syntax that appear to be pulling in opposite directions, the regular line length intoning the claims of conservative reason, while the broken syntax of the colloquial voice graphs the pulse of lawless Dionysiac energy.

In the middle of line six, roughly halfway through the stanza, the meter implodes, the two balanced halves of the line falling into the line center where the repeated word "pushed" supplants the rhythm propelled by the "don't" repeated at the extremities of line four. The whole stanza seems to collapse on itself at shortened lines seven and eight, since the heavy caesura in the middle of line six brakes to a halt the swift momentum unleashed by line four. When the rhythm regains tempo in lines nine through twelve, the regular tetrameters have faded out, displaced by a waveriness of line scale that prevails for the rest of the poem, a viable instrument that, in its exquisitely wrought fluctuations, is a true, sensitive barometer for shifts in mood, voice, pacing, event. In sum, the poem's craft exhibits the versatility and wide range of expressiveness that is the hallmark of all free verse of a superior order.

Lines nine through eleven expand, while the speaker's fantasy—of playing God and tumbling the globe down the cliff side—unfolds. But fantasy, which has outpaced action, is swiftly deflated: the rhythmic speedup stalls, the line ebbing, again, as one stanza quits and the next commences:

> . . . Its monstrous plunge.
>
> I pushed. It was like trying
> To push a mountain . . .

With the rhythm now doubly retarded by "pushed" and "push," the repeated physical word ironically smothers the overtones lingering from the purely mental "crush" and "plunge." Stanza two comprises two distinct rhythms: the rhythm of the spluttery short sentences that begin and end the stanza, both articulating impulsive physical acts of the persona ("I pushed," "I leaped back in terror"); the rhythm of the single long sentence in the middle, which remarkably uncoils, clause by clause, as the persona's deeper mind envisions stages of the globe's history:

> I pushed. It was like trying
> To push a mountain. It
> Had lived through so much, the incessant
> Shove, like a shoulder, of north wind nightlong,
> The ice-pry and lever beneath, the infinitesimal
> Decay of ledge. Suddenly,
> I leaped back in terror.
> Suppose!

The abortive fantasy of stanza one is displaced by the searching mind's eye of visionary intelligence. This sentence assembles a chain of phrases that suggest a supersensory penetration and plumbing of the rock's secret *life* ("incessant / Shove," "ice-pry and lever beneath," "infinitesimal / Decay"). More and more, as the poem proceeds, the rock is perceived to be an organic Being that has survived a myriad succession of life stages and has attained an advanced wisdom, coupled with its astounding longevity in years—by human standards.

The quality of language, the texture of line breaks, and the resilience of sentence syntax molded around the lines combine forces to suggest the deep intuitive centers of a mind's cognition, slowly permeating the innermost laminae and foliations of this metamorphic rock. The efflorescence of the poet's style, here and in the next longer stanza, strikes the reader's eye and ear as a wonderfully apt investiture—or garb—for the intricate mental processes rendered lucid by the poem's crystalline art.

The discovery of the globe's hidden life came upon the persona accidentally, in a moment of frustration as he recoiled— helpless—from the physical exertion of pushing. The discovery of Being, presence, identity in the rock was occasioned by "terror," triggered as much by the unaccustomed flood of cosmic awareness as by the primitive fear of retaliation— the rock, by a will of its own, might push back, toppling, and crush the pusher:

> . . . Suddenly,
> I leaped back in terror.
> Suppose!

But it is the flash of *cosmic* terror, and its lingering afterglow, that lures Warren the pilgrim-wayfarer to return to this magical site, a devotee revisiting a holy place, periodically, in later life.[3] In the second half of the poem, some time has passed—perhaps days, perhaps half a lifetime. The distance he has traveled in the interim is not temporal, in any case, but has occurred outside time. The pilgrim's change of heart is mirrored in the altered pace of stanza three, coupled with a serene passivity of mood. Hot blood has indeed cooled, and the slowdown of metabolism enables the speaker to identify with a master of sluggish tempo, the lichen:

---

3. In a number of poems in *Being Here*, the settings in which sacred or profound events occur—whether in childhood or middle life—are thereafter beautifully haunted sites, to which the aging poet returns, whether to renew the adventure or to deepen his enlightenment. The archetypal poem in this genre is "Speleology," in which the child-protagonist is drawn, again and again, to visit a deep cave that he explores with increasing bravery and greater risk to personal safety until the one occasion—at age twelve—of grand illumination, following a close brush with death.

So some days I now go again to see
Lichen creep slow up that
Round massiveness . . .

No longer "the fool I once was," he comes now *to see,* not to shove, and
to slowly develop phlegmatic second sight:

> It creeps
> Like Time, and I sit and wonder how long
> Since that gneiss, deep in earth,
> In a mountain's womb, under
> Unspeakable pressure, in total
> Darkness, in unmeasurable
> Heat, had been converted
> From simple granite, striped now with something
> Like glass, harder
> Than steel, and I wonder
> How long ago, and how, the glacier had found it,
> How long and how it had trundled
> The great chunk to globe-shape.

The long sentence that composes the bulk of stanza three, one of the most
exquisitely modulated passages in all of Warren's free verse, projects the
enigma of geologic time as a series of profoundly imaged stages in the
conversion of granite into gneiss—a crystallized form of metamorphic
rock. The sentence is a coiled spiral that binds the many interwoven "in"
phrases. The whole stanza moves like a high-powered drill, Warren a
geologist boring down into the rock and deciphering—layer by layer—
each phase of its terrestrial evolution from samples of shattered stone
extracted at graduated depths.

   In stanza two, the speaker was struck by the globe's timescale, radically
different from his own. "It / had lived through so much," he pondered, but
confining his thought to the globe's life span on the ledge. Now, allured
to the globe's previous subterranean existence, he meditates upon the
nature of "Time," focusing the slow trance of his vision upon conjured
images of the globe's genesis in the "mountain's womb," fathered by the
"last / Glacier to live in Vermont," which, in Warren's ecstatic transport
of vision,

> . . . trundled
> The great chunk to globe-shape.

Then poised it on ledge-edge, in balanced perfection.

What an achievement, the creation and dexterous balancing of the globe! We don't think to question that both glacier and boulder were/are alive. The glacier was the last survivor of its species in Vermont, the gneiss its offspring and heir, as if glacier and mountain mated to produce the gneiss-child. Warren's vision of the glacier as artist-progenitor is astonishing in its power to illuminate the enigmas of science, such that we come to feel the creation of the gneiss ball was no less a miracle than the creation, say, of a seventy-five-year-old poet's life, which prepares us for the sudden revelation of the final stanzas:

> Sun sets. It is a long way
> Down, the way darkening. I
> Think how long my afternoon
> Had seemed. How long
> Will the night be?
>
> But how short that time for the great globe
> To remember so much!
>
> How much will I remember tonight?

The tone abruptly shifts as the discourse tilts to a slant of personal intimacy. The circuit of images—tracing the genesis of the gneiss from birth to maturity—is complete; by the most effortless refocusing of the angle of vision, the speaker turns his fluoroscopy—refined and perfected by training its X-ray sights on the inner layers of the gneiss—back on his lone figure starting its twilight descent down the cliff side. The plainness of the poem's final lines and delicate simplicity of syntax belies their freight of accumulated meaning and resonance. As in all true parable, or allegory, meaning has been stored and nurtured, covertly, in images or parts of the story, and a harvest of wisdom now breaks with the force of a hidden swell suddenly tossing up a foamy surf on the shore of the poem's finale. The author, sapiently, trusts the spare plain strokes of the last lines to carry the charge that sweeps, by sheer inescapable force of analogy, from gneiss to man.

Only once before in modern American poetry have we witnessed a similar glacial purity and primitiveness: in the brief parables of Stephen Crane. However, Crane's elegant miniatures—sweeping out into the same precincts of great impersonal Being—could not have foreseen Warren's unprecedented genius for rerouting the vision back to the strictly mortal passions of his own uniquely vivacious personality.

In "Globe of Gneiss," the aggressive human ego of the opening stanzas, stymied, mellows into a saintlike human who can commune with stone on its own terms, as Saint Francis conversed with birds. Unable to budge the globe with brute muscle, he befriends the rock, encounters it with the slow, full, steadfast power of his spiritual intellect. He discovers—by exerting the tenacious grasp of his old man's eagle mind—the beauty and glory of the gneiss's history. Tracing the rock's evolution, he travels backward in geologic time, epoch by epoch, from the gneiss's present perch ("poised on ledge-edge"), downward to its embryonic nurturing in the "mountain's womb." He envisions these prior moments in time with preternatural clarity and incisiveness of detail. A reader, drawn resistlessly into this compelling hallucination back in time and down into the mountain's interior, senses deeply—as he voyages with the poet—the masterful poise of Warren's doubleness of vision, for without sacrificing a vestige of naturalistic detail in portraying the rock, Warren simultaneously finds his own identity mirrored in the gneiss. The gneiss is, by subtle, ghostly strokes, transformed into an emblem for Warren's own aging corpus, his weathered physiognomy, his great staying power and vision of himself as one of that precious handful of robust and hardy survivors of his own many-tiered, much-layered succession of human eras.

Part III.

Stephen Berg

The Passion of Mourning

I.

In *The Daughters,* Stephen Berg's first book of poems, he exhibited virtuosity in a wide range of styles and genres, an assortment of voices familiar in the fledgling author; but *Grief,* his second volume, centers its vision around a single unifying motif—the passion of mourning.[1] The poet has suffered a loss that is *felt aloud,* poem after poem, to be devastating, irremediable—the death of his father. As in a song cycle like Schubert's *Winterreise* or Mahler's *Kindertotenlieder,* the speaker hauntingly orchestrates his grief and pain, sounding out his vacillating moods in all keys of his ever-resilient emotional octave. Hope of recovery from anguish rises, at intervals, "the cure" glimmers its fake promise, seems within reach—hope is dashed, the spirit falls. This cycle is repeated, a wavelike pattern, as the speaker works through the many developing phases of his mourning process.

The best poems isolate and dissect each unique shade, texture, and hue in the palette of *grief,* the author emerging as an exquisite aficionado of the dirge who follows the impulsive and wavery route of his tortured nervous system through a diversity of weathers, seasons, Philadelphia cityscapes, and times of day, at work and at leisure. The pained voice seeks consolation, solace, at every turn, but the struggle for truth of soul prevails, finally, over the craving for relief from *angst.* Indeed, the poems in sequence mount a heroic descent into dark canyons of the bereaved psyche, exploring the caves, grottoes, and fissures of this spiritual landscape, and revealing—en route across the panorama—as remarkable a depiction of the *aesthetics* of the passion of mourning as we have witnessed in the work of any American contemporary (Philip Roth's superb prose journal of his last years' engagement with a dying father, *Patrimony,* achieves a like intensity and emotional range).

Berg's sequence of father poems anticipates, by its careful delineation of all phases of the bereft soul's agony, the amazingly parallel world of

1. This essay originally appeared in two installments of *Denver Quarterly* in fall 1993 and winter 1993.

Anna Akhmatova's grief for her murdered son and husband in Berg's third book, *With Akhmatova at the Black Gates*. And perhaps a similar linkage can be felt between Berg's father sequence and "Heartache," an opening poem in *Grief* based on Chekhov's short story about a Russian cabdriver who, like an exemplum in a medieval morality play, becomes the living image—or transfigured effigy—of grief ("a grief in rags leans up to a thick dirty ear"), a bereft father who has given himself over totally to the verbal dirge of mourning the death of his small son. His chanted passion, like Berg's in the father poems, seems endless and inexorable, first falling on deaf ears of his succession of sleeping passengers, as if—for them—his blurted grief is the perfect lullaby, then finding in his horse the perfect listener. This is a portrait of grief that feeds upon itself, and renews its passion, endlessly—no healing catharsis even hinted in the immortally echoing sound world of the cabbie's pained utterance:

> But a grief in rags leans up to a thick dirty ear
> and speaks and his breath melts a hole in the air
> and the years break like infinite mornings on the faces,
> white, imperceptively shrinking, of men asleep
> that would not listen.

Donning the cloak of this persona, then, Berg secretly trains his ear, his voice, for the many subsequent poems in which he speaks his utmost grief in his own person.

Two poems, "Red Weed" and "Remembering and Forgetting," approach a skeletal bareness of style. The lean tight-lipped line and austerely flat language, in both pieces, keep pace with the son's quiet rage to cope with the appalling fact of cremation, the sudden collapse of his father's body into a tiny "box of ashes." The tools of Berg's craft have rarely been so tautly streamlined, as if the poem's spare flakes or slivers of speech aspire to the diminutions of the shrunk body, mourning the dead by taking on the semblance of vaporized flesh and bone with the form of his art.

The young man who visits the crematory office in "Remembering and Forgetting" seeks advice about finding an apt plot in which to install his sire's remains. The presence of "the director," a perfunctory bureaucrat, does little or nothing to dispel the gloom, and all the burial plots surveyed seem alike: "they're all / friendless, naked to the naked sky." The impersonal exchange that ensues between them seems worse than no human fellowship at all. Oddly, the speaker in this poem seems more isolated and lonely than the chanter of the ghostly soliloquy in

"Red Weed" who takes comfort from addressing his words to the scraggly red weed of the title, which recalls the Russian cabman of "Heartache" funneling his endless tirade of remorse into "the thick dirty ear" of his horse. The Berg of "Red Weed," like that cabbie, finds himself in an extremity of mourning throes that may relieve itself best on nonhuman listeners, who, dependably, are "so wise" as "not to answer." The horrors of a parent reduced to the box of ashes ("a box the size / you'd wrap a wineglass in for a gift / with brown paper and string around it"), which the surviving *only* child must then escort to his chosen plot for burial. These ghastly facts can perhaps be divulged to no human fellow, whether friend, lover, or total stranger, but the poet as mourner may work through his anguish by holding court with the answerless void of the red weed.

The raw power and incisiveness of this poem strike a chord, to my ear, that echoes Shelley's "I fall upon the thorns of life, I bleed." Or we seem to revisit the world of Hamlet's words spoken, in private soliloquy, to his dead friend Yorick's skull:

Red Weed

> next to me on the riverbank,
> I pluck you out of the dirt,
> I hold you
> between two fingers
> because I'm alone.
> I wish I could speak through the invisible
> roots I have,
> not through my face.
> You don't have a face,
> brown roots going nowhere,
> bloody spiked crown.

Like Hamlet, the speaker here has been stricken with an apparently boundless and ineradicable malaise. Each man seems to feel that, to survive in the spirit, he must enact some fundamental revision of his core human nature. Hamlet would wipe out all trace of his memory, the source of his heartsickness, and refashion himself a pure engine of revenge. Berg's heartsick, bereft son would *unface* himself, or efface his overt public ego, unseat his personality, as represented by his face. Hence, like the faceless red weed, he too might speak purely "through the invisible / roots I have." We know the cause of Hamlet's oedipal horror: his father's murder. For Berg, the incinerating of his father's corpse to ash is perhaps felt to be an equivalently devastating assault on his sensibility, for he had drawn succor from the memory of his father's unrazed face, which keeps coming back to haunt him now in dreams. Or in waking visitations, scarier yet! Still seated on the riverbank, where he absently tracks the course of the discarded red weed drifting away downstream, he catches sight of his father's face glaring—open-eyed and sightless—from his own reflected image on the mirror surface below:

> When I toss you
> you sail a few inches
> then fall onto the water
> and drift away.
> There's my father the morning I woke
> and saw him. I see him
> in me, eyes
> open, mouth open,
> drifting away.
> He didn't wake.
> The spot of blood he coughed up on the pillow's
> you, red weed,
> so tiny, so clear when I held you
> up against the sky, so
> wise not to answer, god
> of the box of ashes,
> father.

The fact of cremation is withheld, explicitly, until the poem's final lines. But the chilling dread of the box of ashes itself is felt as a tonal undercurrent from the start. Then, by a surprise turn of vision, grief is transformed into a surreal gesture of worship, as if the mourner would now say his prayers at the altar of this new incarnation of God ("god / of the box of ashes / father").

To my ear, this remarkable ending combines a delicacy and tenderness akin to James Wright with a wry nuance of humor, just enough of a chuckle to lighten the burden and salvage the son's sanity. As in other poems of the father sequence ("I was trying to see God, touch God"), the protagonist clings to his badly shaken faith in God by a mental reversal of great alacrity and risk; it is a brave leap of faith he takes, a restoration of belief snatched, so to speak, from the very ashes that had most challenged his hold on belief. The psychic turns of the screw, here, are intriguing to probe. First, the son feels unbearable guilt for allowing his father's corpse to be torched, guilt reverts to anger as he shifts the blame to a God that would permit, even sanction, such abuse to human flesh, but then, by a final absurd leap of faith that would do Kierkegaard or Dostoyevsky proud, the lost God reappears *as* the essence of the box of ashes itself, his father's spirit felt to be intact therein, after all. So quiet rage is eased, and bitterness toward God is assuaged to gratitude, even worship.

The ongoing struggle and aspiration of the father poems is the son's passion to work his way through the successive phases of grief, to free himself from the father's image—both the father's hallucinatory mask of face that keeps coming at him in dreams and the father's body that he seems to carry within him like an outsize fetus ("I still carry you inside me, Dad, one hundred / and thirteen extra pounds, gray-faced and weak")—then to find a liberating peace and serenity. At this early phase of mourning, he still reveres the "god / of the box of ashes," a stalled plateau in the mourning process.

In "Remembering and Forgetting," he recounts his shock at first taking hold of the actual box of ashes, prior to meeting with the director of the "crematory fortress" to consult about possible grave sites:

> I put my
> hands around it, around *him,*
> and stand there holding it out in
> front of me, staring across the field
> of thin stones . . .

For all his queasiness, he might be grappling with a box of radioactive plutonium. The sheer enigma of the experience is contained in the four words that seem to shudder—by their oddity of syntax—with his trembling: "holding   it   out   in / front of me," as if each word is held at arm's length from the others, while the box is extended outward from his body, his breast. The words sound isolated, or quarantined, from each other—like the units in the line of gravestones he surveys. The speaker's mind drifts, moving in and out of the actual scene, the shock so intense he must shy away, coming at it obliquely. Time is in flux, this moment and the recent past existing side by side,

> . . . like yesterday
> at the supermarket when an old man pushed his cart by
> and we smiled
> and suddenly
> I was studying

> the long shelves of bread,
> crying, lost.

Each time frame makes its rival claim on his consciousness, yanking him this way and that, while the poem's deceptively plain sentences adroitly suspend each phrase, suggesting with the subtly halted syntax and rhythmic seesawing—as in the lines quoted above—a mentality of poised vertigo.

In this earliest phase of grief, the mourner's will hangs back, desultory—suspended between *was* and *is*. His spirit knows it must not rush the healing process, wavery and indirect in its moves. *Poised vertigo,* the delicate balance between "remembering and forgetting," is the right twilight zone of the psyche for now, so he finds he must while away time in this halfway oblivion:

> Recently, five months since then,
> I asked a sculptor I know if she'd pick out a stone
> and carve it into a marker and I'm
> still
>
> remembering and forgetting to remind her to do it.

Although he seems lost, prey to the vicissitudes of the seasons, his inner daimon knows it must wait out its own slow timetable of recovery; he resists—a dynamic, not static, passivity—the temptation to tie off the wound before its time, sidestepping, for now, the premature closure symbolized by the picking and setting of a gravestone.

Marital strife, yet another mode of mourning the father's death, is dramatized in the tumultuous poem, " 'In Death I Know Well Enough All Things End in Emptiness' ":

> I feel wonderful today after a long night
> being naked with my wife.
> For weeks we hated each other, refusing to speak or touch,
> but last night when I got home from work
> there was nothing,
> nothing except the face of my dead father,
> his eyes half open not seeing in or out.

If turmoil during the final weeks of his father's dying took a heavy toll on the relationship of the married lovers, their coming back to love following the rift and rupture of affections is perceived here as a strategy for coping with the pain and bewilderment of death. Their lovemaking is potent therapy, a style of coming to terms with loss and offsetting the void of death, as hauntingly evoked by the ghostly apparition of the father's face, which hovers and whirls between the lovers, gleaming over their conjugal bed: all three faces—the dead and the living—spinning as one composite visage:

> Death does this with people.
> Her face, his, yours swim out of the darkness
> that terrifies us. We can live.
> Three pale blue lights burn . . .

This poem remarkably articulates, with its vervy stop-and-go rhythms, the extreme vacillations of the lovers' passions, from chilled aloofness to happiest merging of bodies:

> I read the letters you wrote me when he was dying
> and wept. You said that what we talked about
> when I'd phone you before he died made you remember
> how you're afraid sometimes of not finding anybody to help you
> when you need it, of how we live trapped between the
>   "clayey walls
> of life," reaching up for a hand.

Indeed, many passages here *read* like those letters, or like panicky impulsive phone calls. This stylistic quality of jagged-edged rawness has been a central mode of Berg's craft from the start of his career, and the mastery of technique in this superb early poem anticipates Berg's later breakout into the capacious incremental sequences of poetic prose, in which the author finds his most electrifying and ideally expressive medium yet for voice riding the fiery edge of overt speech, high-spirited vocal events tonguing themselves out, a medium in which actual quoted chunks of heated phone exchanges and impassioned letters blend with the prevailing versatile rhythm of paragraphs in prose that suavely mimic, or simulate, verse meter.

However, in this compelling marriage poem, the fitful cadence of Berg's line weave handsomely accommodates itself to the energy spurts of the lovers, abrupt rises and falls of emotion, sudden mood swings:

> All those long weeks he was failing I'd call you
> and you listened, so delicately aware of my pain that

it was your pain.
     I feel death's leaning
just outside ready to smash in the door and begin on me.
Life cuts me open, but I do what I want to, mostly.
Last night I came home angry and tired and told my wife to love
 me.

The seesawing hate-love shifts of this poem partake of the mentality—not to say the rapid-fire physicality—of blurted phone calls. For all the surprise turns and swerves of voice, the persona might be standing at a public phone booth in a crowded train station, chanting with vivid hand waves. The voice keeps trying to break out of the form, the snug clamp of even free-verse metrical lines, as if to give the speaker's discourse a heft and wobble of hips moving. This dancelike virtuosity of line moves, as I say, seems to foretell the great release and rhythmic advance of Berg's most recent work in poetic prose.

While the marriage poem hints at "a cure" for death remorse to be sought in the turbulence of sexual love, a pair of quieter poems point the way, perhaps, to a more secure and lasting balm for soul sickness, "To the Same Place" and "Driving Out Again at Night." In both poems, the speaker persuades a male intimate, or soul buddy, to drive with him to sacred locales, magic sites which happen to be quite ordinary places in nature that—for inexplicable reasons—waft a peace and serenity into his brain whenever he visits them. In "To the Same Place," we learn that he came upon the place, at first, quite by accident, and while he discerns there can be "no escape from grief," "slowly again / the peace I felt / when we drove past this place nights ago / spreads through me."

  Finding the right place for healing, the right weather, time of day, and the best companion is largely a matter of accident, happy coincidence; it seems more likely that the lucky events will occur if the grieving man's *will* is suspended. He mustn't aggressively try to force the inner change, but instead slowly wait out his spirit's recovery. Hence, the quiet, unobtrusive titles for these two poems about the uplift and deep succor that may well up, of itself, in the man who finds his own true wavelength for silent communing with nature, the elements, and his dear friend, as in the opening lines of "Driving Out Again at Night":

A full moon tilts over the lawns and trees.
Pale shadows, pockets of heat,
couples humped along the riverbanks,

these and the invisible road cure me.
The arc lights are out for miles.
I still carry you inside me, Dad, one hundred
and thirteen extra pounds, gray-faced and weak,
but out here the smell
of water and leaves fills me and pushes you out.
I'm sorry. I love you. But I have to let you go.
So we drive away again
into a few blurred things,
my friend and I,
most of the time not talking.

In these austerely luminous poems of Berg's lowest voice register (following the more strident brink-of-hysteria pitch of the marriage piece), the restraint of his antidramatic palette grooms the field for the great healing accidents, the random unplanned events, to sink into the agonized psyche and enact their rigors of healing: "these and the invisible road cure me . . . out here the smell / of water and leaves fills me and pushes you out." Such lines tacitly infer the workings of a deep mysticism veiled as relaxed drift, the will held utterly at bay. In moments of stunning revelation, the author has divulged the very time and place on the actual map of our communal dailiness (the outer geography, if you will), whereupon his grief over his father's death, his prolonged and intense vigil of mourning, turned the corner, bottomed out, and the wounds commenced to heal. He pinpoints the instant of letting go ("I'm sorry. I love you. But I have to let you go"), the grip of the dead loosens, and he can resume his life. To illumine the true site of the onset of healing, convalescence, is this art's passion and its durable enactment.

The poem's later lines are suffused with pain's, grief's, and mourning's afterglow:

> When cars rush by us they blind me
> and I like not seeing.

We know he has emerged from the pit, and recovery looms ahead. The few items of setting—the weather, the landscape—so plain and low-keyed, so unaggressive and fleeting, barely noticed by the conscious mind, *are*, in and of themselves, *the cure*. Peace, then, springs from that unlikely source: "out here the smell / of water and leaves fills me and pushes you out."

No passive action in a poem was ever more efficacious, or more final, in its swerves back to health of soul, following the sickness unto death.

We come now to a work that I take to be Berg's strongest poem of his early career, "To the Being We Are," a harrowing confrontation with *the void* that, in its fierce self-purifying negativity and prevision of a ghostly afterlife, points ahead to this author's recent major opus, "Homage to the Afterlife." The poem begins with the severest dose of antipoetic, antiromantic sentiment we encountered in any early Berg works (though the accents of revulsion do harken back to that rigorous exercise in negativity, or nihilism, "Crutches," in Berg's first book, a poem beginning with the line, "Something in me hates being here"):

> Nobody's
> with me this time.
> Gray sky smeared over the gray trees and water.
> Nothing's in it.
> Each word the sages use to describe God
> disgusts me.
> Who cares what exists?
> Driving. The river on my left.
> Long floors of shale cling to the hillsides,
> yellow weeds jut right out of the stone,
> cars, the road, distance,
> they don't stop anywhere.
> I'm not here so I see everything,
> listen and see . . .

From the first word, "Nobody's," we're struck by this poem's power of denials, its relinquishing of all supports for the bereft soul—from friends, from God, from nature: no help from weather, seasons, landscape, or starry skyscape. The work's uttermost puncturing of all such comforts anticipates, tonally, the bleakest Akhmatova poems of political destitution in Berg's next book. It is the one father poem that faces boldly into the unmediated void, braving it out with no hope, no solace. The least forms of nature or human helps are staunchly refused, the lowly "yellow weeds," the road, the lovely river; no spark of life is welcomed, or received.

The speaker, shorn of any last inkling of pity or compassion for himself, in his grief, takes an odd relish, it seems, in letting his soul sink to unplumbed lows, as one who risks a free fall of self, or *being,* to test the bottoms:

> I park and step out on one of the dirt paths
> leading to the water and stretch out
> by the side of the river and stare into the
> cloudless sky until
> that's all there is. Not even
> my heart. I can't feel anything
> except the vast moist breath of the unnamable thing
> we live in, someone's mouth close to my skin . . .
> forget it.
> I know the spirit doesn't exist.
> What dies is hatred, and love, too.
> And you can call anything anything then.

A reader feels that the aura of total risk is genuine and unforced here. The driest, excruciatingly arid pitch of voice is very difficult to bring off, without touching off phony overtones, but the mood of this passage is undoubtedly authentic in its grueling desolation. We behold a bitter, scary plunge into faithless despair, from which there may be no return trip:

> Each word the sages use to describe God
> disgusts me.
> Who cares what exists? . . .
>
> I'm not here so I see everything . . .
>
> I know the spirit doesn't exist.
> What dies is hatred, and love, too.

It's an unfamiliar gloom, a few furlongs lower, perhaps, than this soul has ever plummeted before—or so it feels. We fear there may be no bounce at these levels.

But the voice of the pained soul rings true to its own innate health, for all the guise of willful masochism. This is a rage for utmost truth of soul, absolute and uncompromising, no matter how biting and painful. And indeed, in the course of the descent into this poem's dark purgatory, we learn that a tougher, leanest vision may be the one best formula for survival in the spirit, though the self-immolating voice of the protagonist openly flays and flouts God, the spirit, all human feeling, the heartbeat itself, as he burrows into the tunnel of despair, unflinchingly. His body, flung from the car and stretched out by the side of the river, supine and prostrate, by turns, recalls the Anthony Quinn character—Zampano— in the final agonized moments of Fellini's *La Strada,* while he confesses, here, that "I was trying to see God, touch God":

> Today the river didn't move, or the leaves,
> or anything except us, bodies tossed anywhere,
> held anywhere. Listen. I was trying to
> see God, touch God. I laid my cheek on the grass.
> I could hear that nation I will be joining under me
> celebrating itself, at peace with itself,
> chewing things.
> I stuck my fingertips into the gritty mouth
> of the earth.
> I pissed in the bushes.

Not before the finish is the word "we" in the poem's title borne out, given a ghostly resonance, at last, in a poem for the duration of which the author had vowed at the outset that he would be—for once—severed from all human fellows: "Nobody's / with me this time." In other poems of the sequence, he had taken heart from a companion on these therapeutic drives. But today, he finds himself sunk to a mood of desolation so bleak that it puts him beyond the reach of friend *or* lover. Yet amazingly, in the poem's closing passage, he enters into a mystical brotherhood, a familial kinship of sorts, by bonding himself to the citizens of the afterlife ("that nation I will be joining under me"), thereby identifying "the being we are" of the title with the community of the grave.

So far from any smirching or desecration of his new-minted alliance with the legions of the dead, I find a welcome note of buoyancy, a lift for the spirit, in the erotic self-mocking humor of the last lines:

> I stuck my fingertips into the gritty mouth
> of the earth.
> I pissed in the bushes.

II.

To view Stephen Berg's recent books through the lens of earlier poems, perhaps his second collection *Grief* emerges as his single most seminal volume of verse, laying the groundwork for many later developments. The sequence of poems mourning the death of his father burgeons into the recent cycle of stormy poems about his mother's terminal illness and dying, which culminates in that most ambitious Whitmanesque elegy, "Homage to the Afterlife." Moreover, both the title and the central motifs of his third book are prompted by the poem "With Akhmatova at the Black Gates," much as a fiction writer's short story often provides the nucleus of a novel to come.

Distinguished editor, translator, and educator, Berg is a man whose days are steeped in arduous labors of readership. The act of reading, it would appear, comes second only to breathing, and this early Akhmatova poem enchantingly dramatizes the power of books in his life to rival and compete with his home and family. Evidently, he had reached a simpatico in his reading of Akhmatova's work that was so overpowering, when he put the books aside they continued to engross him and take over his inner life, leaving him dazed and half withdrawn from daily routines:

> . . . my life's somewhere between what it was and what it will be
> this Saturday morning reading you.
>
> On the book, two photographs of you, young and old,
> your suspicious hurt face fogged with sorrow.
> I skim the pages and eat and look out
> at the scrawny branches until they blur,
>
> I shave and stare into the mirror
> as if I don't recognize myself, my eyes caged and vacant
> like a girl's I was afraid of twenty years ago, like my father's.

More so than the mirror before which he shaves and grooms, Akhmatova's work holds a mirror up to his life, and he finds that he identifies so totally with her art and vision that she becomes his ghostly double, such that her *secret* revealed hatches into the key to his own secret life, and he is helpless to prevent the full impact of this revelation, hitting him, as it does, when he least expects it: in his kitchen and bathroom while he eats, shaves, dresses, tries—ah, how he tries!—to put the books aside, to shut them out of his awareness. He's not sure he's ready for so much painful insight, but there's no stopping the process: "there's a secret I can't tell anyone, not even myself," and by the poem's marvelous finish we come to know, as does he, that his secret and Akhmatova's are one:

> My wife and daughters
> work in the kitchen, somewhere the secret white

> stone of happiness and suffering, your dead husband,
> lies at the bottom of a well, and you're cut off
> from everyone . . .

No one can tell this man that reading is a secondary or lesser form of being alive, since, at such moments, the author he reads has become the supreme fount of his own pulse beat, her books so strong in his spirit they threaten to cut *him* off from everyone, to usurp his very being in the midst of the domestic setting. For me, as a reader, that is this poem's most amazing revelation, in what it tells us about the incredible magic life of exchanges between reader and writer, the one feeding life-flow to the other, or draining it away, by turns, as in Henry James's wizardly metaphor of *The Sacred Fount.* That is this poem's implicit message, its *other* secret. But the work's conclusion forcefully renders *explicit* the secret nexus, or linkage, between poets Berg and Akhmatova that predisposes Berg's sensibility to pull off the amazing feat of vocalizing his next whole book of poems through the great Russian woman's larynx.

Much as Akhmatova drew a constant ever-renewing stream of emotion from painful memories of her lost love, her "dead husband," to fuel her art, likewise Berg drew upon a commensurately boundless pool of emotion welling up from his father's memory when he came to write his poems of mourning. The secret he might rather not have had revealed to himself is that the grief wellspring yields "happiness and suffering" in equal parts (albeit the happiness, Berg's and Akhmatova's, is mainly a by-product of shaping and transforming the pain into art). All the same, to openly acknowledge that the process of mourning the dead through art is, in itself, a source of great joy and spiritual uplift for the poet could arouse pangs of guilt and shame; hence, Berg's wary approach to Akhmatova's "secret white stone." But the prevailing thrust of the poem is a great spillover and access of creative energy, Berg recognizing at this juncture that in writing his sequence of father-mourning poems he had served the ideal apprenticeship to take up the mantle of the Akhmatova heroine, and the aesthetic field was tilled for his next whole book.

But I come away from this poem feeling privately haunted most by its poignant revelation of the inner workings of the dedicated reader's double life on the home front. After he stops reading Akhmatova and puts the book aside to address himself to domestic routines, the truly momentous—not to say dangerous—journey into the other world of the author-mentor begins in earnest:

I skim the pages and eat and look out
at the scrawny branches until they blur,
I shave and stare into the mirror . . .
and as I dress I know Akhmatova's deep shyness
with men, her thirst to be touched,
the intimacy politics almost killed . . .
It's a slow, anxious day in Philadelphia, lonely.
I keep seeing your eyes . . .

In this passage, we are astonished by the skillful U-turns and detours taken between levels of awareness: the mundane events of shaving and dressing, the weather in Philly this day, his wife and kids bustling in the kitchen, all these weave in and out of his deepening insight, his obsessive and always continuing drift into the heart and soul of the books he just *stopped* reading, Akhmatova's vision opening its mysteries inside him, her secret holding free commerce with his own fragile and unfolding life moments. We feel that any surprise turn her vision takes may wrench his whole inner life another way—he is so open, raw, defenseless and impressionable; his guard dropped, no way can he dodge the full impact on his soul. Although he goes through the physical motions of putting the book down, carelessly succumbing to amnesia about the contents, its pages keep working themselves out in his deeper mind, and Akhmatova's lines of poetry explode, at last, into clairvoyant truth, éclaircissement, in this poem's powerful finish:

. . . you're cut off
from everyone in a glittering resort town the rich ski
    through, writing,
cooking, screaming, and "I can't and don't want to fight it,"
    you say,
"only the stone age wind beats on the black gates."

And only now do we see that for Berg to find himself taking up—in his own person, time, and place—a position at Akhmatova's side is for them both to face those bitter Stone Age winds together, across time and the continents. Together, two souls braided in one voice of his lines today, they mourn the dead beloved at such a pitch and fury, they are swept back in time to the most pristine era of prehistory, the Stone Age. Has human loneliness ever been imaged more icily than by those subarctic winds?

When Stephen Berg undertook to write the poems of his third book, *With Akhmatova at the Black Gates,* he began by reworking Richard McKane's published translations of Akhmatova's texts, and stage by stage, he gradually moved away from those poems, so closely molded from the originals, toward a new kind of hybrid poem of his own in which two voices—Berg's and Akhmatova's— became twinned or intertwined. First, he called his experimental pieces *versions,* but finally, he came to regard them as strictly his own poems, drawing on the life and voice, even the line-by-line matrix of the other writer.

The centerpiece of Berg's Akhmatova volume—the longest poem, "Memory"—is beautifully structured. The work's collagelike form, unique in Berg's oeuvre, augurs the fragmentary and open-ended mode of his recent prose cycles. The restless energy of the six unnumbered sections creates a zigzagging pattern of stanzas, many units ending abruptly with ellipses, though clarity is never in doubt; the powerful unfolding of ideas, from stanza to stanza, is always fully cogent, despite the many breakoffs of normal syntax. The form of this sprawling rhapsody of Akhmatova's visionary flashbacks—pictured events, hallucinated dream sequences out of her war-torn past—seems disconnected and perhaps a bit muddled, on first reading. Hauntingly evocative phrases that keep cropping up in Berg's later works, "the rescued fragment," "strangely unfinished closure," provide the key to his deliberate asymmetries in such a poem as "Memory."

A number of shorter poems in the Akhmatova book, bearing such titles as "Two Fragments," "Fragment, 1959," "Nothingness," and "Endings," contrive a veneer of sketchiness. Frayed edges, here and there, suggest that the poems are pages snatched from diaries in progress, notebooks, or journal entries. Perhaps a useful parallel can be drawn between the way these shorter poems fit into the network of the book's format and the apparently disjointed fitting of sections into the matrix of the poem "Memory." I find that the long poem does exemplify the principle of structure at work in this entire volume of diaristic and self-revelatory pieces. "Memory" brings together a wide-ranging anthology of vignettes and sketches that add up, finally, to a record of Akhmatova's phases in a remarkable spiritual odyssey. The exiled persona voyages swiftly, backward and forward, across great tracts of Russian geography; she voyages between past and present; but most profoundly, she travels between continents of her own psyche, colonizing, one by one, uncharted territories of her spirit. First and last, these are *migrations of the soul* she notates, and she does so with the fearful exhilaration and innocent daring of any explorer of new worlds.

Not since Roethke's *Meditations of an Old Woman* and Kinnell's *Book of Nightmares* have we witnessed in American poetry anything quite like Berg's verse dramatization of Akhmatova's dialogue of self and soul, for in Berg's work, once again, a reader is astonished by the speaker's genius for consolidating a wholeness of self, and indeed a health of soul, from shattered fragments. I recall conversations I had with Galway Kinnell in 1969–1970 in which he spoke, tremblingly, of the enigmatic way that portions of poems from his *Book of Nightmares* in progress seemed to shift, or migrate, from one part of the sequence to another, live organic fragments of his being seeking a better matchup in the composite map of his unfolding selfhood. He wasn't tinkering with literary artifacts on the page so much as finding the secret key to reassemble parts of his own riven sensibility via the passages of his art. If he got lucky, if the word parts of his disassembled being came together in the right combinations, *who he was* might become indivisible and whole, as never before. If not, he might fall to pieces. It was a scary enterprise, risky beyond measure; the stakes were high, oh high . . . I feel the same high stakes operating in the Akhmatova poems, and in the "Memory" sequence most compellingly.

Akhmatova, in exile, uprooted from her home and fellows, her husband and son torn from her by the war (and *by God,* she says): it would appear that she monkishly renounced almost all human desires and material wants, and gave herself over totally to her art:

> Invisible; visible.
> I don't know what the difference is.
> I don't mean God, religion.
> I've spent my whole life writing
> clear, simple sentences, things that I felt.

At the start of the "Memory" sequence, she has suddenly come, as if by accident, into a magical plateau of the spirit in which the poles of her experience that had seemed forever cut off from each other— apparent dichotomies—the past and the present, "the world, my soul," "invisible, visible," "impossible, possible," these opposites have converged and become alike, so there is no telling them apart:

> I'm here; it's here,
> I'm not sure which is which . . .
>
> All my life
> I've been terrified this would happen.

Most particularly, it's the world of "memory" and the world of today that have merged, coincided, and her doubling of vision has occurred so abruptly, it feels like a miracle. Yet we know that her intense conjuring of images from her past in her poetic art, images out of memory, has gradually brought about this transport of spirit, even though the moment of arrival of the past-in-the-present seems instantaneous ("I'm here; it's here"). She has clearly predisposed her mind, by arduous discipline, for this breakthrough: her power to imagine the past events *as if* they happen again today. But perhaps to regard this phenomenon as a spiritual event at all rings a false note ("I don't mean God, religion"), since her work has been strictly a mastery of lines and "simple sentences" on the page; no pretense of a mystique or otherworldly aura had she ever indulged, or allowed herself. She'd never invited the world of spirits or demons to come to her assistance, stubborn rigorous technician that she was. Evidently, she'd always espoused an aesthetic of solid no-nonsense toughness, having little or no patience with fantasy or mysticism. *Or religion:* "I've spent my whole life writing / clear, simple sentences, things that I felt." She'd always put her allegiance to work on the bare facts and deeds of life, just the irreproachable facts of her enterprise.

So whence cometh this upheaval of the soul? Memories of her past now seem to displace her fond daily world of objects, and it's bewildering for her to have to reacquaint herself with the newborn surfaces of things:

> . . . as if everything I fought against
> inside me all my life
> isn't part of me now,
> is the stone, leaves, flowers
> of these blind walls and this small garden . . .

As one who had been a faithful adherent to the pragmatic world of particulars, she could easily appreciate and identify with Isaac Babel's vision of "the essence of things," who found such uplift in the familiar setting when he wandered "his hometown streets" as a child in turmoil. For him the spirit was immanent in things that contained it, never overspilling its receptacles. But now, inner and outer worlds have blurred, or traded places, in Akhmatova's cosmos, and she finds herself to be a reluctant pioneer dumbstruck by the new world she must decode and explore.

Her baffled attempt to sort out the newly mingled images of yesterday and today, memory and the present sandwiched side by side in her vision, sweeps her back to a time when she was subjected to political interrogation and torture, and her one defense against the oppressor was to achieve a schizoid bifurcation of self:

> Impossible; possible . . .
> they called my name
> then took me to a wooden room.
> I laughed inappropriately; a second Akhmatova went:
> one peeked through neighbors' windows, picked flowers,
> rambled the beach, read all day on a rock,
> waves nibbling at her feet;
> and one, in a chair bolted to the floor,
> said anything. Anything. . . .

In normal times, the disassociation from self portrayed here would be labeled psychosis, but while strapped to the torturer's chair, her divided psyche achieves a saving health of soul; it is a way to survive in spirit and prevail over the worst political debasements. Today, in America, the psychologists have devised for us a prolix vocabulary for illness, for pathology, but we have no commensurate vocabulary for supreme health of spirit. Berg's Akhmatova is hovering on the brink of finding such a language:

> Right now when I look back over my shoulder
> into the room where I sleep and write
> I see my old house following me, its
> one vacant, malicious, hollow eye
> of light all night long gnawing through the wall, the darkness.
> Fifteen years. Forever. Dense as granite.
> Akhmatova: Granite: Time:
> the verge of revelation—that the past
> can't be held or measured, that it changes,
> that it's as strange to me as it would be
> to my neighbor if he could see it, hear it, taste it.

In this passage, we overhear her inventing a vocabulary for transcribing the delicate impromptu shifts between levels of her ever-vacillating spirit, much as this poem has improvised a collagelike structure that is malleable enough to accommodate itself with grace to a motley blend of fantasias and graphic inserts, culminating in the trio of horrific photographs. The photos reveal, at last, images of the atrocities she'd often hinted at but shied away from until the finish; previously, she would break off in midsentence just prior to divulging the harshest facts, excusing the hiatus with such a brusque remark as "What good are details?" But the details of mass murders in the camps and deaths by atom bomb burst forth in the photos, she having attained a psychic level of total clear, no facts too painful to be flushed into the poem's luminous glare, "its one vacant, malicious, hollow eye of light . . ."

III.

The opening couplet in Berg's next book, *In It,* picks up the vision where it left off at the finish of the Akhmatova cycle, despite the radical change of persona, from the Russian bard and heroine to Berg himself:

> More and more often as the years accumulate,
> the life you are living inside you rises until it *is* you.

The inner life of the mind seems to cast a light of its own on the world of objects transforming them, bathing them in an aura that draws a second life from them. These are the dramas of the reciprocal engagement between mind and nature, soul and landscape, that pervade most of the poems in the book titled *In It.* When the life of our soul has been trained and cultivated over the course of many years, as plants are pruned and fertilized and nurtured in the best gardens, the Spiritual Intellect, as Yeats termed it, may "rise" and overspill its container, as a river may overflow its banks. This soulful charge may seem to give off a rarefied light of its own, and if you can harness this pure energy and embrace it, you see all things with second sight, you are yourself the source of this magic luminosity and the recipient of its blazing riches of fluorescence. I take this to be the pervasive underlying theme of the book, and the overtly dramatized *action* of the book's long title poem in particular.

To be *in it,* indeed, is to find oneself swept along on the river of inner soul light, and to find the action of our senses tilted or altered such that our perceptions of all things is permanently new-made. All familiar objects become strange, as if reborn in this light. Such was the soul light in which Akhmatova discovered that every moment she recalled from her past kept changing and changing; the more she dwelled on familiar memories, the more they shifted and grew strange, alive and unfinished, never static or changeless. It is the same light that brought her dead beloved husband back to her from the grave, their two souls twinned in an eternal and inseparable bond:

You stood near me,
glimmer of identity, soul,
whatever makes men free,

we touched, we became one voice

like a lover on whose face
the sad accident of moonlight continues.

from "Memory"

Don't you see us—a soul, a brightness?

On the wall day
splashes a pane of light. Through it
we are taken.

from "Endings"

It is the light of souls that is researched and anatomized in the book *In It*, and the prime labor of the artist's intellect is shown to be the hard-bought skill of *reading* the secrets locked in this light.

While writing this book, Berg's imagination seems to have been especially captivated by the works of artists. He is so haunted and engrossed by particular paintings, Buson's "six-panel screen" and Monet's "cloud," the canvases draw him into their vortex as palpably as the settings in nature that they resemble, such as the embankment beside the Wissahickon River where Berg and his friend Bill went hiking one day to gather rocks. He carries the rocks home in his car trunk, *plants* them in his garden, and broods upon the mysterious actuality of rocks, as revealed to him most alluringly in Buson's work. It seems as if he had never truly learned to feel his way toward the essence of rock before studying the thirteen rocks painted by Buson:

I loved kneeling on them stiff-armed with all my weight,
snugging them tighter into the dirt,
hearing the gritty shifting until each one fit.
Their muddy, unashamed aloneness,
their permanent, homely sorrow soothed me.

We discern, in time, that Berg ascribes aesthetic mood and even spiritual nuance to the rocks, owing to his tutelage under the guiding brush strokes of the master painter:

> My favorite is right out of Buson's six-panel screen:
> fierce, haggard, recklessly free, floating in air
> or earthless, simply there,
> a few touching, merging, all thirteen
> brushed in a kind of accidental
> poise without meaning or purpose.

Finally, the focus of the speaker's enchantment shifts from the painting to the life and working habits of the artist. Buson, himself, is movingly envisaged as he devotes the last four months of his life to the ponderous labor of completing this masterwork. Berg's depiction of the painter grappling with his tools in his studio is powerfully memorable; it is both a vivid realistic cameo portrait and an allegorical emblem of the work of the Spiritual Intellect at full stretch. As we contemplate this lonely brave figure stooped over "the screen" spread before him "on the floor," losing and finding himself endlessly, patiently awaiting the chance arrival of "the next rock" as if the fate of the world depends on it, as if the future of the race hangs by a thread from the next sure strokes of his brush, we come away from the poem convinced that we have beheld a vision of the soul's utmost toil, as embodied, purely, in the mystique of the painter at work saving his soul, *and ours,* in those crucial last months of his life:

> He lay the screen on the floor.
> Just above it was a window clouds would glide across.
> He'd look up at the clouds, then paint. Look up. Paint.
> Drink wine late afternoons, watching the sun slip away.
> Spend some days only leaning over it,
> scouring its five-by-eleven whiteness,
> unfocusing, lost in it, imagining
> shapes live, shapes die,
> flicking the dry bristles unconsciously with his thumb, not knowing
> when, where—four months from his death—
> the next rock would appear, bending abruptly,
> filling, wielding his short-handled brushes faster and faster until
> the ink ran out.

Perhaps as much as any mortal is capable, Buson is here perceived to be totally *in it,* and his projection of his innermost human fragility and selfhood into each of the rocks he paints may explain why his "translucent" brush strokes seem to invest the rocks with his wide range of emotion as he prepares his soul for approaching death:

The sketchy translucent strokes seem to tremble—
you can see through them—as if our fear of time, death, how
temporary we are is what the rocks are.

Following this passage, the poem seems to lose its innate tautness of measure, as the speaker's narration of his family picnic by the river dilutes the resonance of the foregoing account of the amazing phenomenology of rocks. The work's structure is a bit too slack, the line weave in the second half tending to sprawl, and the rich texture of the middle section dramatizing Buson and his art seems dissipated by the relaxed conversational flow of the ending. I have a similar problem with the structure of "Both," another work that ingeniously appropriates into the format of a domestic setting a haunted view of a painting, "Monet's Cloud." Images from the artwork are, subsequently, woven into the poem's ongoing discourse about a marital crisis:

It's almost a month since we touched, or wanted to . . . .
Some nights, trying to kill what haunts us, what is us,
we scream at each other until we can't speak.
Our skin can't bear the touch of the other's hand.
We sleep on the edges of our bed.
The clouds in the middle of the water, going nowhere,
don't know what's happening to us either.

This is an ambitious and imposing work, which reveals the impasse between the married lovers with splendid rhythmic brio and deft cadence; the poem's fierce shifts in energy level handsomely articulate the human struggle. But to my ear, the incursions of detail from the Monet painting simply do not gel with the marital discord they are intended to mirror:

Two blue-white strokes rush through the painting and stay
    there,
raised slashes of anger, scars troubling the scene.

Personally, I am much taken with Berg's implicit thesis in these poems. Images from paintings are primary nuggets of available reality. They may provide us with indispensable wisdom or solace of a kind we can get from no other source, enabling us to carry on with our lives when nothing else may give us the uplift of spirit we need to grow, or even survive. Such artworks are a necessity. There are times when we feel we can turn to them, alone, for nourishment, as to a most steadfast and loyal friend. The poems under discussion here very forcibly invest the paintings with the highest degree of empirical primacy. But the form of the poems does not quite amalgamate the inserts of art visuals with the prevailing human dramas. We are teased into an expectation that, somehow, the urgent pressing questions about how to get on with our lives will be answered by the painted images, or the inherent credo of the artist issuing from the scene.

In the long title poem, *In It,* the form itself seems to shudder with vibrant little shocks of preternatural discovery. The style of breathing and delivery is so assured, uniquely sweeping along with the flow of the car-driver's panoramic vistas, the line rhythms and contours of phrasing feel as if they all uncannily existed before the writing of the poem. From the very first lines, we are caught up in an ongoing experience; the language seems less like a way of uttering or describing those happenings in the life of the speaker than a gaseous medium that has been exhaled directly by the beautifully pictured events themselves:

> I love being here, like this.
> Off to my right, the gold cross of a church,
> dumb, tense, symmetrical, there;
> soft, late afternoon, pink,
> pre-spring Philadelphia light. Beautiful.
> I'm in it now . . .
> Stacks, buildings, wires, billboards, all on the sky,
> all the horizon. Driving like this I hear—
> inside the bubble of the car,
> inside the pure, perceiving, thoughtless calm mind—
> *I know I know it it is there there*

From this opening salvo of images, a reader finds himself drawn breathlessly into a world in which a multitude of tiny revelations, or epiphanies, seems to lurk in every random facet of the scene portrayed. The very singular quality of daylight that endues all objects in the setting with an eerie luster suggests that, at such moments, the most ordinary phenomena may appear to be mirages, to throw off haloes of their own internal radiation.

We are all familiar with the exquisite ghostly light that occurs, however briefly, at distinct times of day, more pronouncedly in one season than another. If we've been indoors, and come outside during the enchanted spell, the light catches us by surprise, it seems to bathe all normal objects in an elixir that transmutes them into strange foreign bodies. We blink, try to awaken from the spooky—if joyous—daydream:

I know that flower of emptiness
when the self touches the world in a deep blur
and the mind opens and is anything . . .
                                    darkness
seeping in turns the sky a vague blood color,
each thing begins to be another.

The special light, as Berg describes it, is strictly a natural phenomenon, a
fact of the atmosphere we can all behold in common ("soft, late afternoon,
pink / pre-spring Philadelphia light. Beautiful. I'm in it now"), but the
contemplative mind, too, seems to give off a light of its own, which may
be triggered or enhanced by the rarefied light of day, and when these two
keen lights—mind's and day's—take fire at once, ordinary things in the
urban scene, such as the Walt Whitman bridge gliding over the car roofs
of this poem, alter into something luminous, hallucinatory; before our
eyes, objects become raw, naked, fiercely alive with a second life:

We glide under the immense, blue, concrete-and-steel
footings of the Walt Whitman Bridge, and feel small.
Black and white wavy bars, like zebra hide,
stamp the blacktop. Light through a grating. Here.
Light fuzzy with smoke and time as it grows dark. Back there.
Driving with you asleep, I see
eye-level red clouds scooting across; raw
seeded hills, scallop-topped, sprouting in patches, washed pale
    brown,
        green, following both sides of the road.
And distance, hazeless after yesterday's hard rain.
I'm in it, as I just said,
and what it is is who I am . . .

As we read such passages, we are reminded that there's another life
lurking beyond our usual borders of awakeness, just over the edge of
our subliminal mind sill, but lying in wait for any one of us to discover
it there, and partake of its fecundity, much as we find ourselves doing
now with Berg. We are *in it* with him. The reader, so much more than a
spectator or amazed witness, becomes a full participant in this vision.

On first reading, "In It" moves like a voluptuous extrovert work, a
poem that abounds in the sensuous pleasures of driving home from work
through the bustling cityscape at twilight, imbibing the rich colors and
noises of the urban setting. The narrator, though he seems on the verge

of some *unwilled* spiritual breakthrough, exults in the sheer physical joy of immersing himself in the gorgeous panorama of his drive, his sleeping wife at his side, and at first, he resists his inclination to analyze or comprehend his happy state, "I . . . know, too, the plain, unintrospective sense / of being here." He is reluctant to let his mind, that aggressive will, impede his direct engagement with the flood of life pouring around him. Relaxed and passive, he invites that sensuous glut to ravish his being, the perfect receptor. But soon he finds himself drifting back to the classroom scene of an hour before, as well as recollecting snippets of talk with friends in the campus office; and the data of recent memory weaves hypnotically in and out of the flux of live tactile events bombarding him as he drives. Twice he encounters mysterious flocks of birds that seem to be signaling a private message to him ("starlings by the thousands vibrate . . . their lewd / meaningless twitterings could be a sign"); but he refuses to interpret. Instead, he contents himself with vacillating between this moment and the recent past moments, a wonderful mental tightrope he walks between "back there" and "being here," balancing, never losing his sharp focus and concentration on the traffic as he safely drives. It is all a juggling act, as I say, of the *extrovert* mind, a giving himself over to the life of action and overt happening though we feel, as time passes, the pressure is building in him to allow his restive intellect some free play to grapple with the multiplicity of events that have been unfolding, and at last, to put forward the big questions that have been kindling in his deeper mind:

> Is there anything we can say we know?
> It's near dark . . .
> small pleasures now; being at one with you.
> I think I know where I am, and who; and turn right.
> Up the hill. Know. Don't know. Neither. At a lecture last night . . .

What a surprise eruption of ideas, this passage, on Berg's most purely impressionist canvas. The drama of thought swings, here—flip-flops of intellect—is as alluring as the tangible world of lights and color that prevailed before, ideas as alive and vervy as pure action. It is surely a tribute to this work's efficacy of form that the usual gap in poetry between ideas and the palpable surfaces of things has been seamlessly bridged.

And only now do we recognize that "In It" has been, from the start, a deep meditation in verse. But so far from a monkish exercise in a woodland retreat, the fullest cycle of meditative inquiry has been conducted obliquely, as if by accident, in the midst of a total engagement with the life of action and sensory excitation. Behind the vivid whirl of the highway voyage, the maneuvers up and down steep ramps, the sweeps under bridge and across overpass, our driver has been more than dimly aware that he is taking a second journey, simultaneously. He has been moving deeper and deeper into the trance of soul light, as he says repeatedly to himself "I'm in it," and though his will and ego have been held at bay, his Spiritual Intellect has been persistently, if semiconsciously, sifting through the mosaic of worldly beauties flying past in its quest for answers to the big existential interrogatives, "where I am and who," and so on. What is most amazing about the poem is that, for all its leisurely and lackadaisical mood, for all the illusion its story line maintains of idle reverie and free drift of mind and heart, the deeper mind of the narrator has been engrossed in an unflagging labor, the great mental and physical work of *becoming,* and this is the task we perceive to have been fully accomplished, as if by subliminal accident, during the drive home. Quite as intensely as Buson pondering his six-panel screen, day after day, in the poem "The Rooks," the Spiritual Intellect of the driver has been doing the soul's high work of coming to terms with the great unknowns of existence.

The big tip-off arrives in the form of a dimly remembered comment a poet made, as reported in a lecture the night before, about the woman who modeled for a certain Vermeer painting. For many lines, the narrator's voice seemed to hover on the verge of revelation, and the spiritual breakout is, indeed, catalyzed by a sudden discovery: the hypothesis that the artist's model "had finished licking her lips just / before the expression she has in the painting. Because of the moisture / you can see glistening— now; because of the strangely unfinished closure." We surmise that the pervasive tone of the whole painting may have been effected by her chance licking of her lips at the crucial moment, such a tiny shift in the tongue of the living woman radically empowering the mood of the major artwork. The insight flashes, and all at once it comes to feel like the missing link in the speaker's half-conscious chain of thought, rippling back to the poem's opening lines and images:

> And, hearing that, something joyful about time came clear—
> because we want to be so alive, because
> we're afraid to be here. Brief, human touches become everything:
> light on an eyelid; clean, blond hair; half-consciously whistling
>   an old popular tune;
> words needed, words received; a warm look . . .

For me, the key phrase here, and by extrapolation, the hidden clue to this unique poem's aesthetic, is "brief, human touches become everything." We noted, at the outset, that the speaker took his delight in the drive home by reveling in the numberless minutiae, the flaring tiny epiphanies, of the sensory panorama spreading around his cruising car, and touching off a parallel chain of minutiae in his memory of the previous hours. In both visions, the "being here" and the "back there," it is "brief human touches" that have been revered, celebrated, and even embodied in the poem's richly variegated imagistic style. So it occurs to us now that the work's pervasive manner, its language and quick-paced energy, has suavely contained throughout, as an incarnation of word choice and phrasing, the discovery that caps the poem's intellectual quest. Hence the idea that bursts forth at the finish both reeks of innocent spontaneity and seems uncannily familiar as well, since the work's innate stylistics has exemplified that very concept from the start.

We do well to recall that, while the other poems under discussion here dealing with artworks incorporated passages of explicit commentary or depiction of the paintings themselves that seemed to digress, at times, from the poem's center of vision, the revelation about the model in the Vermeer painting of "In It" is gracefully blent into the finale of this long poem's structure. We feel a sense of awakening at the end, as if we've known the message intuitively, en route, that was withheld from explicit disclosure until the finish, as if the end was hiddenly inherent in the start. But the genius of the poem's structure kept the secret from the reader's inquiring mind, without a lapse.

In the art of "In It," Berg had found a mode near enough to the perfect vehicle for articulating his sensibility. He took his most adventurous deployment of the extended lyric to a new peak of virtuosity and refinement. He now found himself at a pivotal crossroads in his art, and there would be no turning back.

IV.

"In It" was a poem that tore through the veil between the visible and unseen worlds and bathed both realities in an otherworldly light that revealed the particularized details of objects and divine essences in an equalizing aura. The moony light of mind and light of day found a common wellspring in the flux of the poem's stream of daily observed sights, remembered views, and mental epiphanies; the author's voice achieved a kind of free commerce of movement between present and past, the visible place and the just-vacated place, such that all accustomed boundaries of time and place fell away, vanished—"one light dissolves into another."

For all the undoubted success of this form and scale of writing, Berg exploring in the unshackled mode of the personal lyric a more expansive and fleet-footed momentum than ever before, a snappier ebullience of spirit, a reader senses a restlessness to break out of the limits of the genre. He has stretched the parameters of this form as far as the tautly crafted mold will allow, and some inchoate new pulsing in the breath and measure, a wavery new bounce in the verse rhythm, seems to percolate like so many chanted hooves kicking at the traces of the poetic line itself. Although he'd brought to perfection of a kind his original prototype of the extended lyric, "In It" arguably the single most dazzling and virtuosic of all his poems to date, he now found himself at the most difficult pivotal crossroads of his art and career.

For the next few years, Stephen Berg devoted nearly all his best *poetic* energies to the writing of experimental prose, prose instantly surprising a reader with its highly charged phrasing, a richly palpitant imagery and dense tactile weave of language. That undulant sweep of clauses in supple free-flowing syntax bore no little resemblance to his free-verse poems, especially passages in longer lines. Excerpts from various extended prose works, or works in progress, would appear in magazines from time to time, bearing the titles *Porno Diva Numero Uno, Oblivion,* and *Shaving. Shaving* is, by far, the most ambitious and voluminous work, a sequence of mostly short vignettes and sketches running to hundreds of pages, the expanse of a short novel, say. A representative sampling of these pieces, a dozen-odd works ranging from compact reminiscence of Berg's youth and childhood to portraits of author-mentors he'd met or revered, are included in the *New and Selected Poems.*

While it's difficult to get a full grasp of this poet's new improvisatory medium from the handful of samples, we are immediately struck by the wide scope of subjects and the broader emotional range of the work. The speaker of the tales, sketches, diaristic memoirs, and literary footnotes on artists and authors moves with remarkable freedom and daring across the widest spectrum of sensuous thought, as if the passions of intellect and eroticism have found a viable new partnership in this art. The color palette of this sensibility is so pliant, so diverse, all the passions are vented, given free play in the generous breath of the whirling sentences. The voice of these pieces is dependably resilient; it can shift from whimsy to revelation, clownish farce to anguish, by a single turn of phrase or twist of tongue. We are being escorted through a sonic world with an emotional amplitude akin to Berryman's *Dream Songs.* The mixture of humor and pathos in the heart of the narrator keeps pace with the ever-fluctuant swings between worldly and soulful topics, motifs, flights of imagination, and absurdist fantasy.

But these are prose works, at a glance, not any form of poetry we can easily name or recognize. Why, then, include them in a *Selected Poems*? Certainly, there are prolonged chants and musical fantasias that erupt, here and there, into passages of exquisite rhythmic nuance and lyric pulsing that set our ears on a verge of expectation that the writing will begin, at any moment, to scan itself out in lines and meters. Or often, we feel convinced that we've just been reading well-honed lines of poetry, only to discover when we pause, back up, and reread the cryptic prose clauses, no line breaks have ever impeded or modulated the flow. No verse here, but we are fooled, again and again.

We rummage around in the grab bag of familiar literary modes and specimens, but *poetic prose* and *prose poem* simply won't suffice. We feel, rather, that we've been reading a more capacious, longer-breathed version of the free-verse poetry of Berg's that we met in earlier pages. The surge of the phrasing and surprise undulations of syntax seem more a continuation and amplification of the prosody we found in the strictly *lined* verse than a total new departure. Whatever was most innately compelling in the taut weave of Berg's best long-lined passages seems fully intact in much of this nonlineated work. We keep fumbling for line starts, line endings, that aren't visible (as in the best nonpunctuated poetry, W. S. Merwin, say, we intuit all pauses and spacing of normal punctuation in the brilliant craft and modulation of the phrasing); and in time, like a tightrope walker working for the first steps without a net, one gets a new kind of balance and feels a new trust. Berg seems to be pioneering a mode of *unlined verse* modeled, somehow, after the ideal prescription set forth by Baudelaire and Rilke for the prose poem. The goal of such work in nonlineated sentences is to suggest, hypnotically, that the most intimate pulsations of the artist's voice and breath are captured, as in the best verse, but at greater risk and by wild outreach of the clause, to suggest with versatile turns of syntax and pirouettes of phrasing that the safety helps of line extremities have been shrewdly compensated by the sharp inlets and closures of rhythm. As is obvious here, we don't have a critical vocabulary yet that is fit to explicate this newly palpitant muscularity of rhythm, but the work exhibits an implicit aesthetic throughout that earns its claim to a newly evolving *verse* genre, formulate it vaguely if we must, for now.

"The Coat" is an exemplary prose piece, all its three pages of close-knit imagery condensed in one sweeping paragraph. The texture of the writing is such a thick weave of resonant detail, the style might be patterned after the density of the mellow garment itself, "its nubby random unassuming weave, its hand-loomed itchy grain brimming with dots of pink." The work is so steady, richly flashing with nuance, it reads as if it is all exhaled as one breath, or as a single long line of lyric verse endlessly folding and unfolding, always just escaping the need to complete the "strangely unfinished closure." The piece sparkles, throughout, with a zany sly wit that we'd glimpsed, if fitfully, here and there, in Berg's free verse, but the new scale of laughter in "The Coat" is expansively satiric and Rabelaisian. Berg's gift for the comic in his poetry didn't begin to approach the escalating power of many passages in "The Coat," as in other prose works:

> Russians know coats, don't they? and Jews, those death-
> fearing, Godless, touchy maniacs of the world who need their
> vulnerable, paranoid bodies, ecstatic, wrapped in a heavy
> expensive coat—so gas fumes can't penetrate, so torture
> can't swell their ankles and wrists, so the ideas of clean
> rigid gentiles . . . can't get in . . . .

The speaker, finally, concocts a plan while he stands at the mirror, shaving (and we find ourselves believing he's often inspired to feats of art or mischief via the act of shaving—hence, the title for this longest prose sequence): he'll lecture to his students, today, on coats instead of poetry. "My lecture should explain the coat's power to stop death." So he comes to class wearing one of his bulkiest woolen coats, and by the time he launches into his garrulous spiel, we know the talk will be totally extemporaneous, unrehearsed. He has plunged into the risk of wild abandon, bravely enigmatic to himself, and unpredictable. "Suddenly they're quiet. I'm talking about the coat . . . Brilliant. Euphoric. Letting my mind speak, wandering in all its honest blindness."

As we turn to other selections from the prose book *Shaving*, we find that Berg's characterization of himself, here, as a man lecturing spontaneously to his students is an apt metaphor for his aesthetic ideal in most of the other prose works as well, which erupt into frequent spur-of-the-moment impromptu flights of erotic fantasy or intellectual brilliance. We come to see, at last, why Berg has turned to the broader unrestrictive canvas of this original new genre, since he secures in the wider scope of the prose forms a freedom he found lacking in the self-contained and metrically circumscribed parameters of lyric verse. It is, above all, the added leverage of phrasing, the heightened access of breath, which gives the persona a welcome release from bonds, thereby liberating a passionate exploration of unshackled intellect ("letting my mind speak, wandering in all its honest blindness"), and that is a strong bonus for readers, since Berg's is one of the more imposing and adventurous mentalities on the current poetry scene.

His brilliance shines, especially, when he turns the prose searchlight to the lives of other writers, Robert Lowell (who was his teacher), Rimbaud, and Conrad. The Lowell piece is anecdotal, an affecting reminiscence. It is also an exercise in what Berg calls "wierd master-disciple incense." The work reveals, equally, the two characters portrayed at a distraught bewildering moment in their lives, the worshipful young poet visiting his idol in the hospital during one of Lowell's recurrent *breakdowns.* Berg titles the piece "Lowell: Self-Portrait," and the most touchingly memorable passage is the stunned moment of disciple-Berg's viewing himself in Lowell's horn-rimmed glasses:

> . . . mirrors almost; my tiny seated figure sits in them,
> twin color slides; his expressionless powder-blue eyes,
> faintly visible, seem imbedded in the lenses—it's like
> seeing myself in another, as another who watches me, a
> blanked-out false self sick with identity whose instinct is
> to fix us both into a permanent thing, make seeing and seen
> sacred, one. It must be I worship him.

This condensed fragment of memoir is perhaps more intent on probing the enigma of the author's own youthful identity than affording a telling portrait of Lowell, but the combination of accurate reportage and close scrutiny of precise shades of temperament leaves me feeling that I have come closer to *grazing* the live physical ambience behind the Lowell legend than I glean from reading many chapters of Ian Hamilton's critical biography.

However, we find a more rigorous vehicle for the exhibition of Berg's full range of intellectual resources in the pieces on Rimbaud and Joseph Conrad, "Music" and "Talking." Both works begin as philosophical essays on the root source of human pain and suffering:

> . . . isn't it the one thing you'd rather know than anything—where
> the dread comes from when it seeps into your belly and chest, into
> you, like a stink you hit driving the turnpike—skunk, pig shit,
> chemicals—or like one's poor conscience crying No! No! You can't
> do that, can't say that.

from "Talking"

In the Rimbaud piece, "Music," Berg mediates between the diaries and *Les Illuminations,* searching for an explanation for the French prodigy's early abdication of poetry for "the world of business, where intelligent song doesn't mean shit, where the words 'visionary' and 'apocalyptic' make people laugh, where speech isn't risked to explore mind." But the Conrad piece, a mixture of discourse and soliloquy, cuts much deeper. This free-wheeling meditation draws on Conrad's letters on life and art, his formal essays, his stories and novels (for which Berg has great affinity, he knows them down to the ground), excerpts of phone conversations with his close friend Charlie, and most profoundly, photos and lithos of Conrad, as well as manuscript pages and first editions of the novelist's books that Berg examined in the rare books wing of the Princeton University Library:

> . . . his prissy Vandyke beard and narrow sorrowful puzzled black
> eyes stare, a high collar, white, propping up his chin, his suit
> jackets buttoned to the last, top button, almost to the neck.
> What an incongruous formal figure he cuts in those photos and
>   lithos
> when you think of the pain in his books, his relentlessly etched
> landscapes, his disheveled tortured men being peeled away until
> they see themselves and are left in the abyss of mind, of self,
> of nature, suspicion worming out their brains . . .

The work's structure is a very deftly modulated collage of its wild potpourri of sources, and reading it, I'm reminded that the best literary criticism is a high art, a mode of poetry in its own right. Whenever I return to D. H. Lawrence's illuminating essays on the art of Whitman and Melville's *Moby Dick,* or to Robert Penn Warren's marvelous essay on Conrad's *Nostromo,* I concede that the uncanny wisdom of the artist-critic may seem hopelessly entangled with thefts the critic-as-creative-writer has wrested from the work under review. Formal academic critics will protest that such *impressionistic* discussion of an author is fatally distorted, flawed, because of the critic's personal bias: the reader has projected himself overmuch into his subject. But I maintain, conversely, that such criticism may achieve art status in its own right, often matching the exaltation of the works espoused. I'd rather place my bet on criticism by fellow artists who have a private ax to grind, who put the risk of their own soul's fate on the line when they critique the kindred artist's life or work, as is surely true in the case of Lawrence's *Classic Studies in American Literature,* and likewise, in the case of the Berg plumbing of Conrad's depths, by communing with his haunted photos and personal letters and manuscripts:

The muted tenderness in every copy of Conrad's face, the
dignity in his fear of love, the heavy-lidded oriental eyes
and thin mouth felt alive. He and I were alone in the big
silent room. Some of the books showed a page he had dedicated
or signed. One case held six full-face portraits, all with
the stiff high collar crowding his chin, dark jacket buttoned
to the top, nothing suggesting jungle, ships or oceans.

V.

Stephen Berg's long poem, "Homage to the Afterlife," is groundbreaking
art. This sweeping litany, a prayerful wavelike song in which the chanted
words "without me" begin every unit in the marvelously expansive chain,
belongs, provisionally, to the list-poem genre. But after reading a modest
fraction of this twenty-page rolling sea swell of a verse pilgrimage, we
know that the author has confounded the conventions and is galvaniz-
ing a radical new form, improvisatory and bravely experimental, from
first strophe to the last. In passing, he pays homage to Breton, Hegel,
Sophocles, Rimbaud, Yeats, and Whitman, but his form derives from
Søren Kierkegaard's *rotation method* ("The whole secret lies in arbitrari-
ness according to S.K. . . . The arbitrary in oneself corresponds to the
accidental in the world"). The narrator's entire discourse revolves around
the relentless ongoing litany of self-dismissals, disavowals of myself, as if,
so he says early on, "Whitman's self did in fact commit its very existence
to the space beneath your bootsole." Berg's *Homage,* the familiar oedipal
trauma clothed in a novel garment, is Whitman's *Song of Myself* with its
coat linings turned inside out.

The poem begins casually, its meandering gait a form of play, the
author keeping a loose hold on the reins as he trots:

> Without me, the world became what it was what it always is
> Without me, a huge man beat the shit out of me dreaming but was
>   beaten across the face and chest head smashed until he died
> Without me, cornflowers jack-in-the-pulpits kept flourishing along
>   the east wall tucked between rocks
> Without me, FBI agents raided artists writers confiscated photos
>   manuscripts paintings notes
> Without me, the godless mood of a country deepened . . .
> Without me, whatever gods were proposed spoke were heard faded
>   arose were heard
> Without me, friends enemies opposites equals understood nothing

> Without me, the immense trying broke like waves crying out mercy
> mercy . . .

Berg's mode is the ultimate toy in the hands of a writer who loves to
revise, reorder, and shape his materials endlessly. Early in the verse med-
ley, a deliberate hopscotch of swerves and pivots from subject to subject,
Berg counsels the reader to adopt a cavalier stance toward his poem:

> Without me, one instruction for reading this is jump or stop or
> don't care while you skim . . .

Perhaps he catches us in the act of drift, lulled into reading superficially
by the poem's apparent dreaminess and lack of focus, but now we are
put on guard. Is it to be a battle of wills between us, the author taunting
and heckling the reader to quit outright, or give only half of his mind to
the task? Does he feign laxity of craft, as if to throw us off the mark? Or
rather, is it to suggest that the boorish reader has no right to be snooping
around here, eavesdropping rudely on this private soliloquy, this dialectic
of one soul with itself?

 Homage is a tragicomic enterprise. Many lines and extended passages
commence in a spirit of light banter, horsing around, but seem to stumble
or falter into heart's utmost seriousness. In time, we find that Berg's
relaxed trajectory of movement, his dalliance across a field of random
topics and motifs, emerges as the best mode for his narrator to ensnare
"insight wisdom those wonderful near twins." Only gradually do we
come to recognize that the speaker is, for all his purported aimlessness, a
storyteller in earnest:

> Without me, absolutely is the story I confess is here not being
> hidden really is the story about a great love affair . . .

 In the course of the *tale*, we discern that two clearly separate love
stories are mysteriously interwoven. The predominant narrative is the
history of Berg's stormy relationship with his mother ("my old mom")
that entered a crucial healing phase during the two years of her only
son's performing the rites of caretaker, as she succumbed to the stomach
cancer that eventually took her life. The other story is the drama of Berg's
earliest memories of erotic awakening, the first a haunted encounter with
a classmate in the schoolyard at age ten:

> . . . well there was this girl from a distance I could barely

> see her face how she looked I never did love I mean
> never could love I never have known what love is she
> was standing in the schoolyard when I first saw her
> blond curls little blue dress really such love I guess
> poured out such ridiculously fraught longing for what
> I've only just 45 years later begun to realize I still can't
> quite grasp what it is what need flared but the particular
> scene I remember now . ..

Then the poem, like a video running on fast-forward, cuts ahead to a scene in young adulthood. The second action takes place in a young woman's car, and what unfolds is perceived to be the author's first experience of sex play ("I don't remember tenderness more like euphoric fear or any of the so-called higher feelings"). It becomes evident later in the passage that the birth of Eros and the advent of the soul merged in a single access of awakening:

> . . . I'm not sure which girl it was exactly but the scene's
> the same almost first heaven the expanse of space that seems
> to be over the earth like a dome the dwelling place of the
> Deity and the joyful abode of the blessed dead a spiritual
> state of everlasting communion with God a place or condition
> of utmost happiness . . .

Through most of the poem, the two love stories are disclosed separately, the struggle with a dying mother and first erotic flirtations, each ascribed to clearly distinct planes of the narrator's psychic empyrean. But at particularly haunted junctures late in the poem, one story seems to slide, unaccountably, into the other, and there is little doubt, thereafter, that the "great love affair" memorialized by this poem of homage is the mother-son relationship, for all of its turmoil, agony, and bewildering turns in the labyrinth of the love-hate equation, the parent-child mix of joys and pains (we do well to recall, at this point in my exploration of the text, that Berg, himself, is the author of a highly distinguished original translation of *Oedipus the King):*

> My life is over and so is yours . . .

With these words spoken by the mother to her *only* child, the day her doctor informed her that she was dying of incurable stomach cancer, was launched a psychic upheaval in the son's soul that is so catastrophic and overwhelming, those words and the full brunt of their hidden incestuous import plunged the narrator of our tale into an abyss of voided identity. His ego felt shattered beyond repair, his being shaken to its roots. When he asked his "shrink" why she hated him so deeply, his reply was, simply, "Because you exist."

Suddenly, the spurned offspring recognizes that his presence, and by implication his very existence, has become a nearly intolerable burden to his dying mother:

> My life is over and so is yours let's agree she had no choice she had to say it it was her only authentic release the truth of who she was about her state when she was told about the cancer and then was forced to face without really being aware of it her hellish dependence on me so I listened to it let it in if I did not exist would she have been happier yes almost surely yes then what a different life o conscience fear . . .

His fear reaches apocalyptic proportions, since he feels enormous guilt just to be alive; his life is now perceived to be the main obstacle to her finding any peace or respite from pain, before she dies:

> Without me, she the world my world would not have been an obstacle another consciousness to feed tend worry about know accept Because you exist . . .

This insight, we are to understand, aroused powerful impulses of self-effacement in the son, which grew in time to approximate a kind of psychic suicide, taking the form in the poem of the refrain, "without me." While the source of this key phrase was the son's *selfless* wish to step aside, thus giving the mother relief from the pressure of his pained "consciousness," the relentless chanting of this litany phrase throughout the long poem led to a remarkably wide spectrum of mostly beneficent repercussions.

No reader coming to this poem for the first time could have anticipated the incredible power of this refrain, "without me," to revivify its wellspring of fantasy and emotional learning, from one unit in the poem's litany chain to the next. By a surprising paradox of psychic reversals, the recurrent process of tossing out the *old mes* (evicting the ego from the house of the self), without the least faith that anything whole or healed might grow back in their place, leads to rejuvenations in the narrator's soul. The strategy burgeons, finally, into an inexhaustible labyrinth of fresh starts, inceptions, a process that recalls Hamlet's modus operandi of wiping his dirty slate of self and memory clean, to prepare his template of being for a new mission of personality. From voids of self, then, from the many inspired swerves of self-annulment, spring new inklings, new ramifications of thought and human feeling:

> Without me, the agony threads through it all which is love loss grief and the death of it all awareness of that at some level always without me above all gratitude the lesson
> Without me, heart as if you never spoke never got to say how only the moments of feeling matter the ephemeral myths of truth mean all the rest . . .

Often, we are reminded of the wonderful aphoristic gems, those proverbial nuggets of prose, in Wallace Stevens's *Opus Posthumous:*

> Without me, a word is like a note struck on a keyboard said the famous pioneer in innocent philosophizing . . .
> Without me, the Socratic vanishing moment teaches all now

Homage comes across, finally, as a poem of great leaps of faith, amid still greater lulls of disbelief, oddly aggressive *faithlessness,* if you will ("whatever gods were proposed spoke were heard faded arose were heard"). . . . I find the work to be groundbreaking in its original sweeps of metaphysics and phenomenology.

The allusion to Socrates, quoted above, is a most revealing tenet of Berg's *ars poesie* in this work's epigrammatic structure. For much of the poem, it seems as if each successive unit in the series reaches for ultimacy of saying ("teaches all now"), the many units radiating from a hidden hub like spokes in a wheel. All spokes appear to have been assigned equal weights, provisionally, and there is no telling when supreme consequence shall well up in any one unit or another. The units all embody the "Socratic vanishing moment," in that each is complete in itself, a total utterance. The sequence is random, arbitrary ("the whole secret lies in arbitrariness according to S.K."), defying any expectation in the reader of normal continuity. But the overriding message builds, it's solidly cumulative, despite the poem's refusal to follow any linear chronology, rational linkages, or clear-cut narrative line.

In a few remarkably complex units, the speaker pivots, then skillfully reverses direction halfway through the mini-discourse, and ingeniously sidesteps the negativity of the refrain:

> Without me, no surrealism no 18th century couplets no enjamb-
> ment no acephalic foot none of that prosodic yesterday and to-
> morrow no elision and yet this beauty haunts the hand that loves
> them like one woman's face loved more than anything guides
> the living hand abandons the living hand on the dark margin . . .

To begin, the drift of the passage suggests that the entire substance of the speaker's life career of teaching and readership and composing verse has been dismissed here, obviated; but then ("and yet"), the whole enterprise is rescued *by virtue of the absurd* (so saith Kierkegaard), salvaged in the next breath, which celebrates the hand's saving process in the writing of this poem that has been miraculously nurtured by the author's brooding upon the memory of his mother's face after death ("one woman's face loved more than anything guides the living hand"). And indeed, it may be inferred that the *afterlife* honored by this poem is, itself, the art of composing the work, which merges the act of mourning the dead with the act of paying homage.

At its best, Berg's mode reads like a limitlessly flexible medium. His structure is wonderfully supple, porous, like a semipermeable membrane of words and clauses that lets diverse matter flow in or out as by a linguistic osmosis, depending on the free and open and naked moment's need or caprice. For example, consider the passage in which Berg declares the avowed credo with which he began this poem, then recants in midstride, and finally concedes the work's inevitable failure to eject his stubbornly persistent mortal ego in writing of such pained eloquence that it ironically redeems the excoriated self. Again, the genius of the dialectic is confirmed by the natural grace with which the flow of ideas reverses, abruptly turns back on itself:

> Without me, I wanted this to I have to confess help I mean
> possibly console in some way but halfway through I knew it
> was wrong knew it couldn't too many motives too much blind
> greed stupidity the needs hungers moral violence of having a self
> unable to give beyond its who knows beyond its need to be rid
> of itself . . .

I come away from this poem speculating about how exhausting for the author, how emotionally draining, it must have been to sonically put oneself into jeopardy at the outset of every breath cycle:

> Without me, crippled refrain of absent humanity singing itself to
> sleep now down to sleep . . .

How enervating, for this hurt voice box of a man who is committed to banishing himself, his *me*, from the universe of the litany at every turn! To be told to get out, get out, at the start of every strophe in the poem, mere device or hypnotic chant though it is, must exact some huge toll on the narrator's energy. The credibility of his own being's continuance must be called into question, shaken, by turns, despite the many layers of symbolic overtones. What a discipline to exact upon oneself, a "crippled refrain" indeed, that recurrently keeps knocking the wind out of the voice that bequeaths its song:

> Without me, the story the search for its mortal meaning goes on
> among the lines the absent one I was you you were in this reverie
> of one's own absence forever I will be will be forever not here
> not there in nobody's mind practice . . .

Like Lazarus coming back from the dead to speak in another's ghostly tongue, like Prospero speaking through the mouthpiece of a disembodied Ariel, we have witnessed in Berg's *Homage* yet another true myth of the invisible man who, instead of dying, has undergone "a griefless disappearance." For this is a deep inner fantasy of the race that Berg has inadvertently tapped into. The myth of No Death. Instead, a painless vanishing, instant evaporation, induced by the words *without me*. But look again, folks, it was all a magician's trick. I'm still here, as attending consciousness, a bodiless listener. I'm a third dimension through which the story passes, telling itself, the perfect uninterfering medium:

> Without me, the story has to be its own teller now that the speaker
> is dead . . .

The aggressive ego is gone, even the ego of words expunged. Yet the passive listener works harder than ever before at his art, finding great serenity in silence. He is "the absent one" in this "reverie of one's own absence forever," since quixotically he is still profoundly *present,* a presence everywhere felt—as listener, witness, and at last, feelingful spirit. It is the aggressive male will that has been voided, banished forever, while the pain and horror of a mother's dying of cancer is swept away in the same cleansing dispatch. At the last, a feelingful inner peace has sprung up in its place, filling the void with a serenity he'd never before embraced:

> . . . your face drained
> my heart of all fear hatred that ebbs and drowns

Without me, sitting there with you your face the only peaceful
    silence I have ever known one thinks that way without realizing
    how to use it overall
Without me, how you use it in the hours days and years to come is
    what matters how did I . . .

That unforetold peace, that future in the art of words, we take to be
Stephen Berg's *afterlife*.

Part IV.

From *Unassigned Frequencies*

Selected Essays

Derek Walcott and Michael S. Harper

The Muse of History

Miasma, acedia, the enervations of damp,
as the teeth of the mould gnaw, greening the carious stump
of the beaten, corrugated silver of the marsh light,
where the red heron hides, without a secret . . .
where the pirogue foundered with its caved-in stomach
(a hulk, trying hard to look like
a paleolithic, half-gnawed memory of pre-history) . . .
let the historian go mad there
from thirst. Slowly the water rat takes up its reed pen
and scribbles. Leisurely, the egret
on the mud tablet stamps its hieroglyph.

The explorer stumbles out of the bush crying out for myth.
The tired slave vomits his past. . . .
the mummified odour of onions,
spikenard, and old Pharaohs peeling like onionskin
to the archaeologist's finger—all that
is the muse of history. Potsherds,
and the crusted amphora of cutthroats. . . .
       The astigmatic geologist
stoops, with the crouch of the heron,
deciphering—not a sign.
All of the epics are blown away with the leaves,
blown with the careful calculations of brown paper;
these were the only epics, the leaves.

           —Derek Walcott

In St. Lucia, all secrets of the past are burrowing deeper and deeper under "miasma, acedia, the enervations" of the slow lassitude of the West Indian temperament and metabolism, languishing beneath layers and layers of mold for want of the one true artist-historiographer to discover and interpret the myth of history.[1] To found the myth of history is an act of creative discovery, a courting of the muse; it is, above all, an act of bravery, austere honesty, and searching imagination. The historian, the archeologist, the geologist—all are ill-equipped to deliver the myth of the life of past eras, of lost epochs.

Two outstanding new books by black poets immediately advance their authors to the front ranks of poets writing in English today, and challenge afresh the misnomer "Black Poetry," given such widespread currency by the proliferating institution of Black Studies programs in the universities and by chief spokesmen for the black cultural establishment alike. Since both of these volumes boldly defy the rigid limits ordinarily ascribed to the genre, perhaps they will help us to dislodge not only the name of the so-called Black Poets School, but our specious fixed ideas of the black man's potential scope of vision in the poetry of our language as well. The prevailing trend in poetry criticism is to greet the better work of black poets either with polite silence or, worse, with deadening overpraise, an undiscriminating rave notice that invariably demeans the book under review by suggesting, patronizingly, that though the work is the best of its kind, critical allowances—of an order equivalent to a handicap for second-class entrants in a golf tournament—are automatically extended to black artists.

Luckily for our apprehension of contemporary poetry's range of vitality, neither Derek Walcott's *Another Life* nor Michael Harper's *Debridement* can be conveniently pigeonholed. These are fourth—and best—volumes by both authors. Walcott's reputation in this country has grown slowly, but steadily, since the appearance of his *Selected Poems* in 1963. He is the one distinguished poet-playwright of the West Indies to have acquired, early on, an assured niche in the mainstream of contemporary poetry. Harper, a younger poet in an earlier stage of development, who divided his childhood between Brooklyn and Los Angeles, has produced work of very high quality at the rate of one book per year since 1970. Both poets, noted for a musical richness and density of style in the short, compact lyric, have suddenly exploded their technical resources and extended their range by venturing into the broader landscape of the imagination of history. Walcott's book-length autobiographical narrative is the issue of seven years' labor. Harper's *Debridement* is a trio of poetic sequences,

---

1. This review of *Another Life,* by Derek Walcott, (New York: Farrar, Straus and Giroux, 1973), and *Debridement,* by Michael S. Harper, (Garden City, N.Y.: Doubleday, 1973), originally appeared in *The Yale Review* in 1973.

each exploring the life of a key figure in the black man's valiant struggle to achieve an American identity, and representing three different eras in United States history: John Brown, Richard Wright, and "John Henry Louis," a persona for the black Congressional Medal of Honor winner who was murdered in Detroit.

Both Walcott and Harper, recognizing that the crucial breach in the cultural identity of the black Westerner dates back to the epoch of total blackout of consciousness (the many decades of slavery with their legacy of namelessness: racial and cultural amnesia), set about to fashion a poetic instrument with the efficacy to fill the void of the historical interregnum. Both poets, writing in an alien, bartered language and lacking a viable tradition in poetry of their race to build upon, sought mentors in early career from the sister arts. Harper, in his first volume, *Dear John, Dear Coltrane*, pledging himself in spiritual apostleship to the great jazz master, modeled his rhythms and verse measure after Coltrane's music. His debt to the music was evidently far more pertinent to the annealing—a tempering and toughening—of his own distinctive line and meters than to any literary influences. Walcott struggled for many years of failure as a seascape painter in the company of his gifted friend Gregorias, a painter of impulsive genius, his first master in the arts; together, they paid homage to Saints Vincent (Van Gogh) and Paul (Gauguin). Despite the collapse of his abortive career in pictorial art, he had served his apprenticeship and made inestimable headway in exploring the artistic sensibility that would support his poetry. Later, he would revivify in his poems the early credo to which he and Gregorias swore their vows: they would transmit into paint or words the natural lineaments of their native place, the island of St. Lucia:

> But drunkenly, or secretly, we swore,
> disciples of that astigmatic saint,
> that we would never leave the island
> until we had put down, in paint, in words,
> as palmists learn the network of a hand,
> all of its sunken, leaf-choked ravines,
> every neglected, self-pitying inlet
> muttering in brackish dialect, the ropes of mangroves
> from which old soldier crabs slipped
> surrendering to slush.

Subsequently, this creed was appropriated into Walcott's mature poetics as a ritual first step in the process of recovering the lost history of the native peoples, and forging a poetic craft informed by history and the vitality of its correlative mythos. Already, in these fledgling years, he had unknowingly become conscripted in the service of the muse of history, "that astigmatic saint," whose vision is always impaired, doubled, until the artist unlocks the hidden second life—*another life*—sealed within the memory of events and unblurs her sight.

The youthful Walcott and Gregorias saw themselves as pioneers undertaking, for the first time, the task of naming the forms of life in their habitat:

> For no one had yet written of this landscape
> that it was possible, though there were sounds
> given to its varieties of wood;
>
> the *bois-canot* responded to its echo,
> when the axe spoke, weeds ran up to the knee
> like bastard children, hiding in their names,
>
> whole generations died, unchristened,
> growths hidden in green darkness, forests
> of history thickening with amnesia . . .

The birth of Walcott's art, then, may be traced to his terrible foreboding that, like the many generations of black slaves—his forefathers—who vanished into a void of namelessness, the generations of native flora, too, would fall into extinction with no record, no history, no trace of a past for lack of a language—in words or paint—to christen them and preserve their memory. The modest goals outlined here barely hint at the immense ambitiousness of Walcott's full-scale undertaking, the high claims he would make for his art in the course of this impressive work. The islands of the West Indies were originally populated by tribes of Arawak Indians, and, later, legions of blacks imported from Africa: both cultures, strains of a common stock, were hopelessly cut off from each other by "the estranging sea." To reenvision the events of black history, Walcott is faced with the perplexity of trying to sort out myths and traditions spread out over a scattered island chain:

> There was a life older than geography,
> as the leaves of edible roots opened their pages
> at the child's last lesson, Africa, heart-shaped,

and the lost Arawak hieroglyphs and signs
were razed from slates by sponges of the rain,
their symbols mixed with lichen,

the archipelago like a broken root,
divided among tribes, while trees and men
laboured assiduously, silently to become
whatever their given sounds resembled,
ironwood, logwood-heart, golden apples, cedars . . .

His early vow, a spiritual pact with the land, to render into words the beauties of the natural habitat of a single island would later grow into a quest for cultural solidarity—a unified identity—for all of the islands, viewing the voluminously widespread Indies as a single interconnected archipelago, an aspiration that, not incidentally, parallels the thrust in recent years by many of the separate island governments to achieve political sovereignty and independence from the colonial empire state— England, France, the Netherlands—and to seek a federation of liberated island republics.

Gregorias had an initial advantage over his friend, since the painter's medium was more natural and direct. The colors and pigments posed less difficulty than the finding of a language for the poet, whose medium was pervasively tainted and impure, impossibly overladen with the baggage of English literature, the dialectic and oratory of political diplomacy, the stuffy grammarianism of the British public-school system with its attendant colonial snobbishness and condescension to blacks. All of this freight stuck to the language in his ear, and before he could purge the alien elements from his medium, before "the tired slave vomited his past" in Walcott's psyche, he had to submit himself to many years of indentured service to the smutched instrument of the white culture's hand-me-down mother tongue. He and the painter shared a common objective, to achieve a wholly indigenous Carib-black's art, but the poet would have to arrive at the goal obliquely.

In the first of four sections of this autobiographical work, "The Divided Child," he returns to the abandoned house of his childhood in search of "Maman"—his dead mother—and he discovers her essence at last in the touched edges of objects she always carefully arranged in their home:

Finger each object, lift it
from its place, and it screams again
to be put down

in its ring of dust, like the marriage finger
frantic without its ring;
I can no more move you from your true alignment,
mother, than we can move objects in paintings.

Your house sang softly of balance,
of the rightness of placed things.

He must touch the household utensils, the knickknacks, take them up in
his hands again and again since they are deeply tinged with his mother's
being, her presence. The magic vessels "assess us," and secretly mediate
between us in our homes and families, and if our "radiance of sharing
extends to the simplest objects, / to a favourite hammer, a paintbrush, a
toothless, / gum-sunken old shoe," they, too, in their turn, extend us, and
the touch of ourselves clings to them long after we have left them behind.
The sacred objects imbued with us-as-we-were embalm and preserve our
lost ambrosias, our scents of self: they are the secret crypts and vaults of
memory, both in the private life (the intimacy of family and friendship)
and in the public life (the lineage of race and community). The key he
discovered in search of "Maman" finds its wider application, then, in his
search for the lost memory of his race. The lineaments of racial memory
may best be traced, heritage and authentic myth reconstructed, by con-
necting with the simple objects, natural or man-made, that shared the
life-space of the earlier peoples. They embody the spirits of the dead. This
passage in Section One prefigures the radiant climactic passage of Section
Four, celebrating the recovery of lost identities, personal and communal:
a litany of holies addressed to Walcott's small son—all illuminations—of
the simple elements of setting that surround the Rampanalgas River:

I was eighteen then, now I am forty-one,
I have had a serpent for companion,
I was a heart full of knives,
but, my son, my sun,

holy is Rampanalgas and its high-circling hawks,
holy are the rusted, tortured, rust-caked, blind almond trees
your great-grandfather's, and your father's torturing limbs,
holy the small, almond-leaf-shadowed bridge
by the small red shop, where everything smells of salt,
and holiest the break of the blue sea below the trees,
and the rock that takes blows on its back

and is more rock,
and the tireless hoarse anger of the waters
by which I can walk calm, a renewed, exhausted man,
balanced at its edge by the weight of two dear daughters.

Via the familiar landmarks of his own childhood—hawks, trees, old bridge, aging shops, and finally rock and sea—he is inundated with a vision of history, hidden and secretly waiting in the river and the objects adjacent to it. All meanings of the past, buried with a people who kept few written records, if any, of the crises and trials of identity as they crossed the sea and plunged deeper into the anonymity of slavery, all salvageable history is to be found in the permanent enduring objects— physical structures or natural phenomena—of the locale. To rescue that history, to come into possession of its surviving treasury of myths, is to get sensitively into touch with these living things; if he can charm them, invite them into the music of the poem, translate them into a language and, above all, release the song of their names, they will breathe their wisdom into his pages, effortlessly.

No other West Indian poet, to date, approaching Walcott's stature, has succeeded in nourishing a consistently developed art under the inhospitable conditions and hostile social climate of the island culture. Which was the more insuperable obstacle to the artist's enterprise, a reader is prompted to speculate: the despotism of the British ruling class and their collaborating native flunky ministers of state; or the monolithic indifference of the poet's fellow countrymen, who refused to be shaken out of their stereotypic image of the artist as one of society's derelicts, who ought properly to die young, his early promise unfulfilled, his body to be found in the slum gutter? There are moments in the work in which the contempt that Walcott evidently feels for his own countrymen, "a people with no moral centre," appears to become an obstruction to his mission. In a number of passages toward the end of the book, the unrelieved stridency of his anger devalues the quality of the writing, his tirades lacking resonance or evocative overtones. This vituperative tendency culminates in the nightmarish imagery of Chapter 19, in which he consigns his enemies to perpetual suffering in an updated version of one circle in Dante's *Inferno:*

> . . . I enclose in this circle of hell,
> in the stench of their own sulphur of self-hatred,
> in the steaming, scabrous rocks of Soufrière,
> in the boiling, pustular volcanoes of the South,

> all o' dem big boys, so, dem ministers,
> ministers of culture, ministers of development,
> the green blacks, and their old toms . . .

The chapter is a shattering indictment, but the overt analogy to Dante's masterwork seems pretentious and overtaxes the poetry. The poet arouses expectations in the reader far beyond the rewards that the modest dimensions of the images and pictures in this section can possibly deliver. The diffuseness of materials works to disadvantage, in contrast with Dante's relentless compactness and his pictorial genius; also, Walcott's moralizing tone suggests a pomposity in the author, who appears to be brandishing his credentials in a masquerade of self-importance, as if the linkage to Dante will automatically invest his scene with an elevation, a dignity, and a relevance that is not forthcoming from his poetic resources themselves. Characteristically, the strength of the passage inheres in those lines that draw on the indigenous experience. Walcott is at his best when he exercises novelistic skill in presenting his gallery of West Indian characters, an inexhaustible storehouse of types and classes. The physical details selected in his adroit portraits add up the historical indictment and sociological exegesis with amazing economy. When he lets the journalist-insider's eye speak out directly, he irresistibly persuades the reader. But his baggage of literary allusions and classical references are often stultifying, and they dissipate the driving primal force and energy of his firsthand experience.

For example, the vignette on the wealthy merchant Manoir, a former peasant turned "liquor baron," is perhaps the best of many fine compact story-capsules fitted into the matrix of the predominantly chronological narrative. The story of Manoir's death is a brilliant fable, a moral exemplum with an allegorical impact akin to the psychology of the medieval morality play. Walcott's gift for theatric characterization, an expertise acquired in his very substantial work in the drama, shows to best advantage in these capsule portraits. Whatever his debt here to English tradition, the mode is wedded with such dexterity to his West Indian subject that he both reanimates a dying form and exhibits a firmer grip on the crucial raw materials of his common humanity than is in evidence in most parts of the poem. Conversely, the interlude in the mode of Dante's cantos recoils upon itself, due to the striking contrast with the austerer majesty of the model. The superior style of the Manoir cameo portrait can be illustrated by the close-up of Manoir's hands:

> His hands still smelled of fish, of his beginnings,
> hands that he'd ringed with gold, to hide their smell,

> sometimes he'd hold them out,
> puckered with lotions, powdered, to his wife,
> a peasant's hands, a butcher's,
> their acrid odour of saltfish and lard.

The two identities in Manoir's divided psyche are well dramatized here. His tragedy derives from the way his assumed identity, which governs his lifestyle, obliterates the nobler identity that is permanently stamped on—etched into—his body. Manoir's hands remember the whole man he was. The portrait symbolically reiterates Walcott's central thesis in this book: the muse of history resides invisibly in the body's memory— the human's body, land's body, sea's body, domestic implement's body. Taken together, they are memory's body. There is no unbodied memory. To survive, a race's, or culture's, history and myth must be bodied in art—words, paint, stone.

A final metaphor, near the end of the book, most perfectly gives body to Walcott's vision of his own destiny:

> I wanted to grow white-haired
> as the wave, with a wrinkled
>
> brown rock's face, salted,
> seamed, an old poet,
> facing the wind
>
> and nothing, which is,
> the loud world in his mind.

Balancing at the sea's edge, half-white half-brown, like wave-foam splashing over rock, he would embody and merge the two moieties that are warring in his soul: the inner rock of his African blood, of race; the outer wash of Western culture, art, language.

Derek Walcott emerges in this book-length poem as one of the handful of brilliant historic mythologists of our day, though he is, as yet, a far less accomplished technician than Robert Lowell, who is surely unsurpassed in his genius for imagining the mythos of our historical moment. For many years, Walcott was haunted with intimations of guilt in having betrayed his best friends, his first love, and the very colors and contours of his native land; he felt trapped and somehow victimized by his unstoppable gift for transforming memory into metaphor. Until recently, he imperfectly understood the long-term virtues and rewards of his extraordinary power to crystallize personal memory and public history into myths that carry an astonishing ring of truth in the dense, rich music of their utterance. He has yet to learn to assimilate into a recognizable stylistic blend his synthesis of the spectacular medley of styles and stylizations, manners and mannerisms, vernaculars and dialects, mystiques and mystifications that he has drawn from the tradition of English poetry, the vocabularies of cinquecento Italian art, modern impressionist painting, and West Indian gothic architecture, as well as the idiomatic "calypso" English of his fellow countrymen. I anticipate his next book, in which it is to be hoped that his conflicting "disciplines might / by painful accretion cohere / and finally ignite" in a fully controlled distinctive voice, and he will become immeasurably more adept at his enterprise, much as the present volume has surpassed his previous work, both in breadth of perspective and in magnitude of human vision.

Michael Harper finds his medium and mouthpiece in John Brown, that rare, Ibsenesque hero in the chronicles of history who can stand utterly alone, and whose consciousness will not be compromised or defined by any partisanship outside the inner dictates of his blazing moral passion. When we find him at the end of his career, his resources depleted, his family in jeopardy, there is not a trace of indulgence in the tepid imagination of martyrdom, or self-pity; he continues to take inventory of his accounts in the accustomed plain, bare style—the items of bankrupt supplies, the items of peak spiritual capacity, listed side by side with the same dry efficiency:

> I am without horses, holsters,
> wagons, tents, saddles, bridles,
> spurs, camp utensils, blankets,
> intrenching tools, knapsacks,
> spades, shovels, mattocks, crowbars,
> no ammunition, no money
> for freight or travel:
> I have left my family poorly.
> *I will give my life for a slave*
> *with a gun my secret passage.*

Harper's language in this book is amazingly free of emotive words, his style approaching a tone of dispassionate quietude, in jarring contrast with the intensity of his subjects. He appears to have adopted the same code for dealing with both literary tradition and black American history:

learn from the past, but most lessons are formulas for not repeating past mistakes. The words must be the irreducible few cues, signals, cries, instant messages, dead-center bull's-eye exchanges between men, "rifle ball words / on rifle ball tongue." The language of sentimentality and melodrama has been stripped from Harper's finely attuned medium, but his deadpan style is deceptive; when it most wears the guise of expressionless immobility, just under the chilled surface a cunning of insurgency lurks to spring:

> We made our own "constructive
> treason" at "Dutch Henry" settlement
> in the Swamp of the Swan:
> death by broadswords.
> I took my instruments
> into their camp . . .
> mistook-mapmaker for slavery:
> Owen, Frederick, Salmon, Oliver:
> chain carriers, axman, marker.
> One Georgian said:
> "them damned Browns over there,
> we're going to whip, drive out,
> or kill, any way to
> *get shut* of them, by God"
> while I made entries
> in my surveyor's book
> to strike the blow.

Much as John Brown posed as a surveyor, his tools weapons in disguise, the crisp, spare units of Harper's verse imitate the form of maps, itineraries, blueprints, charts; their contents—plans, messages, orders, directions. All is presented with the spare economy of data, itemizations, agendas. A day's agenda becomes a year's, a movement's ("The Great Black Way"), a generation's, a race's agendas. The author's passions, like his protagonist's, are ordered, shaped, controlled by intelligence; rage, or pain, transfigured by vision. Emotions, as by a woodsman's discipline, are reduced to lean physical details. The poem unfolds with the clean, unwavery succinctness of a ship's navigator's recording logs, as Brown plans the next steps of rebellion, gauged to match the storms in the quick-changing racial weather.

Harper admires the work of Richard Wright, but with strong reservations about his "uneven wattage." He loves Wright's "soulful heart," but inveighs against his inadvertently subscribing to romantic stereotypes of black sex and black violence, myths that act as a cornerstone still in white America's most prevalent image of the black man's identity:

> That parable of black man, white woman,
> the man's penis slung to his shin,
> erect, foaming in that woman's womb,
> the ambivalent female with smirk-shriek,
> daylights of coitus stuck together,
> through the nights the razored solution;
> that the black man is nature,
> the woman, on her drilled pedestal, divine,
> the man with razor an artisan
> in symmetry steel and sharp blades—
> let him melt into his vat of precious metal,
> let the female wipe her face of sperm,
> let the black man's penis shrink to normal
> service, let the posse eat their whips instead.

While Harper gives Wright his due as both man and artist, he impugns him for misrepresenting black history as "hallucination"; his vision contains too much hysteria, not enough clear-sightedness. The novel in English, Harper seems to suggest, is *ipso facto* an unfit medium for the black artist today. Due to deep-rooted propensities bred into the mode, even in the hands of a substantial writer like Richard Wright, both the form and the novelistic language automatically fall prey to formulas that betray the black man, trap him into misreadings of his history. The black novel is handicapped by a thrust—largely uncontrollable—to appropriate into its vision images and psychologies, myths and stereotypes, that are current in the cinema and popular newspapers. Even a superior black novelist may unwittingly set back by many years the black man's struggle to discover the accurate facts and undistorted raw materials of his usable past, the core of authentic history that is needed as a scaffolding to his art. Harper's vision is, above all, a moral passion because the instrument seems relatively free from innate bonds to conform to idols of the marketplace.

"Debridement," the third and final poem, moves into the present historical moment. It recounts the death of one "John Henry Louis," a Congressional Medal of Honor winner who was paraded as a war hero by the government and business corporations in Detroit for as long as he was willing to debase himself by making a sales pitch to prospective black army recruits. After he resigned from the tour in disgust, the government abandoned him; subsequently, he was shot down in the street by a white shopkeeper who owed the black man money, and claimed that he tried to burglarize his store.

In many sections of "Debridement," Harper experiments with a unique poetic language. In "Operation Harvest Moon," the key segment of the sequence, he employs a "found" poetry, a pure cross section of language chosen from the vocabularies of emergency military surgery and the hospital operating room. At first reading, this unit creates the illusion of merely presenting data from the medical chart and log of an operation, set up arbitrarily in the form of Harper's typical spare, short lines of verse. He is adamant in his refusal to make explicit comment in the body of the poem, steadfast in his assertion that the raw data will speak for themselves; he need merely exhibit them, cleanly and luminously:

> Venous pressure: 8; lumbar
> musculature, lower spinal column
> pulverized; ligate blood vessels,
> right forearm; trim meat, bone ends;
> tourniquet above fracture, left arm;
> urine negative: 4 hours; pressure
> unstable; remove shrapnel flecks.

When you compound the language of the military with that of modern surgery, the descriptions of massive human casualties sound as inert, lifeless, and mechanical as the instruction kit for assembling a model rocket ship. The abiding sting of this poetry in the reader's ear is the implication that the dehumanizing vocabularies of the war bureaucracy will be fatal to us if the war wounds are not.

In "Debridement," Harper alternates short prose sections in italics with the verse units. The poem reads somewhat like a film in the mode of *Citizen Kane:* frequent bulletins of prose newsreel are played off against the longer verse passages that re-create the crises of human personality and character that are hidden behind the public data and public scenes. The form creates a dialogue, or counterpointing, of the two voices: history and its metaphor. The form separates and clearly delineates the two major dimensions in Harper's long, semidocumentary genre. This is a brilliantly appropriate strategy, since the poem's essential subject is dramatized as much by the work's structure as by its content. In fact, a major aspect of the subject is an investigation into the process whereby crucial human events in the public sphere are misinterpreted and distorted by social critics who fail to adequately sift fact from fantasy, sanity from hallucination. This theme underscores Harper's thesis that the first task of the poet as historian is to acquire the trustworthiness and objectivity of a good journalist.

The form of "Debridement" follows roughly a chronological linear scheme. The interaction between news bulletins and resonating human episodes invests the poem's unfolding drama with dynamism. We move at the thresholds, the sensitive border zones, between history and poetry as we observe firsthand the delicate exchanges between objective and subjective orders; Harper never lets us forget that the healthy imagination, the aspiring self, of the artist imposes a higher order on his materials in the shaping of form. "Debridement" is easily the best of the three long poems that make up the volume, largely because the form is wide open and invites the reader to witness directly the secret workings of the poet's medium. In parts of the other two poems, the form lacks multidimensional rigor. But all three poems mask an unswerving blooded vision behind the quiet consistency of simple dutiful reportage, events reflected in the cool restraint of Harper's style which is so unobtrusive, at times, in its recording of the bare historical data—the act of notation—that a hasty reader may miss the abiding qualities of the art which selects and rescues the salient moments—quiet urgencies—of history automatically yielding up its metaphor, as the facts are salvaged by the careful eye and ear informed by a remarkable imagination that balances the American present and past.

Jean Garrigue

The Body of the Dream

New and Selected Poems

Jean Garrigue is endowed with a metaphysical temper of mind.[1] Her characteristic fragility is a supersensitiveness to physical experience of the world. In many of her early poems, the obsessive need of her spirit to keep the upper hand over sensory experience defeats her ear and her eye, while the vigorous sensuosity of her language at its best is dispersed in trance, giving way to the language of dreamy essences. But her later development, from book to book, indicates a steady and valiant strengthening of those elements in her art that can secure a foothold, a vital anchorage, in the world of living forms.

"A Dream," an ambitious poem, journeys into an ultrareal awakeness *within* the dream: a deepening trance in which fantasy is slowly divested of its dim outlines, and all that is vague and abstract in our mutual dream life is pared and peeled away, layer by layer, like so many skins. Suddenly we are inside the "tent of cloud or snow / Not unlike a sailing silk," inside the body of the dream looking out, flowing, unable to pinpoint the exact moment when the delicate osmosis of entry drew us irresistibly into the circulatory life of the poem's deep vessels. Whatever seemed blurred, out of focus, in the vision—at the poem's outset—has grown, through a chain of subtle transformations, to be supernaturally clear, luminous, at the finish.

A brash new underground personality emerges in several of Ms. Garrigue's new poems: the catlike, groveling saboteur of "Police of the Dead Day" ("Ignorant of all but my skin, I may be skinned— / And it is possible for the sake of the pelt, alive—"); the homeless and despoiled mongrel of "Proem" ("I turn / And cur-like snarl at what I'd once cherished"); and the owlish solitary of "Nth Invitation." In these poems, there is a

---

1. This review of *New and Selected Poems*, (New York: Macmillan, 1968), originally appeared in *Poetry* in 1968.

hoarse, rasping defiance, with no loss of Garrigue's accustomed feminine grace, that results in a toughening of voice. The most impressive incarnation of her new identity is the guerrilla infighter of a number of successful political poems, most notably "Written in London after a Protest Parade."

Ms. Garrigue was perhaps more skilled than any other poet of her day with the power to dramatize emotional thresholds between jeopardy and renewal. She had a genius for returning to life's viable starting points following defeats, disappointments, hovering over the twin craters of frustrated love and failed art, owning up to the bleakest shortcomings in the self. In poem after poem, her subject is the failure of events in daily life ever to measure up to her spirit's aesthetic craving for perfectibility. In "The Flux of Autumn," the poem that ends the book, her art is conceived as a religion that takes the fierce impact of natural beauty on the senses as a first step in the strenuous discipline of achieving her sensibility. The process involves a series of selective denials of the heart's pleasure, yielding to the higher demands of the dream: "The shadow of a bird has crossed my heart / That we are these, these living things, enough!" She relentlessly subjects her keenest life experiences to the refining "restless eye" of her dream life. It is because she is able to enjoy all living beauties so much, strictly for themselves, that one is assured of the tragic heroism of her deprivations, of the demands her theology imposes on her responsive being. Her triumph is one of restraint, a succession of inured resistances to all pleasures easy of access, delaying and forestalling her natural gift for spiritual uplift until she has reached the supreme moment in which we are able to "think all things are full of gods." She will settle for nothing short of that arrival, and if she has had to sacrifice the more fashionable virtues of poetry in our time—expressiveness and immediacy—to evolve a middle range, a plateau, of vision (halfway between the language of feelings particularized and the language of elusive dream states), we can only be as grateful for the qualities her art withholds as for those it affords, for there are rewards to be secured in reading her best poems of a kind that can be found in no other body of work.

Studies for an Actress and Other Poems

"Studies for an Actress," the title poem of Jean Garrigue's last volume completed shortly before her tragic death and published posthumously, is an anthology of studies, improvisations, five-finger exercises in the theory of poetry, dramatized as a case study or case history of crises—upheavals, triumphs, collapses, ecstasies—in the life and career of a famous actress, the persona.[2] The poem was evidently inspired by, and perhaps modeled after, the actual performances on stage of Galina Vishnevskaya in Dubrovnik. On another level, the poem is a disguised chronology of stages in Jean Garrigue's own career in poetry; some parts are backward-looking and autobiographical, others are a survey of her poetic resources and devices. The author, who had reached a crossroads in her art, was undertaking a strenuous, aesthetic search and mobilizing the implements in her poetic tool kit from which to select the best set of components for a new poetic strategy. Most of the aesthetic theory in the poem is a seesawing between poles, "The dialogue of self with soul, the quarrel of self with world," which she cited in 1969 (in a commentary on her own work published in *Contemporary Poets of the English Language*) as her favorite subject, during the transition between her previous book—an expertly stripped down but comprehensive selection from five earlier volumes plus some new poems—and the last volume.

With the rebirth of her art in this final work, a more energetic, various, and personally expressive collection than any published before it, she won an undoubted victory over the brutal, impersonal muse that, for some time, had paralyzed her creative impulse, as recounted beautifully in the title poem:

> She flees all action now, she has gone in
> Upon a demi-day that sinks towards night
> Under instruction from the strangest powers
> She would appease and cannot, who reveal
> In the most obscure and sinking down of ways
> This that they want which will fulfill
> This that she does not know, which she must do.
> Can she turn back? The path is overgrown.
> Ahead,
> Roads like lines in the palms of the dead
> Now fade.

Increasingly, in later career, Jean Garrigue evidently felt haunted by forces beyond herself that informed her art, as they had in the past—forces that she could seek or implore to come to her aid but that she could not invoke

---

2. This review of *Studies for an Actress and Other Poems,* (New York: Macmillan, 1973), originally appeared in *The Yale Review* in 1973.

at will, or fully control, once they came into play; but now, they often seemed to bind her in servitude to an anonymous lord outside herself whom she felt helpless to satisfy ("Under instruction from the strangest powers / She would appease and cannot"), often leaving her in a state of bewildering cosmic frustration and, finally, spiritual exhaustion:

> And so she falls half out of life,
> Out of the net of things into the dark,
> Who has no strength now for that bright-in-dark,
> That second life those emblemed figures knit.
> Blind fit. Nothing to hold her back from this descent
> Into a void, opaque, unlit.

These conflicts are enacted in her poem by the actress-protagonist's endless vacillation between the masks, disguises, roles she performs in the theater and her own human identity, a chameleon—a shifting multiplicity of selves—in its own right.

In her poem dealing with the characters in Chekhov's play *The Seagull*—a favorite drama she felt compelled to see performed again and again—she finds another stunning correlative in the theater for her inward struggle with the merciless gods, those strange powers. Although her artist-will was strong enough, in time, to break the grip on her spirit of the antihuman demonic forces in the universe that would contract us as will-less hirelings, puppets in their service, the Chekhovian sufferers are helpless to break the spell they are under, because the savage muse who governs their lives by an iron hand of fatalistic emotional determinism is the muse of the truth:

> The boy is all wrung, unstrung,
> For his mother has laughed at the wrong time.
> Were he other than he, he would leave,
> But the truth of her laughter is, and he knows it . . .
> He knows and knows no better
> That clue to the tears she can shake him down to,
> Treading on all his prides
> So obscurely linked to his fears.
> How can he solve himself! . . .
> And you see how in the interests of truth,
> The anonymous truth that respects no one,
> Whether it was intended or not,
> His purpose in life was to be broken.

She is allured both by the tragic beauty of their fidelity to the "anonymous truth" of their spirits, the invisible world within, and, more consequentially, by the mirror they hold up to her own divided psyche in its struggle to reconcile the rivalry between the actress and the live sufferer in her own poetics. It is as if the Chekhov players fool us twice: first, his characters achieve perfect verisimilitude, true-to-life credibility; but second, by the oddest inversion of convention on the stage, the lifestyle projected by the play's hypnotic mimesis is one in which all the flesh-and-blood subjects behave as if life were a theater, in which the necessity to brilliantly act out every sensation and extremity of feeling with the utmost intensity seems more important than breathing. Life must be *performed* to be life ("as if it were very life performing her") and performed "at breakneck speed of remorse" if it is to keep up with the very timetable of survival. At this pace, the mind will be driven by the heart until the mind snaps, which accounts for the poem's title, "Why the Heart Has Dreams Is Why the Mind Goes Mad."

The very short poem with the long title, "Movie Actors Scribbling Letters Very Fast in Crucial Scenes," is a more comprehensive, though exquisitely compact, illustration of the schism of the poet-actress in whom the mask and the face, the role and the person, the disguise and the guise it veils become indissolubly fused, or blended, in moments of crisis:

> The velocity with which they write—
> Don't you know it? It's from the heart!
> They are acting the whole part out.
> Love! has taken them up—
> Like writing to god in the night.
> Meet me! I'm dying! Come at once!
> The crisis is on them, the shock
> Drives from the nerve to the pen,
> Pours from the blood into ink.

The humorous overtones of this piece give it enough buoyancy and lightness to deliver without strain a complex set of equations, or parallels, between the actor-audience contract and the reader-writer contract. All boundaries between art and life—whether on stage, on screen, or in the poet's verses—are swept away, extinguished, in the illuminations born of shock.

Ms. Garrigue's engagement in politics emerged as an important theme in a few poems of her previous book. In *Studies,* her political interests move to the forefront of her concerns, and in the new political poems she codifies an original and enlightening set of guidelines for the relation between poetry and politics in our age. In "Resistance Meeting: Boston Common," she discovers the viable roles that her own ceremonial and emblematic art may play in the theater of the politics of resistance without violating the integrity of her unfashionable elegance. She would restore to our vision of ourselves something of the lost glory of the classic portrait virtuoso's skill in apotheosizing the most noble and beautiful elements in the handful of sublime models among us of a man of parts, a woman of parts, in the active life of politics; she would revive the lost art of celebrating and defining, for our unique age and moment in history, "the dream of fair men and women":

> April in the Public Garden.
> The boys who will be drafted are here,
> some bearded like disciples,
> others with the large dark eyes of *The Volunteers of 1792*
> as painted by Thomas Couture,
> horsemen-like as a painter might see them,
> stilling, instilling their fire
> of so much being to be praised by the future.
>
> No point in going on about handsome people
> with their thick hair glittering in the wind
> about which we have had much comment from ads
> so that we are less free to think of Titian's *Man with a Glove*
> or a Degas portrait of some olive-skinned pride,
> the élan of the painter and subject met at the point of imagination
> where the magnificent being
> garbed in the full dress of his civilization
> completes in himself by his beauty
> the rose of every expectancy.
>
> For those lounging and lolling here,
> what painter will arrest them in their gear,
> at their height of time?
> Not hardened yet or tarnished.

A veteran of several decades of distinguished work in the poetry of romantic lyricism, the rich embroidery of mythic scenes and emblematic figures, she is now able to import the expertise formerly ascribing grandeur to classic works of sculpture, tapestries, great cathedrals, to contemporary heroes—her friends and colleagues in the resistance movement. They achieve stature and mythic grandeur in her portraits. Moreover, this poet, whose phantasmagoric otherworldly bent would seem too rarefied for an active role in politics, perceiving that the concepts of *power* and *order* have become equated in our country's ad mind-set (which passes for imagination in most quarters) with the proliferating armories of nuclear missiles and moon rockets, vows to make her art assume the full burden of guardianship and caretaking of the language of the inner order and the power of the mind's soul life. She would mobilize a counterarsenal of life-giving words, an artillery of vocables of resistance, to fend off the new faceless vocabulary from the ballistics' pantheon of demigods, an invasion of our language that subtly undermines us by poisoning the roots of common speech:

> Now we need not go mad on abstractions
> about Power, Fire Power, Garrison, Arsenal
> Fire Power, Power, Poseidons
> (giving a "multiple warhead Navy Missile" the name of a god)!

Her political poems lose their authority and verve when they subscribe to explicit virulent judgments attacking the state; her language, at times, sinks to a propagandist journalese with accents embarrassingly akin to the political jargon she abhors:

> Escape artists, fed on swill,
> Wanting more and more, forever more.
> Not one "improvement" will we let go by,
> Still cuddling picture postcards of the ideal. . . .
> But who will judge the victor? Might's still right
> In this our swollen pigsfoot of a state.

The poems in the political mode are most arresting when she dramatizes the inner struggle of noble individuals—solitaries—caught, willingly or unwillingly, in the pythonic coils of the political juggernaut, recalling Yeats's emblematic portraits of Irish revolutionaries. "For Such a Bird He Had No Convenient Cage" is the record of a spiritual rape:

> Her dreameries had been raided.
> To the utmost rag and bone they had been hauled
> Over the coals and up the flagpole for inspection,
> To their limits they had been exposed
> And all but sneeringly investigated.

This woman had achieved a rare triumph of exalted being, her whole sensibility trained to a scale of refinement that could never be measured by the brutal calipers of the political mentality. ("Hers was not of the same case. . . . It was less erect and more elect than that.") Not that the devastation of this woman's elevated consciousness by government committee is, in and of itself, more tragic, or more unforgivable, than countless other crimes by the state against innocents. But the poem transfigures her into a heroic, mythic emblem. She had given all of herself to the life of the Yeatsian spiritual intellect and had grown to exist wholly in a state of purer mind. Hence, she embodies in her own person the sector of the inner secret life of all intelligent beings that must be irreparably poisoned by the blunt instrument of the committee. Since her whole mental life is a reduction to the secret working mind of her creative reverie, a phantasmagoria of images and living forms curiously akin to Garrigue's own interior landscape, "her dreameries had been raided" is a postmortem statement, the poem an epitaph to a crucifixion. She is emblematic of the solitary, mysterious inwardness in each of us, which is losing ground with each passing hour to the political machine.

Throughout her bountifully productive career, Jean Garrigue consistently adhered to and deepened a poetics in which the invisible or unseen world of the self and soul—a world apparitional, mythical, and palpable to supersensory, by turns—figured as the mainstay of her faith, as against her distrust of "the strange untrue of the real":

> You believed in a world that has never come
> With or without hope of this one
> And therefore you would say
> "I believe in what I do not see."

In fairness, she was always eager to give the unsatisfactory, incomplete material world its due, and in times of intense human experience she was not unwilling to allow her faith in the preeminence of the visionary world to be tested, or challenged, by the visible world; and characteristically she adopted a posture, or stance, poised midway between the two superpowers, "assailed by knowledge of a plenitude / the dense, packed world refutes in paining ways," inviting the poem's field of interplay to act as a forum for peaceful or embattled negotiations between them, as in the title poem of this volume. Never before, however, had she subjected her visionary reality to so harrowing a test as the massive frontal assault upon it by the "brute

Sublime" beauties of the Grand Canyon, and never had her bravery in risking her unmasked sensibility to bombardment by the world of nature led to art of such magnitude, a panoramic sweep of vision rare in American poetry. "The Grand Canyon" is the outstanding masterwork of her career, a triumph of an order that could not have been foreseen from her usual nature encounters. The work explores a fantastic inundation from the outside world that becomes mysteriously and helplessly transformed into a metaphor for the world of the psyche, with no loss of the geological marvel's exact multitudinous particularity of detail.

In the title poem, she had explained her aesthetic crisis in late career, and her slackening of creative energies, as a temporary loss of the "binding element," the power to make swift leaps, associative jumps, connections between distant corners of the psyche:

> And she has lost the thread that let
> Those emblems forth, that rich connecting
> Between their powers and broad awaking . . .

In "The Grand Canyon," she restored her genius for "that rich connecting," the power to mediate between inner and external worlds. The key to her best life and best love, then, as poet-actress was neither the open expression of personality nor the effacement of personality to become a perfectly empty medium, or vessel, into which any role could be poured, though she grew to be equally adept in this last book both at projecting her own personal voice directly and at playing the ventriloquist for other voices—whether mythical or realistic dramatis personae. She came more and more toward the last to identify or characterize the *real* of herself, her most enduring best gift, as the Ariel sprite, the elf of the spirit that could balance on the high wire between mind and matter, moving swiftly and decisively between materials and the immaterial—the power to become bodied and disembodied, by turns, never to be trapped for long in this statue, that painting, the natural scene or locale, the human character, but like "the gold of the light nervously darting" up and down the eight strictly delineated and distinct geological layers of the Grand Canyon, or "the eye . . . a long-legged insect on a windowpane" that "slithers and shudders up and down" the canyon walls, or like "the violet-green swallow stitching its leaps and arcs / over the gliding raven, / over the camber of columns, tawny rotundas of ruins . . .": she would *be* the light, the eye, the swallow; she would be a voyaging essence, contained and uncontainable, hitching a ride—a cosmic hitchhiker—on forms, animate or inanimate, that would allow her to travel in buoyancy and pure freedom of weightlessness, to span vast chasms in time and space, the noble distances, in a single instant: to be swept along on the currents of "a large, impersonal strength / beyond herself and borrowed from the race."

James Wright

Words of Grass

Shall We Gather at the River

There is a stubborn, manly honesty in James Wright's new book of poems.[1] He is beautifully resolute in his refusal to make any bargains with life or art. The man in these poems (and we can never forget he is inside their skins) has an unquenchable craving to find "my secret, my life" and to say it in poems. This last, pure demand of his spirit speaks from the very roots of his being; the words have the finality and unshakable authority of self paying its dues, and claiming its total due:

> But my life was never so precious
> To me as now.
> I will have to beg coins
> After dark.

Nearly every poem in the book contains lines that bespeak a man who has been so lost, so hurt, so dumb, so wrong . . . and he knows it to his bones. Now, in his fourth and best book of poems, he is at last able to say it out and nothing can stop him, not even the words. Indeed, he is at war with the very words of his poetry. They will never be enough. If he could, he would change them to grass:

> The earth is hard now,
> The soles of my shoes need repairs.
> I have nothing to ask a blessing for,
> Except these words.
> I wish they were
> Grass.

1. This review of *Shall We Gather at the River*, (Middletown, Conn.: Wesleyan University Press, 1968), originally appeared in *Poetry* in 1969.

But I mustn't mistakenly suggest that Wright is exclusively taxed with introspection—a squaring with his personal demon—in this book; rather, he reaches out to others, and achieves a passion of common humanity, a commonality of fellow feeling for the least of mankind, to a degree not witnessed in his earlier work. In this book, Wright is obsessed with the lives and dyings of people from whom life has taken everything except the inner life of spirit: the arthritic man who "takes coins at the parking lot / He smiles with the sinister grief / Of old age"; the old woman in the gambling casino who "has been beating a strange machine / In its face all day"; Uncle Willy Lyons, who "was buried with nothing except a jacket / Stitched on his shoulder bones"; Wright's father who, though his life was "caught among girders that smash the kneecaps / Of dumb honyaks . . . He came home as quiet as the evening"; Jenny, who "has broken her spare beauty / In a whorehouse old. She left her new baby / In a bus-station can"; as well as the whores of Wheeling, West Virginia, who "could drown every evening [in the river]," yet each dawn "they climb up the other shore, / Drying their wings." Is it possible to doubt the scoured authenticity of such lines, lines that have won their ductility and steely durableness from being eaten into by the acids of living pain; lines that, despite their pared-down, wiry tautness, are stained with the irremovable residue of lived terrors as surely as particles of soil cling to tree roots?

Irresistibly drawn to the souls of beings who have wasted their lives— or who have been devastated *by* life—Wright's soul becomes, at last, hopelessly and lovingly entangled with theirs. He has the largeness of heart of the great empathizers, and worse, a mind suicidally honest, a mind hellishly bent on stripping away all self-protective devices. His best poems enact the drama of a mind struggling, usually with punishing success, to resist the temptation to take solace from its own compassionating ardor. The pain he feels for another never becomes a disguised way of cheering himself up. It is a tougher thing. The poems in this book are nearly identical in form to those of Wright's last book, but they have advanced to an altogether new spiritual magnitude. Perhaps the most serious obstacle to the new life of spirit is brevity of form. I feel that this tendency has become a handicap that impedes a full blossoming into the massive, raw-boned jaggedness of form that, as in the superb *Minneapolis Poem*, can provide the structural leverage needed to render the fuller sense of life newly available, but somehow left unbodied in many of the short poems. The best work in this volume demonstrates clearly that Wright has the skill and fortitude needed to rid his art of the leaning to premature closure that often stifles his ablest, most incandescent vision.

Two Citizens

One afternoon,
At Aetnaville, Ohio,
A broken goat escaped
From a carnival,
One of the hooch dances
They used to hold
Down by the river.
Scrawny the goat panicked
Down Agnes's alley,
Which is my country,
If you haven't noticed,
America,
Which I loved when I was young.

That goat ran down the alley,
And many boys giggled
While they tried to stone our fellow
Goat to death.
And my Aunt Agnes,
Who stank and lied,
Threw stones back at the boys
And gathered the goat,
Nuts as she was,
Into her sloppy arms.

In "Ars Poetica: Some Recent Criticism," the long poem that opens James Wright's volume *Two Citizens,* this shrewdly recalled anecdote serves as an intermediary between fragments of family history and Wright's searching diagnosis of America's soul-sickness.[2] Employing his memory of childhood, then, as a go-between, Wright traces the origins of family tragedy and links its genesis, enigmatically, to the roots of various catastrophes in the current national life. We witness the two tragedies in tandem, a river of recollection and deep human sympathy flowing back and forth between them; Wright aching for the waste, brooding over the desolation of squandered beauty and human resources—so much promise, so much endowment of natural gifts depleted in a single generation; Wright

2. This review of *Two Citizens,* (New York: Farrar, Straus and Giroux, 1973), originally appeared in *The Yale Review* in 1974.

agonizing—not without bitterness, not without a few flare-ups of raw hatred and plotted vengeance—over the downfall and the ruins of his two beloveds: his family ancestry, his country.

Out of this duet of heartaches Wright fashions his new *ars poetica,* which takes shape as he tours through France and Italy in the bewitchment of a second duet, the *Two Citizens,* he and his wife Annie, unfashionably and unabashedly falling deeper in love with America—as with each other—the more they find she has betrayed her citizenry, the more they discover her to be despicable in the quality of her national character as they wander and sample the glories of classical antiquity that beset their wayfarings down public roads, country paths, and mountain trails alike, two citizen-exiles bewildered to find how much they continue to love the ugly matriarchy of their native land. As Wright savors the fragrance of each new language on his travels, he recalls how his United States squandered its wealth of language on the hokum and sentimental claptrap of the history books and all the specious myths in general journalistic currency about the superiority of the American way of life, our language devalued far more quickly than our dollar by its debasement in the service of a fraudulent mythos:

> Reader,
> We had a lovely language,
> We would not listen.
>
> I don't believe in your god.
> I don't believe my Aunt Agnes is a saint.
> I don't believe the little boys
> Who stoned the poor
> Son of a bitch goat
> Are charming Tom Sawyers.
>
> I don't believe in the goat either.

Our freedom of religion, our canonizing of the common man, our permissiveness in child-rearing and our epidemic hero-worshiping of the untutored juvenile mentality, our pretense that animals—wild or domestic—suffer less brutality here than in other countries: in this brief litany of dismissals, Wright repudiates all of the favorite myths, even those that had been patently endorsed by his reverential anecdote—a disguised fable—about Aunt Agnes rescuing the goat. He acknowledges his own taint of false sentimentality in attributing even a modest glory to Aunt Agnes, suggesting that our language is so inured to sponsoring such falsifications that American poetry cannot help falling prey to it.

One of the handsomest overall exhibitions in the present volume of a happy mixture of Wright's usual dependable virtues and the most attractive features of his newer style is "Prayer to the Good Poet," addressed to Quintus Horatius Flaccus. Characteristically, Wright converses with the dead poet, having developed over the years an ambassadorial grace and expertise in the art of diplomatic relations with the ghostly world. With a surprising mixture of humor and high seriousness, in tone both arch and stately, he *prays* to one dead father to receive the dying other one comfortably, easefully, in death. He wishes to lessen his ailing father's pain. The two fathers are secret kinfolk after all, not only because each sired poet James, but also because the craft of poetry and exacting physical labor are equivalently difficult "bitter factories":

I worked once in the factory that he worked in.
Now I work in that factory that you live in.
Some people think poetry is easy.
But you two didn't.

The problem of negotiating a post-obsequies friendship, an exercise in supernatural matchmaking, between his dying father and his dead first mentor in poetry's immortal estate, the classical poet Horace, is an ingenious tour de force. It is a strategy for marrying the two families that have enriched his spirit and provided him with his chief abilities as man and artist, two complementary and allied spheres of intelligence— the world of art, the world of the common laborer. Clearly, Wright knows to his bones that his successful laboring in the craft of poetry is a legacy inherited from his years of apprenticeship—both a physical and a spiritual discipline—in factory work. Thus, his "Prayer" extols this charming triangle of kinships among men, living and dead, who, apart from their specialty of skilled laboring, are immoderately blessed with the power of human warmth. The trio are distinguished humans less because of their artistries than because of their fatherly benignity of spirit, their mutual capacity to "give the gift to each lovely other."

The rhapsody of giving extends, finally, to Wright's own son, in a passage of gentle, lilting rhythms, the tender lullaby cadences of Wright's easy-speaking quatrains more a music drawn from natural speech than spoken idioms implanted into verses:

Easy, easy, I ask you, easy, easy.
Early, evening, by Tiber, by Ohio,
Give the gift to each lovely other.
I would be happy.

Now my son is another poet, fathers,
I can go on living. I was afraid once
Four loving fathers meeting together
Would be a cold day in hell.

Quintus Horatius Flaccus, my good father,
You were just the beginning, you quick and lonely
Metrical crystals of February.
It is just snow.

The divergent streams of paternal ardors merge into a single confluence of brotherly spirits. In the outer limits and upper reaches of Wright's humanity, all delineations and classifications of family ties fade away. There are no nephews and uncles, teachers and students, mentors and disciples, master-craftsmen and apprentices: there are only brothers, brothers!

In Wright's main line of defense of his father's credentials to join the elect friends to Horace in Elysium, the logic for arguing a basis for affiliation is, of course, seriocomic:

Now, if I ask anything, I would ask you
How to gather my father to your bosom.
He knew, after all, how to love Italians.
Others said dagoes. . . .

Every time I go back home to Ohio,
He sits down and tells me he loves Italians.
How can I tell you why he loves you,
Quintus Horatius?

The rich overtones of this passage point to a dramatic frame of reference beyond the context of this poem to the larger scheme of the whole volume. If Wright is taxed by his efforts to put his father over as a great unacknowledged friend and kindred to Italians, how much severer are his anxieties lest the Italy of his European travels turn a deaf ear to his prayers for his own spiritual passport, in retaliation for the vulgarity and outrageous incivilities of many of his fellow countrymen who visited or emigrated to Italy before him, as in "Names Scarred at the Entrance to Chartres":

> P. Dolan and A. Doyle
> Have scrawled their names here. . . .
> I have no way to go in
> Except only
> In the company of two vulgars . . .

Wright's forerunners—maybe rich aristocrats in America—think they can earn a place in Olympus by hacking their names at the entrance gate to the cathedrals. But the poet knows himself to be, at best, a second-class citizen here, a full cut below the peons. Arriving with virtually no baggage—of class, of ancestry, of nobility, or of peasantry's natural grace of person—he pleads his humble case for admission. The poet waits and waits, his country's ugliness and dishonor weighing down his head, his spirit's shoulders hunched, America's disgraceful bad manners under-scored by the scars of "scrawled" signatures, "P. Dolan and A. Doyle," whom he cannot repudiate without forfeiting his American heritage. So he must carry the burden of his countrymen's disreputable acts, as well as the weight of his own crippled prosody ("the crude / Rhythm of my time"), with no help but his pride in his love, Annie, to solace and support him:

> The cracked song
> Of my own body limps into the body
> Of this living place. I have nobody
> To go in with
> But my love who is a woman,
> And my crude dead, my sea,
> My sea, my sepulcher, the crude
> Rhythm of my time.

> This cracking blossom is my second America.

His true passport among the Olympians is the authentic, vast awe he feels before the indecipherable magnitude of beauty in the cathedral. How can his mere stripped-down humble song do homage to this masterwork of scores of anonymous—Xs, nameless and forgotten—geniuses? By finding its modest life in the form of no more than a "cracked song," a broken-voiced mortal prayer to the immortals.

In a number of poems revering great works of sculpture and architecture, Wright guides the reader through an exquisite chain of paradoxes. How can we tell the monuments from the native people they were modeled after?

The Last Pietà, in Florence

> The whole city
> Is stone, even
> Where stone
> Doesn't belong.
> What is that old
> Man's public face
> Doing sorrowing,
> Secretly a little,
> A little above and
> A little back from
> A limp arm?
> What is that stone
> Doing sorrowing
> Where stone
> Doesn't belong?

Wright's ardors to the statues and the people are indistinguishable. Works of sculpture and cathedrals burgeon into supernatural life. The stone trembles and breathes. The stone erupts. It is flesh, and the poet feels embarrassment, shame—at moments, horror—before so much naked exposure of beautiful, soulful bodies in public.

How appropriate, then, for the archetypal woman to greet him unbidden from the eyes of the saints. In Bologna, Mary Magdalene is the muse whom Wright entreats to "give me this time . . . a poem about gold." Arrival in Italy, finding his true place and center at last, is a matter of raw encounter with the presiding supreme holy woman of the place. She rewards him with one of his best poems, "Bologna: A Poem about Gold." In a wonderful passage celebrating Mary's secret earthiness ("her love / For the golden body of the earth"), Wright swiftly composes a synthesis of sublime women: the Wife of Bath, Cleopatra, and his own privately mythic Jenny, all perceived as offspring of Mary, the prototypic complete woman who subsumes her descendants much as Yeats's Maude Gonne is canonized as a spiritual heir of Helen of Troy:

White wine of Bologna,
And the knowing golden shadows
At the left corners of Mary Magdalene's eyes,
While St. Cecilia stands
Smirking in the center of a blank wall,
The saint letting her silly pipes wilt down,
Adoring
Herself, while the lowly and richest of all women eyes
Me the beholder, with a knowing sympathy, her love
For the golden body of the earth, she knows me,
Her halo faintly askew,
And no despair in her gold
That drags thrones down
And then makes them pay for it.

Mary is sublimely guiltless and undespairing. Self and soul are balanced in her, the human and goddess comfortably wedded in the poet's vision of her icon.

W. S. Merwin

The Church of Ash

The hard edge of W. S. Merwin's scrupulous negativity is the fiercest poetic discipline around.[1] Readers can hardly fail to assimilate into their ears the violence of vacancy—the exacerbating vacuum—produced by shorn parings of our excesses he leaves behind him, littered on the path following his poems. In the ten years since the publication of *The Moving Target*, the first of four volumes developing his radical new aesthetics, Merwin's artistry has steadily deepened in the anger of an uncompromising honesty that pares away falsities, layer by layer, always leaving him in a condition of final exposure, vulnerability, nakedness. As in his style of writing, so in his style of spiritualizing—an utter divesting of defenses, the risk of more and more perfect defenselessness. He would denude himself of all possessions, all conceivable forms and modes of ownership, even stripping away the charter to his name, his face, since to own anything is to be enchained, shackled, to be owned in turn.

The soldiers have burned down all our churches of wood, whether our names were carved on the doors or written in the humble black of the charcoal floors. The only church left *standing* is made of ash; nobody owns it, and beautiful nameless spirits worship in its pews:

> we have a church where the others stood
> it's made of ash
> no roof no doors
>
> nothing on earth
> says it's ours
>
> from "Ash"

Merwin would found the church of the poem, then, from imperishable materials, words of ash. It is to be a poetry of no signatures, no

---

1. This review of *Writings to an Unfinished Accompaniment,* (New York: Atheneum, 1973), originally appeared in *The Yale Review* in 1973.

possessorship, a stamp of impersonality on the timbers of every line and stanza. Once complete, the poem is set free from the hand of its maker, its word-carpenter, to be owned by no one, by no place, by no time; thus, like the free nomad-spirit that breathed luminous, unconditional life into the art, the works will be indestructible, and inexhaustible in their power to nourish free spirits of countless readers who partake of their bounty.

Merwin's aspiration is to become an empty nobody, an impersonal, expertly trained thing—a tool, an instrument, a pure vehicle for the "one truth," the vision that suddenly fills the fertile, incubating emptiness: the state in which the spirit has completely freed itself from comforts, needs, habits, freed from a human personality, freed from the body's claims, freed from the demands of other beings, freed from the brand marks of colleagues, family, country:

> If it's invented it will be used
>
> maybe not for some time
>
> then all at once
> a hammer rises from under a lid
> and shakes off its cold family
>
> its one truth is stirring in its head
> order order saying . . .
>
> from "Tool"

This is the state of uttermost self-purification, disaffiliation, dispossession that Merwin has cultivated with unwavering tenacity in his last four volumes of original poetry and throughout his prodigious career as this country's foremost living translator of verse from other languages. It is a condition of maximum plasticity and availability, a priming and predisposing of the receptive ear to become a psychic medium for the poetry of foreign tongues, as well as for deep images springing from the subconscious mind, or from the racial preconscious: images germinating in the visionary dream-life that have the authority and unshakable finality about them of last basic necessities; images that are as indispensable to survival in worlds of the spirit stretching to its outer limits, on the verge of breaking into new uncharted territory, as the barest physical necessities—a little water, roots, scant body-covering—are crucial to survival in the desert.

Regrettably, he cannot sustain this level of peak accessibility, since the habits of our cumbersome sensory apparatus operate in most of our routine daily living at levels of imprecision and inefficiency far less sensitive, less in touch with the hidden spirit in words, images, or objects than is necessary to support the scrupulous fidelity to quantities, nuances, shades, hues, lusters—quieter brilliancies, faded grays, softer delicate radiances—that Merwin's spirit of aspiring perfectibility demands for his art. Hence, the disturbing perplexity, approaching a cosmic vertigo, of psychic states in which we have fallen hopelessly out of touch with the spirit centers, registered in poems such as "Habits" and "Something I've Not Done." Suddenly, we may feel alienated, or dissociated, from our own delicate—if unwieldy—senses. Our eyes, our ears, our tongues, our hands, our lungs—yes, even the most intimately undeliberated act of our breathing itself—every breath we take, or give back, may seem to work against us, to be at war with our wills, or to operate in a dimension so far removed from our conscious awareness, we may feel as if our sense organs have been invaded by alien identities, beings, presences:

> Even in the middle of the night
> they go on handing me around . . .
>
> even when I'm asleep they take
> one or two of my eyes for their sockets . . .
>
> when I wake and can feel the black lungs
> flying deeper into the century
> carrying me
> even then they borrow
> most of my tongues to tell me
> that they're me
> and they lend me most of my ears to hear them
>
> from "Habits"

This state of the psyche seems linked to the immense frustration, borne of a relentless perfectionism, in "Something I've Not Done":

> Something I've not done
> is following me
> I haven't done it again and again

so it has many footsteps
like a drumstick that's grown old and never been used

In late afternoon I hear it come closer
at times it climbs out of a sea
onto my shoulders
and I shrug it off
losing one more chance . . .

To be always obsessed with doing, making, crafting—as is this inex-haustibly prolific writer—is to be perennially haunted by the ghosts of the "not done," to be possessed by the demons of the one failure, the one forgetting, the one loss amidst a horde of gains: it is an aesthetic of tirelessness, forbidding rest or ease of spirit, much less gaiety, exuberance, or comic ebullience.

Behind all our words and acts, behind each very signing of names, lurk absences, vacancies, emptinesses. Active, not passive, voids. Dynamic silences. Alert negative spaces. This mysterious sector of our mental life, usually hidden from us, is vivified with astonishing poignancy in a dozen-odd impressive short poems of a strikingly new species in Merwin's proliferating canon. They are stark, direct in delivery, coolly remote and stingingly intimate at once, like daggers of hot ice: raw, naked, brutally overexposed in the sense of a photo with too much glare drowning the outlines of things, but so hypnotic in their quiet chanting that we cannot look away, or even a little to the side to shield our eyes, and we can't keep our gloveless, perishable hands off of them. The missing things embraced behind the lines of the poem exert an immense negative pull working invisibly upon the reader's ear. If we examine the few words and lines that are present, with much white space surrounding them on the page, we can hardly locate the source of the great suction that freezes a reader's ear to the poem, invisible like the lines of force of a powerful electromagnet.

The remarkable artistry in this cluster of poems is no idle exercise or mere exhibition of verbal legerdemain—the poems make an unmistak-able impact on the conscience of our unique American generation. In the peculiar way they make moral designs upon us, I have never read any-thing like them. They would shock readers into illumination of the slow, irreversible dyings of the true spirit within us, within animals, within things: the slow retreat of the mysterious inner beauty of each thing and being that *is* its life, its identity, its sole reality; the slow withdrawal from us of the spirit because of our neglect, our innocent blindness to all the inner secret life that we fail to recognize and that enacts its slow judgment upon us by simply turning away forever, turning its back on us, as in "The Place of Backs":

> When what has helped us has helped us enough
> it moves off and sits down
> not looking our way
>
> after that every time we call it
> it takes away one of the answers it had given us,

Or by staying hidden, locked inside our helpless waiting pencils, as in "The Unwritten":

> Inside this pencil
> crouch words that have never been written
> never been spoken
> never been taught
>
> they're hiding
>
> they're awake in there
> dark in the dark
> hearing us
> but they won't come out
> not for love not for time not for fire,

Or, again, as in "Something I've Not Done": "Every morning / it's drunk up part of my breath for the day," and the spirit is eaten up from within us, and eats ourselves up, bit by bit, during all our most unnoticed, ostensibly harmless, daily routines:

> while we sign our names
> more of us
> lets go
>
> and will never answer

In the consistent moral vision that informs these poems, a prophecy builds: Merwin foresees the total desertion, or secession, of the spirit from our inner life-space; not that the spirit will cease to exist on the planet we'll soon have depopulated of every animal species but our own—the spirit will simply take up its residence in exclusively nonmortal dwellings, and quite happily flourish without our feeble collaboration:

> While we talk
> thousands of languages are listening
> saying nothing

In another cluster of poems—"The Current," "Surf-Casting," "The Chase," "The Way Ahead"—the metaphysical keystone is the dissection and anatomizing of our age's cosmic greed, our measureless possessiveness and need for conquest. In these poems of the most bitter moral and political indignation since the antiwar poems of *The Lice*, Merwin translates the international politics of grasping into a personal, spiritual condition that can be satisfied by nothing short of the dream of total acquisitiveness: a vast, illimitable gluttony that seeks to swallow everything alive, that would empty the sea of all forms of life in one or two great gulps; and the swindle is all a disguised projection of our human identity onto the extrahuman world, at bottom, the most devastating self-betrayal that can be imagined, in a barren attempt to fill the void in the self left by the spirit's mutiny.

We are "surf-casting," having "practised a long time / with the last moments of fish." We employ our own irreplaceable toes for bait ("you have ten chances"). Our quarry is "the great Foot." The utter futility of the quest blinds us to the obvious barren terms: it is the vain, blundering attempt to repossess willingly amputated parts of our very being, squandered segments of the body of the self. Having depleted all of the available game in the world, we continue the obsolete charade of the hunt, our own foot for prey, which we do not recognize as a projected hunk of ourselves any more than we have recognized for centuries that all the animal legions we have decimated and all but exterminated were of the one spirit with our flesh, sharing our life, an extension and continuation of our own bodies, like our limbs. The current that surrounds the fish and also partakes of their body fluids is continuous in spirit with the blood currents that flow in our arteries and veins, though "for a long time" we've been "forgetting that we are water." Our blindness to our closest familial kin in the animal kingdom—flesh of our flesh, blood of our blood, of the one family—has progressed to the bizarre extremity of the terms of the last hunt. It must be the last, since we fish for our own "great Foot" using our toes as bait, and we will win, we know it, we'll always win:

> if only the great Foot is running

> if only it will strike
> and you can bring it to shore
>
> in two strides it will take you
> to the emperor's palace
> stamp stamp the gates will open
> he will present you with half of his kingdom
> and his only daughter
>
> and the next night you will come back
> to fish for the Hand

There are bewildering ambiguities of tone in "Surf-Casting," as in "The Way Ahead." The process that unfolds in the poem resembles, in many of its particulars, the spare, exacting discipline of Merwin's own most advanced aesthetic of the poem: the painstaking rituals practiced in pursuit of the perfecting of skill, mastery of both the mechanics of a craft and the profound, intimate awareness of the best conditions, the most suitable climate for its flourishing, are, it would seem, set forth sympathetically, and ironically, at once:

> It has to be the end of the day
> the hour of one star
> the beach has to be a naked slab
>
> and you have to have practised a long time
> with the last moments of fish
> sending them to look for the middle of the sea
> until your fingers
> can play back whole voyages . . .

The prophecy of "Surf-Casting" foresees the next stage in "The Way Ahead," envisioning a time in the near future when all nonhuman creatures will have been removed by us, but in our demented fantasy lives a hierarchy of larger and smaller creatures, an entire undiminished encyclopedic animal kingdom, will continue to flourish and populate our dreamscape:

> A winter is to come
>   when smaller creatures
>   will hibernate inside the bones

of larger creatures
and we will be the largest of all
and the smallest . . .

"The Way Ahead" is an agonizing oracular performance—all prophecies, all riddles, seemingly optimistic on the surface, but ringing hollow at the center. The poem has Orwellian overtones, true to the tenor of our American present historical moment. What is so disturbingly powerful in the poem is the way its visionary apparatus—the exquisite images, the authentic oracular tone persuading the ear by hypnosis, incantation, persuading the imagination with genuine fabling, mythologizing, riddle-making—all these immaculate skills flawlessly participate in the sellout that hangs us, an aesthetic soft-sell matching the political machinations of our day. The poem's power is enhanced, I feel, because Merwin dares to let his own instrument, his visionary medium at its most heightened pitch of clarity and revelation, fall under the grimmest judgment:

A Monday is to come
    when some who had not known
    what hands were for
    will be lifted and shaken
    and broken and stroked and blessed
    and made

The poet spares neither himself nor his most exalted art from the ferocity of his denunciation. The poem's valiant risk is in resisting the temptation to take comfort in the aloofness of an aesthetic remove from the crimes of innocence, of allowing ourselves to be violated, brutalized, mutilated, our spirits butchered, as we absentmindedly hasten the progress toward our own genocide, and Merwin invites the poem's craft to illustrate how our profoundest visionary myths and arts may be twisted to serve the fatal ends:

Feet are already marching there
    fields of green corn and black corn are already
    throwing up their hands
    all the weeds know and leap up from the ditches
    every egg presses on toward those ends
    for this the clouds sleep with the mountains
    for this in the almanacs of the unborn
    terrible flowers appear

one after the other
giving new light

A light is to come

How much rage is contained in the parody of political optimism in this passage, closing the poem. All living things left—the few survivors of each diminishing species—are fooled by the Nixonian cant of the propaganda machine preaching better times in "The Way Ahead," advocating escape from the pain of the present into the future. All flora and fauna, then, are tricked into hurrying into the premature void of extinction, mistaking their doom, their "first day of ruin," for a "new light" that "is to come."

Our misdeciphering the tragic events of our time goes hand in hand with our misreading, or mishearing, of the words:

When the pain of the world finds words
they sound like joy
and often we follow them
with our feet of earth
and learn them by heart
but when the joy of the world finds words
they are painful
and often we turn away
with our hands of water

Merwin instills a profound belief, here, that everything depends on our learning to find our way back into touch with the true spirit behind the life of words. Our tragedy is our hopeless disaffiliation from the saving, healing powers of our own native tongue, and what could be more desolately mistaken than misreading joy for pain, pain for joy?

However, I find Merwin's new voice most attractive when the quality of intellectual rage, the impulse to scathing moral judgment, is transmuted into a drama of the lone spirit battling with itself, the full intensity of judgment turned inward that, for all its censuring of failures to measure up to standards set by its highest aspirations, is tempered by a compassionate acceptance. In "Division," an austere myth resonating with overtones from American Indian folklore, a dominant saving quality of whimsy, caprice, archness invests the vision with a fortification of human warmth that is, I feel, the most welcome new emotional undertone in a handful of the best new poems in this book—a quality of tempering mercy and self-forgiveness, a willingness to fail:

People are divided
because the finger god
named One
was lonely
so he made for himself a brother like him
named Other One
then they were both lonely

so each made for himself four others
all twins

then they were afraid
that they would lose each other
and be lonely

so they made for themselves two hands
to hold them together

but the hands drifted apart . . .

There are surges here of the human light of feeling radiating from humility before weakness exposed, indeed, weakness exalted beyond all spite that mistakes its whimpers for meagerness of soul. What abides in these lines is the refreshing quality of quiet ardor, a gentle self-mockery, with all mere human negativity purged out of the judgment, that assures me that this poem could utterly charm the shrewd ears of children, whose infallible capacity to detect some varieties of fraudulence has never been adequately explained or acknowledged. I can only hope that this emergent quality of gaiety and buoyancy, which approaches ecstatic generosity of spirit in the beautiful new poem that ends the book, "Gift," consummate in its serenity and happiness of earned spiritual independence, is the forerunner to the next major rebirth in the work of this poet of many radical self-restylings, this prince of alchemists:

I have to trust what was given to me
if I am to trust anything
it led the stars over the shadowless mountain
what does it not remember in its night and silence
what does it not hope knowing itself no child of time . . .

I call to it Nameless One O Invisible
Untouchable Free

I am nameless I am divided
I am invisible I am untouchable
and empty
nomad live with me
be my eyes
my tongue and my hands
my sleep and my rising
out of chaos
come and be given

Still another remarkable new development in many poems of this volume is the power with which ordinary inanimate objects—a wharf, a house, a room, a hammer and nail, a door hauled on someone's shoulders, a burning plank of wood—are endowed with supernatural presence, or haunted being:

O venerable plank burning
and your pegs with you
the hordes of flame gaining
in the marks of the adze
each mark seven times older than I am
each furthermore shaped like a tongue
you that contain
of several lives now only a dust
inside the surfaces that were once cuts
but no memory no tree
even your sparks dust
toward the last some of your old pitch
boils up through you
many children running
into a shining forest

The objects are pictured—or silhouetted, rather, so few the details selected—with hallucinatory clarity and maximum suggestiveness at once. I'm reminded of the drawings of Matisse, in which a single curved line of subtly varied sharpness and intensity suggests intricately not only the shape and position of the model's neck, arch of back, buttock, calf, and a possible gesture, or swerve, of movement, but also hints enigmatically the exact mass and density and texture of the missing precincts of flesh—flank, loin, shoulder. By a secret power, by invisible craft, the few lines and dots and fleck marks hint—but to hint with precision and exactitude is to inescapably command the viewer's eye—the larger, weightier, missing quantities of the figure that blossom in the vacancy, the eye's masterfully controlled hallucinated versions of forms filling in the blank white space, the explosive negative areas, which make up immeasurably more of the canvas than the *positives*, the areas literally filled with pencilings.

As the draftsman the eye, so does the impresario-poet command the reader's ear. To a degree surpassing every other poet of my acquaintance, writing in English or any other language, W. S. Merwin has developed with increasing mastery in his last four volumes of verse a Matisse-like notation, a fantastic linguistic shorthand, in which the few irreducible lines and images chosen (or has he mastered, rather, the power of perfect submission, passivity, in allowing the inevitable lines and images to choose *him*, the translator's genius?) guide the reader's ear by unerringly exact bridges across the very hinges—invisible overlaps and interlockings—between the words to the silences behind, or surrounding, the spoken utterances. This wizardry is accomplished by chains of sound and echoes, the echoes of echoes, the tones and overtones—all matings that tie or bind sound to silence, tongue to its dumbness, voice to its muteness; and always, in Merwin's art at its best, that which is given, or revealed nakedly, releases by invisible art those quantities that are withheld, buried, concealed, but *contained* in the silence, and therefore inescapably picked up by the reader's ear, and poignantly heard, leading the reader into the heart of a vision of quietly gathering intensity, balanced halfway between sound and silence. Or rather, not vision—the scores of eyes and eye-images in this book are always closing, or going blind—but *audition*, an integrated totality of incantatory chantings, the insistently felt and intensely heard presences of sound building cumulatively in the silences, the apparent voids of voice, as orchestration builds into a central awakening and reverberation within a listener's ear, resonating wholenesses of the heard and ultraheard. But no, Wallace Stevens anticipated me by exactly fifty years in the search for an alternate word, beyond *vision*, to take account of an utterly new music in the poetic art of our American language: a *harmonium*.

Mark Strand

The Book of Mourning

Reasons for Moving

Some readers of Mark Strand's *Reasons for Moving* will dismiss the book as being merely an assortment of clever stories set up to look like poems.[1] For poetry to be as obviously interesting and readable as the pieces that open this book ("Eating Poetry," "The Accident," "The Mailman") is apt to arouse the intellectual reader's suspicion. Even the most difficult poems ("Man in the Tree," "The Ghost Ship") have a deceptive simplicity. They seem so perfectly transparent on first reading that it is puzzling to find, on repeated readings, that they wear as well as they do. Despite their initial sudden impact on our emotions, the poems deliver their full import to us slowly, after many readings. Trying to get under the skin of these poems to experience them more deeply is like trying to get inside a disturbing dream from which we have just awakened. We remember the dream, usually, as a sequence of events in time, and then put it out of mind, vaguely sensing that memory has cheated the inquiring self by reducing a powerful symbolic complex of being to a mere time sequence. But the searching intelligence is not content to be cheated by memory's tricks, not when a dream, or dream poem, has struck like an ax into the deeper mind. As in the most powerful dreams, the events of the story in Strand's poems serve as a frame for a rich complex of symbolic images, gestures, human encounters.

The beautiful strangeness of "Man in the Mirror" and "The Last Bus" derives from the dual effect of an austere simplicity of events combined with an inexhaustibly rich overlay of images. The naturalness of Strand's verse movement allows for a maximum quantity of radical imagery to be carried without making the reader's ear feel overburdened:

> I was walking downtown
> when I noticed a man in black,

---

1. This review of *Reasons for Moving*, (New York: Atheneum, 1968), originally appeared in *The Yale Review* in 1968.

black cape and black boots, coming toward me.

His arms out in front of him,
his fingers twinkling with little rings,
he looked like a summer night full of stars.

It was summer. The night was full of stars.

from "The Man in Black"

The splendid transition between the last two lines of the passage demon-
strates how Strand's imagination characteristically seizes upon a meta-
phor to suggest a just-hidden mystery behind the forceful appearances,
the bright exteriors, of everyday things. The next moment, the scene is
transformed by the metaphor into a new identity, one that retains the old
clarity of outline but clothes it in the unsheddable garment of the poet's
inner life. The poetry moves so swiftly and effortlessly from ordinary
reality into dumbfounding spirituality that a reader is taken by surprise.
And the surprise may not be lessened after several readings—the poem
will catch the reader off guard every time. Somehow the lines sweep
from day into night, waking to dreaming, humor to horror, serenity to
hysteria, safety to ruin—to doom, with no appreciable shift in the plane
of vision. Emotional and spiritual opposites of every sort exist side by
side, and join hands, in the poems: "The end of my life begins," Strand
reasons with absurd clarity, as if he were inhabited by two men—the
living being and the dying being—and the birth of his extraordinary art
is the progeny of the marriage between them.

The poems in this book are defined within a field that is governed by
such clear-cut rules that any flaw in language or rhythm will show like
an inkblot on white linen. No tricks will work. The poet has deliberately
divested his style of every means to fool the reader. Everything he makes
the poem do is inescapably in the open, in plain view. The cost of this
method is an unfashionably thin book of finished work. The reward is a
kind of elegantly flawless art—in a few poems—that bespeaks a perfect
tuning of the instrument.

The Book of Mourning

By all odds, Mark Strand's *The Story of Our Lives* has far less immedi-
ate sensuous appeal than his earlier volumes of poetry.[2] The virtuoso

---

2. This review of *The Story of Our Lives,* (New York: Atheneum, 1973), originally
appeared in *Poetry* in 1974.

performer of *Darker* has been supplanted by an elegist. *Story* is chiefly a book of mourning. Strand mourns the deaths of his father ("Elegy for My Father"), his mother and his childhood ("The Untelling"), his marriage ("The Room," "The Story of Our Lives," "Inside the Story"), and finally, the demise of the aesthetics that informed the spare, compact poems of his other books ("To Begin"). Evidently, for the moment, he has abandoned the assured popular instrument that appears to have acquired a school of followers—imitators and parodists—much as did the prototypical short, intense lyric of Merwin, Kinnell, Wright, and O'Hara of the generation before him spawn a coterie of idolaters and apprentices. *Story* is a haunting book, though not as disheartening as its prevailing timbre of somberness on first acquaintance suggests. The book culminates in a quiet joy, an intellectual ecstasy of a kind we would never have anticipated from the poetry's characteristic gravity. However, readers who were allured by Strand's elegant charm, as well as by the fabling gnomic terror and humor of his phantasmagoric dream poems, may be disappointed by the expansive sprawl of the long new poems that, by a slow effervescence of incantatory rhythms, cast a gradual hypnotic spell over us. The new poems make far greater demands of our powers of concentration, but the rewards, after many readings, are equivalently greater.

In *Darker,* Strand had employed the mode of chanted litanies for the first time, a form that accounted for an important widening of imaginative range, releasing him from the strict contract of the stanza form, the exclusive mode of his first two volumes. In *The New Poetry Handbook,* he explored the associative logic of serial image chains, an experiment related formally to the list-poem genre developed exhaustively in the brilliantly funny poems of Kenneth Koch, and in scores of cheerless imitations by poets of the New York school. It was an ostensibly non-programmatic structure, mystifying the reader with the illusion that the open-ended poems started or stopped at purely arbitrary points in an endlessly stretchable series of imagistic statements, as in Strand's two quasi-fragments deceptively titled "From a Litany." Yet Strand baffled the form, inveigling the reader's ear with a mastery of tonal resonance that left the aftertaste of an organic unity all but impossible to locate or account for by conventional inspection of the structure, while a few passages of lavish imagery contained a more elevated pitch of musical opulence than he had ever approached in his previous work.

In "Elegy for My Father," the stately, slow-paced, hypnotic dirge that begins the new volume, Strand amplifies the serial mode of litany. Exhibiting a remarkable range of technical virtuosity, he adapts the device of image chains to six widely varying fantasias. In each, a simple statement—

flat and blunt—is repeated at irregular intervals, and operates less like a conventional refrain than an aria or leitmotiv in an opera. The statement tends to fade, to become hidden, vanishing into a chanted monotony, but it subtly builds resonance in the reader's ear and accumulates a force of quiet, but irreversible, authority. "Nothing could stop you. You went on with your dying."

In "Your Dying," the midsection of the poem, the father's unswerving complicity in his progress toward death exalts the process of welcoming death into an austere discipline, an artistry that by its propulsive force of negation, by its revulsion from nature and human society, sends all things into orbit around itself. He achieves an absolute solipsism of dying, which is mirrored by the son's solipsism of mourning. The total psychic withdrawal from life, paradoxically, adds a dimension to being alive, a deepening and heightening of spirit, which threatens the comfortable world of the living, the friends and neighbors who "doze in the dark / of pleasure and cannot remember." The living are shocked into a panic of opposition—they are wavery, unstable, flighty, aimless. The act of dying easily imposes its higher will and design on the chaos of life, its deathly order on the disorder that is prevalent everywhere.

The whole book is a profound act of mourning; hence, the aptly grotesque irony of the fifth section of the elegy, titled "Mourning," a Kafkaesque caricature of conventional funerals in which the mourning process, so indispensable to healing the psychic wounds of bereavement, is debased and betrayed by self-pity. The common blind refusal to accept death is parodied as a procession of beggarly kin pleading with the corpse to come back to life, perverting the funeral rites into a litany of gamy ruses to pamper and coddle him into not dying, as if a complex gymnastics of undying could undo the death:

> They mourn for you.
> When you rise at midnight . . .
> They sit you down and teach you to breathe.
> And your breath burns,
> It burns the pine box and the ashes fall like sunlight.
> They give you a book and tell you to read.
> They listen and their eyes fill with tears.
> The women stroke your fingers.
> They comb the yellow back into your hair.
> They shave the frost from your beard.
> They knead your thighs.
> They dress you in fine clothes.

They rub your hands to keep them warm.
They feed you. They offer you money.
They get on their knees and beg you not to die.
When you rise at midnight they mourn for you.
They close their eyes and whisper your name over and over.
But they cannot drag the buried light from your veins.
They cannot reach your dreams.

So far from resisting, or denying, the reality of his father's death, Strand's own mode of mourning is to follow his father into dying, taking as many steps down the path toward death as possible short of dying himself, and though this process culminates in a valiant entreaty invoking the invisible powers for release from the bondage to his father's corpse ("It came to my house. / It sat on my shoulders. / Your shadow is yours. I told it so. I said it was yours. / I have carried it with me too long. I give it back."), it is clear from the other poems of the present volume that the elegy is only the first milestone in an interior odyssey in which he follows a long, intricate course in developing a new poetics that recapitulates his vision of his father's dying. Strand is obsessed, in poem after poem, with absence, vanishings, disappearance of parts of his own psyche. The opening litany of the elegy, "The Empty Body," suggests that the author's obsession with disappearance grew initially out of the shock of witnessing his father's dead body. He could not fathom or accept the emptiness—the spiritual evacuation—of the corpse:

The hands were yours, the arms were yours,
But you were not there.
The eyes were yours, but they were closed and would not open. . . .
The body was yours, but you were not there.
The air shivered against its skin.
The dark leaned into its eyes.
But you were not there.

The two dominant human situations in *Story*—the dying of a father, the dying of a marriage—are not simply fictive correlates, but clearly the occasions in the author's life that demanded for their successful embodying and execution in the poetry a commensurately barren, arid, desolate vocabulary. Strand subjects his style in this book to a severe cutback—approaching a strangulating *cutoff* in some passages—of his most dependable resources, and he adopts a starkly austere and reductive diction. In each of the central poems, the persona has come to a hopeless spiritual impasse—the necessity to change his life is as crucial to continued survival as the act of breathing. The author has reached the point in his career at which the full stretch of his technical powers, all the mastery of craft he can muster, is needed to accomplish an extraliterary goal, a task outside language. He must change his life. He must move beyond a life that threatens to suffocate his spirit into another life, and he will mobilize all human and artistic resources to achieve this—hence, this book's radical shift to a lean poetics of expediency. The process of writing is an act of heroic struggle to stay alive in the spirit against terrible odds, to maintain the life of a beleaguered sensibility. Thus, the stripping away of all but the most subtle artifice, and the divesting of all stylistic flourish, all superfluities. Literary success is an accidental by-product of this enterprise.

The language in this book has grown so refined, so flattened and subdued, that it resembles ordinary poetry—or indeed, literature—less and less, and one may look for parallels to explain its technique more readily in other arts, such as painting, a discipline to which Strand submitted himself years before that of poetry. In "The Room," Strand creates the illusion that the high drama between the lovers at a time of crisis is dictated simply by the interior design of the room's furniture, by spatial and temporal arrangements of objects, by pacings—to and fro— of the two human bodies; but the poem's design is covertly propelled by movements of the characters' inner lives. Everything that happens between them appears to depend on moves toward and away from the few plain objects. I'm reminded of how much spiritual power of the kind that enables people to change their lives radically—to choose or leave their mates, to find their life's work, to risk and perhaps sacrifice their lives for love or some other faith—is contained in the subtle color shadings and spatial placements of pieces of fruit in a still life by Cezanne. Or rather, like the objects in a painting by Magritte, the objects in Strand's poem are so bare and plain and unembellished by ornament that a reader is dumbfounded by any effort to locate the source of the fierce supernatural energy that surrounds them:

> The room is long.
> There is a table in the middle.
> You will walk
> toward the table,
> toward the flowers,
> toward the presence of sorrow
> which has begun to move

> among objects,
> its wings beating
> to the sound of your heart. . . .
> I know by the way
> you raise your hand
> you have noticed the flowers
> on the table.
> They will lie
> in the wake of our motions
> and the room's map
> will lie before us
> like a simple rug.
> You have just entered.

We are persuaded that the activity of writing such long poems and studying the enlarging drafts of each poem between writing spurts, by a slow unfolding of stages, was clearly the *only* way left—whatever others may have been undertaken—for a human being named Strand to survive in the spirit. Any careful reader must discover, unmistakably, that for their author the process of composing these mournful threnodies was not so much an act of writing them down as of slowly begetting and weaning them, coaxing and beguiling the lines out of a near-implacable muteness, a dark interior mausoleum of the soul in which the spirit's pulse has slowed down so much that its tiny flickerings are barely perceptible, and he must carry these slowest, quietest flickerings of the spirit's life through an almost unendurably long gestation from first mumblings into audible voice, and finally, the building into resonant utterance.

In "The Room," as in the two longer poems about the languishment of desolating love ("The Story . . ." and "Inside the Story"), the prevailing mental weather is anxiety. In "To Begin," the poem that I take to be the axis about which the artist slowly and agonizingly rotates from the poetics of his earlier books to his new metaphysics, the climate is a crippling dose of malaise:

> He lay in bed not knowing how to begin. . . .
> There was no reason to get up.
> Let the sun shine without him.
> He knew he was not needed,
> that his speech was a mirror, at best,
> that once he had imagined his words
> floating upwards, luminous and threatening,

moving among the stars, becoming the stars,
becoming in the end the equal of all the dead
and the living. He had imagined this
and did not care to again.

When so much radiance has faded ("The sun and moon had washed
up / on the same shore"), so much ambition and limitless aspiration
played themselves out and been quenched, and youth's inflated dreams
of infinite solipsistic power been punctured, a writer's disillusionment is
total and spreads to every precinct of his being. His refusal of speech and
the preference for silence go very deep, and the failure to summon up—or
mobilize—enough energy to break the deadlock, the stranglehold on his
speaking voice, reduces him to a state of vast spiritual torpor and lethargy:

It took no courage, no special
recklessness to discredit silence.
He had tried to do it, but had failed.
He had gone to bed and slept.
The phrases had disappeared, sinking
into sleep, unwanted and uncalled for.

The last step in an unbroken chain of failures to endow faltering speech
with consequence before the plunging descent into muteness—utter
speechlessness—is the writer's attempt to "discredit silence," but this is the
one failure that will save him. It is by sinking far enough into the silence,
the sleep of language, that language may be restored. Finally, the poet will
honor the silence, not rival it, and celebrate silence in speech that is torn
from immense avoidance of speech, a fierce intensity of passion contained
in the unspoken, the untold. To resist the impulse to tell falsehood, and to
master the counterimpulse of the *untelling,* is to revitalize the art of writing
into a noble mental discipline, a discipline by which he may become
wedded to the silence, transforming it from a rival into an ally. His lost
dream of absolute solipsistic power will return, but in a different form; he
will be absolute monarch and sovereign lord of the manor of his interior
landscape, a possible topography for the rebirth of his deposed aesthetic
reign glimpsed for a few shaky moments in the midst of his struggle to
shake off the bonds of the dying love relation in "Story. . . .":

A bleak crown rested uneasily on his head.
He was the brief ruler of inner and outer discord,
anxious in his own kingdom.

But to rediscover exalted being, to come again into possession of the deep, passional self, necessitates a slow, step-by-step chain of negotiations with nothingness borne of a powerful, ruthless stripping away of all versions of ourselves forced upon us by human society, by occasions in a life—anniversaries, pacts, honors—all those data that the world assumes are the loci for treaties and contracts between the private life and the public theater that beget self-definition. The popular confessional school in our poetry supports this despiritualizing of identity, but Strand's radically opposed strategy of self-discovery challenges the narrowness of the public ego running naked through the avenues of our verse, and aspires to restore to contemporary poetry something of the lost multidimensionality of Yeats's "Dialogue of Self and Soul," by fashioning a self toughened in the crucible of its warring with the timeless human spirit.

Perhaps the most remarkable single poem Strand has written to date is "The Untelling," the very long poem that ends the new volume. The poem revisits a haunting scene from Strand's childhood, as the persona tells the same story, again and again, in his struggle to reconcile—or reconnect—his adult identity with a missing part of himself locked in the past. The poem begins with maximum distance, remove, between the adult and the child, the twin moieties—or doubles—of the same psyche. The doubles move closer and closer, and by a cyclic progression—toward and away, toward and away—they finally coincide. The persona is training himself, by a sequence of scrupulously delicate entries and exits, to achieve a dialogue between the worlds of present and past, and thus to learn expertise as a traveler in the interior landscape of the self. He finds he must rehearse the recital many times, each time stumbling at different points in the script, the audition, the scenario, and beating a retreat to correct his blunders, then beginning again:

> Maybe something had happened
> one afternoon in August.
> Maybe he was there or waiting to be there,
> waiting to come running across a lawn
> to a lake where people were staring
> across the water.
> He would come running
> and be too late.
> The people there would be asleep.
> Their children would be watching them.
> He would bring what he had written
> and then would lie down with the others.

> He would be the man
> he had become, the man
> who would run across the lawn.
> He began again:

In writing a long poem, it is not unusual for the writer to make a good number of partial forays, or tentative excursions, into the field of his vision, withdrawing again and again to retune his instrument and alter his grip on his materials, picking up the weighty opus and laying it back down again in exasperation many times before striking exactly the right key or pitch for executing the vision. But I know of no other poem that dramatizes and explicates this very process, revealing the artist's many approaches and withdrawals, his to-and-fro rhythm of becoming attuned to the map, the layout, of his inner landscape, as exhaustively as this poem does; in fact, the slow discovery of the aesthetic outlined above is quite as much the poem's subject as the reengagement with an experience of childhood that occupies the front of the stage.

The persona of "The Untelling" is an updated spiritual pioneer akin to the hero of Bunyan's *Pilgrim's Progress,* though in Bunyan's work, a chief ancestor of the modern novel, the external lineaments of plot are far more complex. But in both works it is the story within the story, the drama of the spirit's progress, that is always felt to be dominant, though subtly masked by the translucent overlay of the narrative line. The events of consequence are always internal, and must be inferred obliquely from the play of figures and scenes that populate the surface. In "The Untelling," the constituents of nature are a few ordinary, bland stage props of setting—the lake, the woods, the lawn; the human events recounted are pedestrian, colorless, pale. Strand divests all surface glamours and sustains an utmost faith in the power of the barest scene, robbed of all picturesque trappings, to assert a hidden emotional turbulence, avoiding at every step the expected opportunities to exploit strong overt feelings. He explores, instead, the cataclysmic events in the self that occur only when the life of intense personality appears to have slowed and slowed, nearly dying out, like the pulse of a hibernating bear. The active life of ego and consciousness is etherized into a slow lento, the music a stately, dispassionate minuet that, toward the end of the poem, approaches a rhythm of somnolence, a meter that mimics indolent breathing:

> It was late.
> It did not matter.

He would never catch up
with his past. His life
was slowing down.
It was going.
He could feel it,
could hear it in his speech.
It sounded like nothing,
yet he would pass it on.
And his children would live in it
and they would pass it on,
and it would always sound
like hope dying, like space opening. . . .

Hesitant, slow, halting. Slower and slower, from andante to larghetto to largo. The short, end-stopped one-line sentences, especially, bring the poem's rhythm near to a dead halt, the meter all but standing still. The music is holding its breath, and in listening, a reader finds that if the tone of poetry is superbly well modulated, a poem can stop breathing, but its life continues, as it probes for a hidden inner rhythm of the heartbeat. Another music—subliminal—imperceptibly emerges and overtakes the fading tempo:

. . . he was alone in the dark,
unable to speak.
He stood still.
He felt the world recede
into the clouds,
into the shelves of air.
He closed his eyes. . . .
He felt himself at that moment to be
more than his need to survive,
more than his losses,
because he was less than anything.
He swayed back and forth.
The silence was in him
and it rose like joy
like the beginning.
When he opened his eyes,
the silence had spread, the sheets
of darkness seemed endless,
the sheets he held in his hand.

As a child, Strand had felt alienated—as if the scene did not belong to him, nor he to the scene—because he witnessed the events from a clairvoyant and enchanted darkness. He had seen beyond the natural world, through the bodies, past the faces, heard beyond the voices, and penetrated into the mysterious heart of things, but tragically he could not recognize the sacred beauty he saw and heard, much less share his revelations with the adults. Later, in the process of writing the poem, these visions are recalled, revivified, and given a public form in the writings; hence, this poet's power to share his most private and intimate recollections with readers. But to do so, he had to find a way to be in the scene and outside it looking in, at once, to be himself as a child and adult, simultaneously, to see through the eyes of both, and thereby to repossess—by the genius of his art—the leap of spiritual transcendence that had occurred in childhood:

> . . . I shut the window
> and saw them in the quiet glass, passing
> each time farther away. The trees began
> to darken . . . The shapes among the trees kept changing.
> It may have been one child I saw, its face.
> It may have been my own face looking back.
> I felt myself descend into the future.
> I saw beyond the lawn, beyond the lake,
> beyond the waiting dark, the end of summer,
> the end of autumn, the icy air, the silence,
> and then, again, the windowpane. I was
> where I was, where I would be, and where I am.

The Untelling is a Wordsworthian vision of self reborn, as in *The Prelude*, from dwelling on the few enigmatic and haunted moments of childhood in which the natural world flooded our being with an annihilating quiet—half ecstasy, half terror—lifting us out of the net of human society, both its protection and its constraint, and shaping our hidden core of identity. These events occurred at mystical, unforeseen moments, but each at a definite locus in time, in place. The child in the poem, though dazed, poignantly contained, and carried away within him, the scene, the locale in which the mysterious psychic events occurred. To walk away physically was in no sense to leave that geography ("Though I walked away, I had no sense of going"), since the scene had been miraculously ingested and transformed into an inner landscape of himself. For the grown man to recall those moments, and that scene, within the vision, by a disciplined and controlled tautology of self-hypnosis, is not simply to relive or reexperience them, but to reenter the vivid flux of total spiritual elasticity of childhood, that utmost availability for change. Those deep situations, stories begun but left unfinished in our inner lives, may be resumed, continued as if the two or three decades of young manhood have never intervened or interrupted the process of their unfolding. Thus the powerful rewards made accessible by this aesthetic of reentries into an earlier life of being, born accidentally of itself in childhood.

A. R. Ammons

Of Mind and World

Northfield Poems

Not the least of A. R. Ammons's virtues is that he is an original philosopher in his poetry, though often he parades in the guise of poet-as-antiphilosopher, much as Plato wore the guise of philosopher-as-anti-poet.[1] In "Uh, Philosophy," he cuts deeper into the subject the more he pretends, with graceful offhandedness, to dismiss its importance:

> I understand
>   reading the modern philosophers
> that truth is so much a method
>   it's perfectly all
> right for me to believe whatever
>   I like or if I like,
> nothing:
>   I do not know that I care to be set that free:

He comes at each idea a little from the side, obliquely, with a chuckle of ridicule in the voice of the poem every time the meandering river of the speaker's mind inclines to become trapped by any one idea or perspective, or threatens to take ideas in and of themselves as having supreme consequence:

>   philosophy is
> a pry pole, materialization,
>   useful as a snowshovel when it snows;
> something solid to knock people down with
>   or back people up with:
> I do not know that I care to be backed up in just that way:

1. This review of *Northfield Poems,* (Ithaca, N.Y.: Cornell University Press, 1967), originally appeared in *The Hudson Review* in 1967.

231

> the philosophy gives clubs to
> everyone, and I prefer disarmament:

The irony masterfully saves the poem, always reminding the reader that ideas are so many disinterestedly linked events in the circuitous drama of the poem's argument, which ends exactly where it began:

> what are facts if I can't line them up
>   anyway I please
> and have the freedom
>   I refused I think in the beginning?

The poem's secret, which is revealed subtly and implicitly in its movement, is that the mind finds truth—is truest to itself—when it is released into the self-discovering rhythms of a good poem. To be true to the voice and line of the poem—an ever-changing field of play—always captures the speaker's first allegiance, never the ideas themselves. Most ideas would remain inert if not for the vivid life the poem's artistry imparts to them.

Ammons's knack for self-mockery saves the studiedly philosophical poems from self-conscious straining, as in "Zone," in which matter-of-fact remarks about the time of day, and such, interrupt the flow of formal scientific discourse. Ideas, in the poems, are quantities of form, shape, design; they are not vehicles for conveying logic, truth, validity. Ideas have texture, color, size, weight. To Ammons, they have the quality of physical objects:

> A symmetry of thought
> is a metal object:
> is to spirit
> a rock of individual shape . . .
> a crystal, precipitate

Ammons treats ideas as so many jointed bodies colliding with each other and with observed natural phenomena interchangeably. Conversely, actual objects may be decomposed into substanceless vapors by the intense play of the mind. The interchange of form between ideas that have grown solid and objects that have turned gaseous, or bodiless, may have been suggested to Ammons by Einstein's formula $E = mc^2$, demonstrating the relation between energy and matter. (Ammons, indeed, was schooled in the sciences, and this background served to broaden the scope of his poetic imagination from the start.) Whatever the source of his idea/thing inversion, one may more profitably inquire into the use he makes of it, the way he fits it to his unique sensibility. I see it as a particularly apt formula for embodying Ammons's original view of the relation between mind and world, between inner and outer reality. Although ideas and things may exist separately, they can have no importance or vitality for Ammons unless they disturb each other, interact. When this interaction is carried to the point of total engagement, the poet achieves his vision, a state in which elements of thought and elements of nature mix freely and exchange identities in a kind of ecstatic flux of poetic imagination, as in "Peak":

> Everything begins at the tip-end, the dying-out,
>   of mind:
> the dazed eyes set and light
> dissolves actual trees:
>   the world beyond: tongueless,
> unexampled
> burns dimension out of shape,
> opacity out of stone:
> come: though the world ends and cannot
> end,
>   the apple falls sharp
> to the heart starved with time.

The peak experience is defined and demonstrated. Mind stretched to its utmost limits (the "tip-end" of consciousness), after acute concentration on particulars of concrete experience ("actual trees"), casts into "the world beyond." Paradoxically, a scrupulous attention to the thing itself, its precise identity, begets a mental state in which the most solid things lose their form, become dimensionless, apparitional ghosts in the poet's vision (trees dissolve, stone loses its opacity). Ammons's genius is most evident in the transition into the final stanza: "come, though the world ends and cannot / end." Invitation to the reader to take the final step, to throw himself fully into the world of the poem without holding anything back, is a frequent device; in this poem, it is perfectly timed and has the disarming simplicity of a handshake. The reader was at the point of recoiling from the experience, because the poem had shown that mind's peak is a sort of mindlessness in which the lovely things of this world fade away into shadows of themselves, but Ammons now assures us that we shall return from the "peak" (as Frost swings back on his birches) to find a world of things more solid for having undergone his visionary dissolution: "the apple falls sharp." One must be willing to sacrifice the world completely, in faith, if one is to get it back whole, regain it to the peak of mind's embrace.

Ammons, the craftsman, often declares that he will risk everything, technically, to avoid the temptation to take refuge in the safety of pregiven forms, and, from time to time, he discards methods, devices of his own, that have proven successful, as in "Muse":

> . . . how many
> times must I be broken and reassembled!
>   anguish of becoming,
>   pain of moulting,
> descent! before the unending moment of vision:

In learning to write all over again, he stumbles, gropingly, the lines of the poem "inching rootlike into the dark." Since he must slog through many failed poems "to find materials / for the new house of my sight," he takes his place beside D. H. Lawrence and Whitman in the Anglo-American free-verse tradition of blessedly "uneven" poets. Probably that sort of unevenness will always be the sacred trademark of the most gifted and revolutionary poets, since most of our good writers seem satisfied, if not compulsively driven, to maintain a constant of external polish in everything they write.

Ammons is pursuing a theory of poetry that radically departs from the theory advanced by the poetry of Yeats and the criticism of Ezra Pound, who occurs as an advocate to be resisted or revolted against in a number of poems in this book and in the previous collection:

> I coughed
>   and the wind said
> Ezra will live
> to see your last
>   sun come up again . . .
> the wind went off
>   carving
> monuments through a field of stone
>   monuments whose shape
> wind cannot arrest but
> taking hold on
> changes
>
>> from "The Wind Coming Down From"

If Pound is a monument of stone, Ammons chooses to identify with the lowly weed. If Pound advocates the poem of permanence, the indestructible art object, Ammons prefers the poem as a way of being, of being in touch. While Pound affirms what is most tough and enduring in man, the ruthless will to immortality of the conventional major poet, Ammons reveres a delicate, sensitive transitoriness of being. The best of Ammons's poems point, finally, away from themselves, back to the most evanescent motions and vicissitudes of wind, leaf, and stream that first enchanted the poet and finally stole his heart. The gentlest motions of things touch him most deeply, speak to him with a sort of ultimate, if nonhuman, intimacy. He is vulnerable, nakedly exposed, receptive to the touch of feather, pebble, birdsong; in fact, these phenomena have such command over him as to leave him looking helplessly struck (or struck dumb), as by indecent or obscenely overpowering forces:

> I turned (as I will) to weeds and . . .
> weedroots of my low-feeding shiver

Ammons is far from forcing or contriving his vision, his awakening, in his best poems. In "The Constant," for example, he struggles to resist, even to suppress, the *onset* of revelation, with the air of a man who has been used overmuch, exploited, by his admittedly favorite mistress.

> When leaving the primrose, bayberry dunes, seaward
> I discovered the universe this morning,
>   I was in no
> mood
> for wonder,
>   the naked mass of so much miracle
> already beyond the vision
> of my grasp:

If formerly the mistress of experience, of miracle, consented to be a passive, supine guest to his advances, in "The Constant" she has become the aggressor: the poet, helpless and reluctant, allows himself to be overpowered by her mastery.

In a number of poems, Ammons unleashes surprising resources of power in himself by a sort of feminine submission to experience. In "Kind," "Height," and "The Wind Coming Down From" there is a fierce insistence on lowliness and passivity ("preference sends me stooping / seeking / the least"). This is his answer, his refusal, to the male challenge addressed to him by the massive antagonist in each poem—the giant redwood, the mountain, the wind; in each case, he recoils. Like Saint Francis (and unlike Ezra Pound!), he savors the strength of weakness. Strangely, all three poems seem facile, the dialectic merely clever and fanciful, perhaps archly whimsical. The poems are all statement, all philosophy, despite the illusion they try to advance of drama and dialectic. I don't believe the wind or redwood as antagonists, because their *being* in the poems lacks the solidity of a felt presence. They exist only as foils to the persona, and the poems never extend beyond direct emission of "message." They desperately need extension into the world of substance and event.

The weakest poems in the book suffer from overwriting. "Sphere," like "Discoverer," is all writing: the subject—a voyage through the dark waters of the womb—recedes, as the dense filigree of language drives it underground. The subject is so self-limiting and the language so overtaxed that a reader has no sense of traveling any distance across its sinuous contour. Only the agility of Ammons's rhythms can induce a reader to proceed from one end of the poem to the other. A succession of weighty phrases, strung like clothes on a line, smothers the poem's life-breath: " . . . amniotic infinity . . . boundless in circularity . . . consistency of motion arising—annihilated . . . infinite multiplicity, in the deepening, filtering earthen womb. . . ."

"The Constant" succeeds precisely where the other poems fail, because the poet's experience of the world, even though felt to be a "drab constant," is so intense it forcibly invades the poet's mind and takes possession of the landscape of the poem. Although the opening and closing lines (quoted above) are clung to by the speaker's intellection, those lines are the feeble, defeated cries of a lover ravished by his mistress, who inhabits the dominant central section of the poem's battlefield. The war between mind and world, though a losing battle for mind, yields fantastic life to the poem. The mind's defeat is the poem's victory. Yet the speaker's dissatisfaction of mind, resentment even, at the end of the poem, is a valid redirection in itself. In "Corson's Inlet" and "World," poems of the previous volume, Ammons had already fully mastered the plateau of experience successfully revisited in "The Constant": the apocalyptic stroll along the dunes, the Blakean discovery of an entire universe in a clamshell-enclosed "Lake," the sense of totality and self-containment balanced by the sense of fragility and temporariness, likening the clamshell universe to the poem:

> . . . a gull's toe could spill the universe:
> two more hours of sun could dry it up:

a higher wind could rock it out:

the tide will rise, engulf it, wash it loose:
utterly:

Perhaps the only distinctly new element in "The Constant" is the recognition that the poet has been here before and is anxious to break out of the enclosure of old experience, to escape into a fresh territory. I suspect there is a hushed cry of frustration at the heart of *Northfield Poems*. The author senses that most of the good work in the book is a repetition of past success.

Some of the very short poems indicate a remarkable new direction in Ammons's work. At first reading, there is no clue to a significance beyond the purely pictorial and imagistic. Suddenly, one word or line will touch off an astonishing number of overtones. In "Trap," one is at first merely enticed by the visual clarity of the mating butterflies:

> . . . they
> spin, two orbits
> of an
>
> invisible center:
> rise
> over the roof
>
> and caught on
> currents
> rise higher
>
> than trees and
> higher and up
> out of sight,
>
> swifter in
> ascent than they
> can fly or fall.

The poem's surprising force comes from the last lines. The spareness, cleanness, sharpness—the absence of ambiguity or overtones—all contribute to the astonishing impact of the finish, which transforms the entire poem, at a single stroke, into symbol. The reader is left stunned: where did all the hidden propulsion spring from? The restraint with which most of the poem is rendered allows the body of the piece to serve as a perfect conductor of the charge that travels between the two poles—title and last lines—as swiftly as lightning takes the tree.

The most impressive poem in the volume is a long one that achieves a new scope emerging unexpectedly in the familiar setting of the best former poems: the shore. In "One: Many," after the slightly stilted and heavy-handed philosophy of the opening lines, Ammons resumes his favorite technique of cataloging brilliant ephemera along the creek bank: "When I tried to summarize / a moment's events along the creek. . . ." Following a delicious summary, the sentence concludes: "I was released into a power beyond my easy failures." At this point, the mind leaps into a new dimension of world, as the catalog extends suddenly from the familiar imagery of shore to the free-ranging geography of the American continent. Ammons finds himself, for the first time, in the company of Whitman's wayfaring and wandering, or that of Roethke's last North American meditations. But the imagery is uniquely Ammons's; it has been revived and retuned to his most sinuous lines and rhythms:

> I think of California's towns and ranges,
>   deserts and oil fields;
> and of Maine's
>   unpainted seahouses
>   way out on the tips of fingerlands,
> lobster traps and pots,
> freshwater lakes; of Chicago,
>   hung like an eggsac on the leaf of lake
> Michigan, with
> its
> Art Museum, Prudential Building, Knickerbocker Hotel
> (where Cummings stayed);
> of North Carolina's
>   sounds, banks, and shoals,
>   telephone wire loads of swallows,
> of Columbus County
>   where fresh-dug peanuts
>   are boiled
>   in iron pots, salt filtering
> in through the boiled-clean shells (a delicacy
> true
> as artichokes or Jersey
> asparagus): and on through villages,

along dirt roads, ditchbanks, by gravel pits and on
>to the homes,
inventions, longings:

He started in his own backyard, and fumbled into the impossibly new ground, into "unattainable reality itself." At his best, Ammons is willing to stake everything on the full health of the single imagination, cut loose from history and the genius that labored the language into monuments, to begin poetic art afresh.

Selected Poems

I have spoken at some length of the originality of A. R. Ammons's verse technique in other reviews, but in all my attentiveness to the ingenuities of his line, I seem to have missed—or just barely touched on—the more abiding quality of his language that transcends all questions of style or prosody:[2]

I raid
>a bloom,
spread the hung petals out,
>and surprised he's not
a bloom-part, find
>a moth inside, the exact color,
the bloom his daylight port or cove . . .

So many of A. R. Ammons's poems are such raids, his lines fingers and tongues harmlessly loosening the fallen leaf, the petals of the flower, to surprise the hidden yucca moth who is secretly "lifting temples / of bloom." The words, like those intricately delicate moth wings, would "go in to heal" our days. They have a spiritualizing power. The poetry glides with a lingering, light-fingered savoriness over the shades, tones, and hues of sensory experience. Ammons's language, disciplined by attending to the minutest motions in nature with the intensest caring for the "lowliest" forms of life, exhibits a precision and a quality of quiet spiritual rejoicing that carries over from his eye to his verbal ear. He has won his way through to an imperishable quiet at the heart of words,

---

2. This review of *Selected Poems*, (Ithaca, N.Y.: Cornell University Press), originally appeared in *Poetry* in 1969.

and he has infused more of this quality, this quietness—this one of the available essences of all language—into his poetry than is to be found in the work of any other poet now writing.

The spirit Ammons embodies in his poems is "the mode of motion," a mischievous imp that clothes itself in objects—or words of a poem—only to divest itself at whim, disposing of all forms, racing spryly from one incarnation to another. Its favorite condition is to sidle at the threshold between matter and nonmatter and to tease its faithful servant the poet by exercising its impulse for sheer caprice:

> I change shape,
> turn easily into the shapes you make
>   and even you
>   in moving
> I leave, betray.

Ammons's absorption in ephemera of nature is so enticing in itself that it is doubly rewarding to find, as we do in most of the poems, a veiled metaphor for the poetic process running through the description. The central drama of Ammons's poetry is the quest of the Ariel self to escape the enclosure of materials. But these words are too heavy, for they miss the gaiety and lightness and buoyancy of spirits shaking off the bonds—the chains—of matter. This drama complements the struggle in Ammons's line to free itself from any formal pattern, any stricture of form exterior to the immediate line-by-line determinant. The poem aspires to remain open-ended, resisting closural devices at either extremity. It is a poetry dead set against the tendency to close off thought or language, the tendency to lock up a chain of ideas *or* words: "I have reached no conclusions, have erected no boundaries . . . so I am willing to stake off no beginnings or ends, establish / no walls."

The anticlosural gesture is one of the central impulses of art in our time, and Ammons's best poems ("Corson's Inlet," "Strait," "Expressions of Sea Level") do not simply participate in the pursuit of a freer poetics, but rather they afford a definition of free verse that goes beyond the art of poetry to render more intelligible, more conscious, more *visible*, a mode of craft that partakes of the confluence of all the contemporary arts. Ammons carries on the adventure of aesthetic formulizing inside the body of the poem itself, and usually without self-consciousness. What his poetry demonstrates for us all is that the highest degree of critical self-awareness—a total consciousness of the possibilities and limits of medium articulating itself explicitly in the poem—is not incompatible with a total art.

Briefings: Poems, Small and Easy

"Always I hear wings." "He described his trip very well." You may recall these lines of *poetry* from the *Peanuts* comic strip one Sunday last summer.[3] Charlie Brown has been watching (and overhearing!) the flight of a butterfly. The first line appears in the first frame, the last in the last frame, and in between all the saying is left to those fluttering wings.

The short, delicate flights of A. R. Ammons's new poems resemble those buoyant, nearly weightless butterfly wings. The book's abiding spirit is one of humor, ease, and lighthearted and lightheaded playfulness—in part for the sheer pleasure of it, in part for the discipline of staying loose, open, fluid, responsive, available. As in "Square," Ammons refuses to square off or round out his perceptions or his poetic forms:

> I thread the
> outskirts of mandate,
> near enough
> to be knowingly away &
> far enough away to
> wind and snap through
> riddling underbrush.

In this collection of eighty-odd poems, titled *Briefings: Poems, Small and Easy*, most of the poems and the perceptions they articulate are partial and fragmentary by design, since the lucky moments of grasped spiritual wholeness that inform them spring from a self held lightly and uneasily in balance. Subject to momentary fits of change: wakings, dyings, clarities, opacities—waveriness is espoused as a way to findings, allowed failures and fumblings as a way passively to court renewals.

To be constantly on the watch for possibilities in nature for being struck into awe and wonder is a very exacting discipline, and Ammons's fourscore of "small and easy" poems suggest clearly that to maintain this discipline—to keep its gears well oiled—requires daily practice in tuning up, to be constantly in training. The eye, rivaling a high-powered

---

3. This review of *Briefings: Poems, Small and Easy*, (New York: W. W. Norton, 1971), originally appeared in *The Yale Review* in 1971.

telescopic rifle, must train for perfect marksmanship ("My eyes' concision shoots to kill"), and the imagination must train to stay available for enchantments, to be ready always to respond with wonder, to be lifted by such beauties as that sniper the eye has picked off:

> pick a perch—
> apple branch for example in bloom—
> tune up
> and
>
> drill imagination right through necessity:

In a good many of the short shorts of this book, either the sniper fire has flown wide of the mark or the imagination picked too high or low a perch, but nearly every poem contains some moments—flashes of loveliness—that ricochet from arrested points of fire in nature to the eye, from eye to verbal ear, and from there—why deny it?—straight to the heart. And in the best poems, the whole delivery bursts forth with the surety and ease of a supreme word acrobat who can juggle the beautiful simplicities of the natural heart as though such artistry were mere play.

Ammons's pleasures, like his vision in this book, are all, by predilection, tenuous, fragile, temporary, mortal—not mystical or otherworldly; life is an affair of abrupt reversals. "Briefings," if they stay on their graceful, imagistic toes, can dance in step with life's ups and downs— they might even get good enough or lucky enough to stay one step ahead ("only above the level of most / perception"), lazily lofted on the liftoffs, riding easy on the splashdowns. Ammons is content just to keep in pace with the natural event most of the time and oh, how grateful— tickled, even—now and again, to come out on top! Even to break even, or perhaps to fall a little behind, to be *under* the weather—his mind's or the world's—is secretly to stay ahead, since "uncertainty, labor, fear" are "the rewards of my mortality," and he bids a kindly, but mistaken, Providence *not* to take them away, his weaknesses, his failures: *not* to grant him comforts, or fame, or faith, or mission, or belief in a poem of heroic denials ("This Black Rich Country") as profoundly moving and authentically radical in its negations of the transcendental tradition in nature poetry, of which Ammons himself is the most distinguished living exponent, as was Shakespeare's sonnet "My Mistress' Eyes Are Nothing Like the Sun" in its deflations of the hackneyed images of romantic love poetry:

grant me no mission: let my
mystical talents be beasts
in dark trees: thin the wire

I limp in space, melt it
with quick heat, let me walk
or fall alone: fail

me in all comforts

If I'm often a little suspicious that Ammons, out taking his nature walks, is just a bit too deliberate about pouncing on any and every instance or insect or incident (as if words and bugs and events are, finally, just various equally assimilable species of poem parts) as occasion for reconceiving and saying out his aesthetic theory, the good poems always correct me. *Theory* is too theoretical a notion for ideas in poems that transfigure idea- making from a formal enterprise into a primitive natural process. Words never merely talk about or symbolize nature: bugs, ticks, mites, weeds, leaf/stem/root—all are reborn *as* words in Ammons's poems. The words are so sticky, musky, and sodden with smirch and soilures that we forget the poems are made of language at all.

After laying aside this book, we wonder: Is it that we are left feeling that the pricklings from thorn and briar have infiltrated and contaminated the words, or is it rather that we would find words fallen like so much loose change and clinging to stem and creeper in the fields of the "City Limits" of Ithaca where "the radiance . . . does not withhold / itself but pours its abundance without selection," and where Ammons has wastefully strolled away his time, spilling the coin of his ardent gabble through forever patchless and unpatchable holes in his literary trousers' pockets? We wonder, and wander, and when we take up the book again and begin to read, we know we have taken both walks.

Josephine Miles

Josephine Miles's new poems contain great moral beauty.[1] Their abiding generosity of spirit would seem to prescribe a socioreligious faith that is rare in our times—the belief in a community of the heart. The credo I find in these poems advances a more comprehensive theory of oneness than the credo of the mystic, who is so often merely a social escapist. Hers is a religion of ordinary human commitments: the kind of affection she puts most store by is the kind that admits—requires, even—"measureless distances" between people. Like Arthur Gregor's empathy, it is a tenderness and caring that may easily occur between people who are perhaps no more than strangers. In fact, a degree of acknowledged strangeness is necessary to support this kind of affection, so that any possible meshing of personalities—in conflict or in harmony—will be kept to a minimum, freeing the individual's attention from the emotionally charged demands of personal involvement, as in "love at a distance." The more the love is refined in "filaments of thought, in lines as thin / As the lines latitudes rest upon," the more available it will be for worthy and productive tasks:

> In a morning of clarity and distinction
>> Students and I exchange questions and answers about a book
>> As if we had all been reading it.
>
> Then stepping over a rough place
>> I hold out my hand for balance, and someone gives it.
>> And someone writes a letter for help I can give.

Above all, these poems celebrate each "day's simple fact," the small kindnesses that effortlessly occur—in mutual supportiveness—between people who busy themselves with a common task, each giving of himself to the utmost in concentration of being to the common labor, to workmanship "so austere, thank or praise / Only by use."

---

1. This review of *Kinds of Affection,* (Middletown, Conn.: Wesleyan University Press, 1967), originally appeared in *The Yale Review* in 1968.

Frugality is her mode for experiencing emotion; at times, she can't help admitting that she is sacrificing something of value by denying herself extreme passion, but she will not—perhaps cannot—let herself be drawn into the oblivion of mindlessness, the risk taken by the emotional addict:

> Addicts progress from saturation
> > To saturation, ache, thirst, slake,
> > To a plentitude, an oblivion, then they wake
> > And ache, until gradually as the sun climbs the heavens
> > They thirst again toward that oblivion.

Miss Miles's frugality of being extends gracefully from her inner to her outer resources: conservation of spirit is complemented by conservation of language and syntax. Unlike the political conservative who protects and preserves accumulated interests, her conservative spirit is a daily, moment-to-moment dutifulness toward human exchange, a conservation of the frail beauties and liberties that arise spontaneously in talk with friends and associates, beauties that are usually missed because we are in such a rush to get to what is important that we pass over what is ourselves, the *real* of us:

> When I can be
> A moment glad, repletion
> Lasts me the day through, or so I say.
>
> Nibbling greed . . .

Miss Miles's mind moves delicately between two poles—the will to surety, the will to doubt all positive surety. Many poems attain a rare seesawing buoyancy from the difficulty of balancing these two extremities of thought. Her handling of lines and meters, too, achieves a teetering effect, a rhythmical vertigo set in motion in the reader's ear by her technique of framing "lyrics of speech or talk" in sentences with inverted syntax and grammatical ellipsis. The easy-to-hear speech idioms give the poems a very readable surface, despite a highly compressed and compacted style:

> Grievances . . .
> > I keep one or two and press them in a book,
> > And when I show them to you they have crumbled
> > To powder on the page. So I rehearse.

But I do not believe. I believe rather,
The stems of grievance put down their heavy roots
And by the end of summer crack the pavement.

The movement from surety to doubt—the cost of honesty—is dramatized here. Miss Miles is an expert in the art of puncturing false comforts. She loves to catch her mind, as one might pounce upon a thief, in the act of evasion, duplicity. Her intellect is the shrewdest of culprits, and the contest in her between the artist-censor and the mental gymnast—a conflict that parallels her twin careers of scholar and poet—is one of her favorite subjects. The aspiring self's struggle to break out of all mental enclosures, to tear down the mind's defenses, limits, to remove obsolete habits of self-protection that carry over from the past—these themes are appropriately complemented by a new fluidity of line movement, a free play in the management of lines and stanzas unlike anything in her earlier work, with no loss of Miss Miles's customary precision and conciseness, or the depth of her absorption. Whereas most of her earlier poems were as symmetrical and as tightly wound and coiled as a watch spring, in the new poems, though she continues to lean toward lines of middle length—three to five accentual feet—now she can adroitly maneuver into the very short or very long line. She frequently employs the new metrical agility to suggest the careless to-and-fro pacing of spontaneous talk, or relaxed conversation between friends:

Dear Frank, Here is a poem
   I dreamed of you last night;
   It makes me happy
   Because it makes sense to me.

   We went to the Greek Theater to see a play
   And as we entered were given elaborate menus
   Of the players' names.
   Dinner was three dollars.
   It was served on the little round tables from cocktail lounges.

   I kept leaning back against your knees,
   Because of those backless benches, and you kept moving
   Further and further away in the amphitheater,
   I following, until finally you said,
   Jo: I am having the six dollar dinner.

Often, in reading these poems, I am pleased and surprised to find it is the sounds and tremors of my own breathing that are mysteriously being returned to me. The poems do not simply speak *to* me, but they somehow manage to talk (or whisper) directly into my ear; and when I stop reading for a few moments, it seems as though the poem's discourse continues, survives, in my mind's ear, since many of the poems don't begin or end in a conventional way, but are more likely to be framed at either end by chance remarks. They are informal, though intensified, cross sections of talk—lifted from street corner, kitchen, or classroom—and sagaciously trapped on the page.

Richard Hugo

Richard Hugo merely needs to arrive at an enchanted place in nature to recognize the primitive spirits lurking in water, trees, rocks, and immediately he starts to cross over the mystical barriers to make contact with all the hidden gods of the place.[1] They all begin to sing in his hand at once as he writes, rows his oars, or casts his fishing line:

> Spinning hymns downstream is fun. The worm spins
> warm to German Brown, and warm to bad sight
> Rock Creek splits the day in hunks a hawk can't count.
> A fragment of a trout, half tree, half elk,
> dissolves in light and could have been a cliff.
> Current and a cross can blind a saint. . . .
> All sermons warp with one slight knock.
> Eyes are hands. Nylon sings and reassembles day
> and day is cracked in silver jokes: whip and tug
> and whipping rod, red ladder and white play,
> a mottled monster ages down the net,
> brighter than answer, big enough to see.

The Northwest landscape that Hugo knows best is haunted by the spirits of many generations of dead American Indians, and in poem after poem he touches the deep roots of memory in the ghost town, the ghost ranch, the fallen mine or mission, the neglected graveyard. He knows he can trust the spirit of each place, setting, locale—if accurately rendered—to breathe its own hidden life into the image cluster that whirls and spirals down the plunging columns of his verse. No other recent American poet of my acquaintance shares Hugo's power to evoke the magic of place-names: the American Indian names assert a quiet intelligence in his poems, carrying a musical authority as well as a hidden Indian mystique into the very texture and integument of the poem's action. A name may be repeated several times for its sheer musical and rhythmic beauty, while the core of

---

1. This review of *The Lady in Kicking Horse Reservoir,* (New York: W. W. Norton, 1973), originally appeared in *The Yale Review* in 1973.

meaning latent in the name may be revealed late in the poem, suddenly emerging in a surprising new context that releases a hidden river of associations:

> They named it Sweathouse Creek because
> somewhere way upstream from here
> the Indians built houses over hot springs
> where the sick could sweat bad spirits out.

Indian names are demonstrated to be irreplaceable avatars of the spirit of a place or region. The gods asleep in the names are wakened in the "Indian wind" of the poem's physical climate, as weather, too, is revealed to be supernaturally alive, the primeval wind, or rain, or snow becoming a dominant symbolic motif that orchestrates the varied elements of a poem's voluptuous music.

The rhythmic intention behind Hugo's poetry, the impetus and thrust behind his meters, is to achieve a lean, spare prosody, streamlined to accommodate itself to a stylized illusion of conversational rapids, words tumbling like water and heavy currents traveling at very high velocity, shattering over rocks. Or, as in "Driving Montana," his identity is projected as a constellation of live receptors. His total receptiveness is a fervor to take in whatever the landscape and weather may be pleased to bombard him with:

> The day is a woman who loves you. Open.
> Deer drink close to the road and magpies
> spray from your car. Miles from any town
> your radio comes in strong, unlikely
> Mozart from Belgrade, rock and roll
> from Butte. Whatever the next number,
> you want to hear it.

To throw the car throttle wide open, flooring the gas pedal ("Never has your Buick / found this forward a gear"), is to accelerate the rate of bombardment. He hurtles down the speedway of those plummeting stanzas of variable decasyllabics as if he would strip away all traces of artifice and ornament, all harnesses of literary convention, to achieve a pure, unshackled flow of loquacity:

> I got three bulls and a native cutthroat, lover.
> I'm phoning from the bar in Victor.

> One drunk's fading fast. The other's fast
> with information—worms don't work in August.
> I found a virgin forest with a moss floor.
> You and I can love there. Pack the food.

Many poems erupt with ardent impulsiveness, blurted messages phoned in haste and breathless passion from a noisy bar. The visitation has struck. Here. Now. You better listen, reader. Lover. This may be our only chance. Listen with all your heart in your ears—over the bad connection, the jukebox, the snores of the drunk Indian laid out on the table. Listen to the priceless, sage lore veteran drunks and wizened Indians (those "aging eagles") squander on the undeserving likes of me. This is the moment, this the place. The world is all rich, trembling voices; they all speak to me at once—a wonderful, aching music of human misery and ardor. This moment and this place are ever-changing, perishable, fleeting in time. Come share it with me while it lasts ("You and I can love there"). He has won the sweepstakes of the human spirit, the daily double, struck oil, hit a gold lode, and is burning to report and share the lucky claim.

The other world Hugo explores is the cosmos of inured boredom: the small-town mountain communities, has-been boomtowns wrecked by the "Silver Bill repeal"; or rest-cure havens ("Hot Springs") that cater to the imagination of convalescence, a psychic condition of chronic half-aliveness supported by a total hospital-ward world:

> You arrived arthritic for the cure,
> therapeutic qualities of water
> and the therapeutic air. . . .
> You have ached taking your aches up the hill.
> Another battery of tests. Terrible probe
> of word and needle. Always the fatal word,
> when we get old we crumble.

It is a world of all faint grays, the "Degrees of Gray in Phillipsburg." There are no decisive whites or blacks ("with so few Negroes and Jews we've been reduced / to hating each other, dumping our crud / in our rivers, mistreating the Indians"), no exploding lights or darks, only pale and fading neutrals—neutral colors for sexless humans. All the senses have atrophied, not just sight; but the psychic malaise is expertly portrayed as a chromatic wasteland, a world robbed of its color, reduced to bland, diluted fakes of color. Hugo suggests that the greatest poverty, in Stevens's phrase, might be to live in a colorless world; the surest antidote to our impoverishment would be to restore radiance of color to the world by retraining the faculty of color perception, and discovering—with Hugo—the remarkable spiritual aliveness that lurks just below the brilliant, iridescent surfaces of wildlife, woods, rivers:

> . . . he comes lightning
> out of nothing at your egg. Best of all,
> the color. It could be the water, but the bulls
> are damn near gold and their white dots
> stark as tile. The orange spots flare
> like far off fires. The body's tubular and hard.
> Cuts are rose and peach, all markings definite
> as evil, with a purple gill.

Stanley Kunitz

Again! Again!
Love knocked again at my door:
I tossed her a bucket of bones.
From each bone springs a soldier
who shoots me as a stranger.

Stanley Kunitz has had to go away further to exile, and to stay away longer, than perhaps any other major poet of his generation.[1] *The Testing-Tree*, Kunitz's first book in the thirteen years since the publication of his Pulitzer Prize–winning *Selected Poems*, resounds with the upheaval of a spiritual recluse coming back to the world, to voice, after a long self-banishment: the voice surprised at its own return from muteness with intense shocks of awakening like those of a body amazed to have exhumed itself from a premature burial. It is the body of a sixty-four-year-old ghostly stranger he sees mirrored in his collegiate daughter's eyes:

Outside your room
stands the white-headed prowler
in his multiple disguises
who reminds you of your likeness.
Wherever you turn . . .
he waits for you,
haggard with his thousand years.

Kunitz's repatriations in his new book are wrenchings of the "creature self" ("he is not broken but endures") out of its stony sleep of slow recovery from the ravishment—which drove his friend Mark Rothko to suicide—by the worlds of country, family, "adversaries." His recovery occurs with the violence and rage of a self-disinterment, no less than a full return at the age of sixty-four to the "fugues of appetite" of his lost youth.

---

1. This review of *The Testing-Tree*, (Boston: Atlantic-Little, Brown, 1971), originally appeared in *The Yale Review* in 1971.

In "King of the River," a small masterpiece in a Roethkean vein and worthy to stand beside much of Roethke's best work, he sighs from the body of the spawning salmon (now his body!) nearing its hastened death, following its remarkable two-week escalation of the aging process ("the same geriatric process in humans takes some twenty to forty years").

> Nothing compels you
> any more, nothing
> at all abides,
> but nostalgia and desire,
> the two-way ladder
> between heaven and hell.

In "Journal for My Daughter," he blurts out a message to the beloved daughter estranged during the years when "the resentment weed" grew "in the crack of a divided house," hoping to rebuild lost affections: " 'What do I want of my life? / More! More!' " By turns, in another short poem ("The Mulch"), he communes with the "indefatigable gull / dropping a piss-clam on the rocks / to break it open. / Repeat. Repeat," and he feels enticings of empathy for the old man who loves to roam the seashore "gathering salt hay / in bushel baskets crammed to his chin" to take home and spread out on the earth in his garden—even though his garden "prepares to die," " 'Try! Try!' clicks the beetle in his wrist." And he unhesitatingly throws himself into the ravages of love, "Again! Again!"

Nostalgia and desire, heaven and hell, More! More!, Repeat. Repeat, Try! Try!, Again! Again! These paired outcries, crackling like pistol shots in poem after poem, are the systole-diastole heartbeats of a man who, though he admits "I spoiled . . . my own left ventricle," is far from ready to throw in the towel in the tournament of his "unshattered, unshatterable" life passions:

> In a murderous time
> the heart breaks and breaks
> and lives by breaking.

> It is necessary to go
> through dark and deeper dark
> and not to turn.

Kunitz is so powerfully drawn to the imagination of estrangement into that "deeper dark"—"What's best in me lives underground, / rooting and digging, itching for wings"—it is a marvel that he *ever* returns from exile. Note his tone of emulation in speaking of Dante's unshakable exile, as well as his sympathetic participation in both Mark Rothko's escapist suicide and Pastor Bonhoeffer's political suicide, that failed plot to assassinate Hitler.

Despite a recurrent impulse to regain his lost affiliation with the community of mavericks by joining his daughter in the youth movement— "Oh to be radical, young, desirable, cool!"—he is an incorrigible loner, and part of him must always hang back: "Demonstrations in the streets. / I am there not there, / ever uneasy in a crowd." He knows his repatriations must always be partial, incomplete. He is fatally condemned, and perhaps secretly blessed, to a life stance poised halfway between exile and return, between banishment and inheritance. In "King of the River," he hovers at the threshold between these antipodes. Midway through each of the poem's four symphonic stanza movements, the *impossible* steps over into the *actual,* man alchemizes into animal and angel, by turns ("you are changing now / into the shape you dread / beyond the merely human"), generating the remarkable incandescence—half-demonic, half-ecstatic— of this poem's vision:

> On the threshold
> of the last mystery,
> at the brute absolute hour,
> you have looked into the eyes
> of your creature self,
> which are glazed with madness,
> and you say
> he is not broken but endures,
> limber and firm
> in the state of his shining,
> forever inheriting his salt kingdom,
> from which he is banished
> forever.

For all the pain, the loneliness, the helplessness of having chosen "a damnable trade / where winning is like losing!" his happiest moments of exalted vision come to him as he balances, survives, on the edge, belonging neither to this world nor to the other world, but instead vacillating between them:

> The sands whispered, *Be separate.*
> The stones taught me, *Be hard.*

I dance for the joy of surviving,
On the edge of the road.

There are a handful of masterful poems in this book, but the collection taken as a whole lacks body. Too many pages, I feel, are given over to translations from the Russian poets that are scattered, rather arbitrarily, over three of the book's four sections. "Hand-rolled Cigarettes," after Yevtushenko, is a splendid political spoof on the Russian custom of rolling cigarettes by hand in old newspapers; the charming mixture of humor and political allusion is rendered with gusto in Kunitz's crisp, rhythmical quatrains. One gathers from the quiet austerity of tone that the translations are diligently faithful to the originals, and a whole volume of these vignettes, which we are told is soon to be published, will clearly be an engrossing and readable book. The abiding clarity and restraint of his style, spread out over an ample range of selections, will enhance the majesty and dignity of the Russians.

Theodore Roethke

Theodore Roethke had just begun to write his major poems in the late fifties, and wrote his very best poems near the end of his life—one waits in vain for the final flowering of his genius.[1] I shudder every time I think of the poems he might have written had he lived just another year or two. I am reminded of the premature deaths of John Keats and Kit Marlowe. These poets were in their twenties, whereas Roethke was fifty-five when he died; and yet, like them, he was just beginning to reach his creative prime.

Apparently Roethke had some foreboding that death was near. In his last collection, *The Far Field* (published posthumously), there is a very touching poem to his wife, "Wish for a Young Wife," that sounds like a last will and testament:

> My lizard, my lively writher,
> May your limbs never wither,
> May the eyes in your face
> Survive the green ice
> Of envy's mean gaze;
> May you live out your life
> Without hate, without grief,
> And your hair ever blaze
> In the sun, in the sun,
> When I am undone,
> When I am no one.

In another piece, "Infirmity," he has the air of a man who has been ill for a long time, a man who struggles to find a meaning and even a kind of fulfillment in disease of the body:

> Sweet Christ, rejoice in my infirmity;
> There's little left I care to call my own.

---

1. This review of *The Far Field*, (Garden City, N.Y.: Doubleday, 1964), originally appeared in *The Antioch Review* in 1964.

> Today they drained the fluid from a knee
> And pumped a shoulder full of cortisone;
> Thus I conform to my divinity
> By dying inward, like an aging tree . . .

For me, Roethke is strongest in moments of tenderness. Curiously, his many poems depicting sexual experiences do not reveal the profound humanness and tenderness in the man nearly as well as those describing subtler love experience, such as the gentle endearment he feels toward his wife and even toward his own body in the poems discussed above, and the strange, quiet compassion he speaks over the grave of his student thrown by a horse (a student to whom he had never spoken a single word) in the well-known anthology piece "Elegy for Jane."

Perhaps the most moving expression of tenderness in all his writings appears in one of the last poems, "The Meadow Mouse." The poem begins with directness and naturalness of expression:

> In a shoe box stuffed in an old nylon stocking
> Sleeps the baby mouse I found in the meadow,
> Where he trembled and shook beneath a stick
> Till I caught him up by the tail and brought him in,
> Cradled in my hand . . .

The images Roethke uses to describe the mouse suggest an amused tenderness and a keen sensitivity to frailness:

> A little quaker, the whole body of him trembling,
> His absurd whiskers sticking out like a cartoon-mouse,
> His feet like small leaves,
> Little lizard-feet,
> Whitish and spread wide when he tried to struggle away . . .

The end of this poem extends the poet's tender concern to include all vulnerable and fragile forms of life:

> But this morning the shoe-box on the back porch is empty.
> Where has he gone, my meadow mouse,
> My thumb of a child that nuzzled in my palm?—
> To run under the hawk's wing,
> Under the eye of the great owl watching from the elm-tree,
> To live by courtesy of the shrike, the snake, the tom-cat.

> I think of the nestling fallen into the deep grass,
> The turtle gasping in the dusty rubble of the highway,
> The paralytic stunned in the tub, and the water rising—
> All things innocent, hapless, forsaken.

In another mode, the long series of meditations on North America, Roethke tries to identify with the American Indian ("Old men should be explorers. / I'll be an Indian. / Iroquois."). These poems combine life-enhancing descriptions of weather and landscape with the poet's psychic responses ranging from despair to joy. The moments of praise and affirmation outweigh the gloomy passages, and even death becomes a way back to life, as in "The Far Field":

> I am renewed by death, thought of my death,
> The dry scent of a dying garden in September,
> The wind fanning the ash of a low fire.
> What I love is near at hand,
> Always, in earth and air.

The meditations are his most powerful works. In them he pursues a spiritual reverie that, at times, borders on a too personal abstractness but usually erupts into distinct images out of the poet's urgent past, such as the picture of his father lifting him over the "four-foot" rose stems in the "six-hundred-foot greenhouses," and his memory of reckless speeding over gravel and rock roads of America. The search for self and beyond self in these poems is the prevailing motif in Roethke's later work.

Theodore Weiss

In 1939, by an absurd leap of faith, Yeats could look past the political nightmare of his time and take solace in those spiraling gyres, the cycles of history, to rebuild the fallen empires: "All things fall and are built again, / And those that build them again are gay."[1] In 1965, Theodore Weiss, foreseeing a catastrophe beyond all reassemblage, disavowed both the legacy of culture and the historical cycles that bequeathed it to us, "To hell with holy relics . . . More shambling about / in abandoned clammy churches / and I abjure all religion, / even my own." Such towering disavowals—amounting to a self-incurred exile from the very language of his craft—come at a high cost to a scholar-poet who, in his eminent work over the last twenty-five years as editor, professor, and man of letters, has himself dedicated immense labor to perpetuating that bequeathal.

By his forty-ninth year, Weiss had reached a major aesthetic crisis and crossroads, as avouched in the poem "Ruins for These Times," which I take to be the pivotal statement of his middle career, a declared manifesto for the future. He had grown contemptuous of mining the ruins of the past:

> I, plundered, plundering,
> out of these forty odd bumbling
> years have heaped up spoils
> with spells compelling
> enough, my own.

"The Medium," another poem of the same period, is a humorous dialogue between He and She that, in developing a serious aesthetic philosophy through exchange of repartee, is Yeatsian. Through excesses in the discourse of the male speaker, Weiss parodies the ponderous allusive style of his early work. The poem is an act of conscious, painstaking self-criticism. It demonstrates Weiss's rage, in midcareer, to purify his language, to learn to listen for deeper voices in his psyche than those of his education, and

---

1. This review of *The World Before Us: Poems, 1950–1970,* (New York: Macmillan, 1970), originally appeared in *The Yale Review* in 1971.

to wait for the silence to deliver its speech. He must withhold his limitless verbal skill, his sprawling talent:

> Cleansed of words,
> my fears and doubts cast off, the fears
> that words invent, I see each thing, free
> at last to its own nature, see it free
> to say exactly what it is.

This poem challenges the integrity of language itself, as if the very essence of things is somehow beyond language, and the words, no matter how scrupulously they are used, somehow always corrupt and impurify beings, feelings, events. All things, to approach their pure essence, then, must escape, and thereby transcend, language. But what appears here as an attack upon all language as an unfit medium to transmit sacred or mystic experience is tempered in later poems to a quest for a raw, open, intimate, and direct language.

Weiss's most recent short poems have advanced to a more acute raw-boned gauntness of style than any earlier work, approaching stridency in some passages. The new poems resume Weiss's faith in the undiminished efficacy of today's language as a medium for poetry, a faith first voiced in the youthful poem "The Hook," the brilliant exemplar of his early style that introduces *The World Before Us,* this meaty selection—ample in bulk as well as substance—from four previous volumes, plus a complete book-length sequence of new short poems.

As I leaf through some three hundred pages that do not even include the superb long poem *Gunsight,* published as a separate volume in 1962, I am reminded that Weiss's longest poems are usually his most impressive and memorable works. They form a continuing cycle, from book to book, and in them a reader may chart the milestones of Weiss's extraordinary search for a more viable poetic language:

> Read to him,
> his face among the pictures—the animals gentle
> in their alphabet—like something princely
> blossomed there, naming after me
> with first clear breath flowers, birds, and beasts.
> Day by day his mind more avid, lighting
> up whatever feeds and brightens it . . .
>
> from "The Generations"

The genesis of all language—in the ear of the preliterate child and, by extrapolation, in the ear of primitive man, the racial vestiges echoing in the modern voice—is in the *naming of things.* At the pure beginnings, the need to enchant (yes, a chanting!) the ear with beautiful names was indissolubly linked to the need to control things with words. The religious and aesthetic functions of language evolved concurrently with the physical, all collaborating in survival. Through language, self-preservation extended effortlessly and naturally from the hunt and the kill to the inner dream life. Weiss's poems, especially the long interior monologues—"The Generations," "Gunsight," "Caliban Remembers," "Wunsch-zettel"—reenact this drama for us, as the poet participates with intense sympathetic involvement in the mental life of adventurers in language, following them through each stage of the love affair: from first infatuation with the sound and feel of words, through the deaths of language as it becomes cut off from its origins in natural process and man's dream life is divorced from his daily life of action, to those high, rare marriages of language and mission—the true calling—that come as a beatitude of fulfillment to the lucky few who fight their way back from exile (language abused banishes us from its country) to find the true heartland of the self in human love.

The first poem in the series, "The Generations," appearing in Weiss's second volume, is trapped in the middle stage of this journey. The problem of losing and finding the language again is hopelessly entangled with the sin of self-righteousness. The iron-willed female protagonist is the sort of gardener who tramples her flower bed to keep the weeds from growing. This attitude extends to her method of child rearing, as well as to books: "Silken words . . . Rip them out and rip though some good go." Her vision is monolithic, totalitarian—resembling the doctrines of Maoism as satirized in a new poem, "The Little Red Book"—and her lifelong failed genocidal war on the weed population carries over to her sons. She would tear the human tongue out by the roots rather than risk a few weeds in the garden of speech.

The gardening motif in "The Generations" is an obvious repetitive symbol. Weiss masters the garden metaphor in the far superior recent poem in the same mode, "Wunsch-zettel." The art of gardening, like the art of mountain climbing explored in the ambitious "Mount Washington," is a complex metaphor that both lends itself to a richly developed personality portrait and advances Weiss's theory of language arts. The heroine, a German war expatriate now living in New Hampshire, recalls a six-week stay in Switzerland during which she taught gardening to child refugees of World War II, many of whom had lost their families to the concentration camps: "Nature, I told them, can be / trusted. Though how they, plucked from the wreck / of Europe, could trust to trust me I do not know." Despite her skepticism, she succeeds in transmitting to the children her sensitive gift, learned as a child, for expressing a wide range of human feelings through plants, and she restores them to some measure of human community: "I've striven for this: / A garden to be implanted in each mind, / with fruits for others, blessed community." Thinking of the plight of the children, she recalls her own childhood in a passage that develops more exquisitely than in any other poem Weiss's remarkable theory of the way the healthy mind discovers language:

> Till three I said no single word. My mother
> worried, by the tinkling goat-bell father
> tied to me soon reassured.
>
> "That child,"
> he smiled, "only when she can put her words
> in perfect sentences will speak."
>
> What other
> namings needed I? Clear voices they were,
> the animals, wings, petalings, voices
> like the sun in heather loud. Each day
> I took him to our flower-beds to show
> each fragrant task the seedlings were performing . . .

Instinctively, the child knows the words must be held back. Words must wait for the natural forms to choose them, to embrace them in her own auditory imagination—the inner ear or mind's eye of the poet. Namings are emblems rooted in the beings of plants and animals they inhabit, and the wise child, a poet in her way, knows it is best to wait for her body's knowledge of living forms—"wings, petalings, voices"—to unlock the mystery of words. The intimacies of touch, allurements of the eye and ear, if learned first, carry over to the words and endow them—for speaker and listener alike—with feelings. The child knows how to wait for the life of feeling to resume the language slowly in her ear; she discovers her own best pace for receiving the seeds of language in the garden plots of memory. Then, when she first takes hold of the words with her voice, she truly makes them her own: they belong to her, find a new life in her use of them. They are reknown and kept alive in her saying.

Language is sterile and lifeless if it is absorbed mechanically. A poet must periodically rage to return the words from books to plant and animal beings. A poet must be a gardener or a mountaineer first, a word maestro second. Most of us learned the language too fast, and if we get lucky, we spend the rest of our lives learning to slow down, to wait for the words to reconnect with those avatars that enshrine them: things of this world.

William Stafford and
Frederick Morgan

The Shocks of Normality

The shocks of normality.[1] Of healthiness. To be an ordinary man today. To be alive now, to spring awake in the night, what a lucky coincidence! It is the great reward, the greatest privilege of all:

> Sometimes we wake
> in the night: the millions better than we
> who had to crawl away! We borrow their
> breath, and the breath of the numberless
> who never were born.

In William Stafford's poems, the shocks of steadiness, the great stillnesses of his quiet, reserved voice—innocently surprised at its own depths of silence—are just one step, one line of verse, one breath away from registering the whole earth's shudder as our own:

> When the earth doesn't shake, when the sky
> is still, we feel something under the earth:
> a shock of steadiness. When the storm is gone,
> when the air passes, we feel our own
> shudder—the terror of having such a great
> friend, undeserved.

One of the rich, unexpected rewards of Stafford's maturity was the discovery that the many years of cultivating a bare, plain idiom capable of the widest range of expressiveness in the lowest registers of the quiet

---

1. This review of *Someday, Maybe*, by William Stafford, (New York: Harper and Row, 1973), and *A Book of Change*, by Frederick Morgan, (New York: Scribner's, 1972), originally appeared in *The Yale Review* in 1974.

tones of language—the low-pitched key of our human voice (consider the narrow range of the bass viol, but the unearthly overtones sung by the instrument in the hands of a virtuoso performer!)—have produced a medium in which his own great calm would be a fit conductor for violent hidden movements of the earth, quaking in concert with deep temblors of the human spirit. Stafford celebrates the common bonds—the mediating site—between the earth and the single frail human vessel, astonished to find that any one of us in depths of "our stillness" can *contain* such magnitude of subterranean currents:

> We know the motions of this great friend,
> all resolved into one move, our stillness.

Stafford is inundated with the ecstasy of beautiful surging communion with the land, and he is so stubbornly committed to thinking himself an average simple person, his experience ordinary and shared by everyone, by anyone else—any reader, certainly—why, he petitions, isn't each one of us this very moment out running on the hills of night, of day, to become swept up into this love affair with our great benefactor, this marriage to our most faithful patron:

> Why is no one on the hills where they
> graze, the sun and the stars, no one
> clamoring north, running as we would
> run to belong to the earth. We come, we
> celebrate with our breath, we join on the curve
> of our street, never lost, the surge of the land
> all around us that always is ours,
> the beginning of the world and the end.

Stafford's voice is so quiet, so low-keyed, that his taciturnity may be mistaken for frailness, timidity; his humble cries for self-diminishment, or self-depreciation. Yet he makes the highest possible claims for his humanity and his art. He is a man who knows how to stand utterly alone and let the heart of the world shudder through him. In the most intimate communion between one soul and the earth, there is no friend, no companion, no beloved who can follow or accompany this pilgrim, *"Oh friends, where can one find a partner / for the long dance over the fields?"* That path is immitigably a lonely one (this is his poem "So Long" in the earlier volume *Allegiances*):

> At least at night, a streetlight
> is better than a star.
> And better good shoes on a
> long walk, than a good friend.
>
> Often in winter with my old
> cap I slip away into the gloom
> like a happy fish, at home
> with all I touch, at the level of love.
>
> No one can surface till far,
> far on, and all that we'll have
> to love may be what's near
> in the cold, even then.

This poem is aimed at the unpeopled zones of the planet. There is an arctic chill lining the verses. In this book, as in the others before it, Stafford is of two minds: a loving, generous, outgoing brother to all human fellows, dear ones and strangers alike. Not accidentally, he addresses remarks in his poems to *friend,* or *stranger,* by turns; or a militiaman of the wilds, a guerrilla woodsman constantly in training to *provide, provide* for a foreseen era of extreme shortages of supplies, an age of severe poverty and drought (guess how soon, reader). On one wavelength, all the saying favors a life of giving and belonging to the human community. On the other, he would give himself up irrevocably to the wilderness:

> At caves in the desert, close
> to rocks, I wait. I live
> by grace of shadows. In moonlight
> I hear a room open behind me.
>
> At the last when you come
> I am a track in the dust.

Stafford's enduring resources of human warmth and personal intimacy are revealed in the short masterful poem, "Father and Son":

> No sound—a spell—on, on out
> where the wind went, our kite sent back
> its thrill along the string that
> sagged but sang and said, "I'm here!
> I'm here!"—till broke somewhere,

gone years ago, but sailed forever clear
of earth. I hold—whatever tugs
the other end—I hold that string.

The kite metaphor skillfully mediates between the worlds of paternity and authorship. In so few lines, aptly low-keyed, undertoned, Stafford merges the two aesthetics—the siring of poems, of sons—and demonstrates with effortless grace and agility the stark interwovenness of his vision. The trick is to keep holding the string years and years after it breaks, and to keep feeling the infinitesimally faint—but invaluable—tugs from the lost kite of fatherhood through the feeble, paltry conductor of thin air. To continue to traverse that gap across a near-vacuum in the thinning filial atmosphere is a feat of mental radar, thoughts and feelings so delicately balanced and held by so light a grasp, contact with the other being—father to son, writer to reader—is maintained by subtle echo-location.

A large unwritten chapter of the book of our "Origins" is locked in the racial memory of our hands—the key site, or locus, of our body's subconscious mind passed over by Jungian psychologists:

So long ago that we weren't people then
our hands came upon this warm place on a rock
inside a high cave in the North, in the wilderness.
No light was there, but "Homeland" glowed in that dark. . . .
Now along walls, over quilts, by locks, our hands
retell that story. Wherever touch finds hope again,
these hands remember that other time: they are lost;
they hunt for a place more precious than here.
Who will accept us wanderers? Where is our home?

In many new poems, Stafford explores the frontiers of the hands' powers of remembering. A friend of mine, an expert craftsman of the short story, doggedly insists on the rule of thumb—not of tongue—"I never know what I think about anything until my hand tells me." Stafford is a poet who espouses that aesthetic. His art is lavishly extemporaneous and unpremeditated. He is poetry's zealot of improvisation. Moreover, with a childlike innocence, he profoundly trusts what his hand tells him is true:

This is the hand I dipped in the Missouri
above Council Bluffs and found the springs.
All through the days of my life I escort
this hand. . . .

Summits in the Rockies received this diplomat.
Brush that concealed the lost children yielded
them to this hand. Even on the last morning
when we all tremble and lose, I will reach
carefully, eagerly through that rain, at the end—

Toward whatever is there, with this loyal hand.

Stafford's lines of verse are felt to be a perfect extension of his hand's
natural moves and gestures, as exhalations of our breath are inescapably
tinged with our lungs' odor. The lines charmed and escorted across
the page by the maestro's conducting hand are the intensest and most
irreducible expression of our human reality. They are *the authentic:*

The authentic is a line from one thing
along to the next . . . It holds
together something more than the world,
this line. And we are your wavery
efforts at following it. Are you coming?
Good: now it is time.

To live well in the world, to write the poem that rings true, follow
the hand's right leads, the hand's wisdom. Aristotle was a great thinker
because he correctly assessed the hand's sensitive intelligence. Its genius
inheres in its flexibility, the instinctive rightness of its moves, not in its
power—athletic or military prowess, a lesson that his student Alexander
failed to learn (from *Allegiances):*

Aristotle was a little man with
eyes like a lizard. . . .

He said you should put your hand out
at the time and place of need:
strength matters little, he said,
nor even speed.

His pupil, a king's son, died
at an early age. That Aristotle spoke of him
it is impossible to find—the youth was
notorious, a conqueror, a kid with a gang,
but even this Aristotle didn't ever say.

William Stafford has continued, unwaveringly, for the last thirteen years, following the publication of his first volume of poetry at age forty-six, to develop and refine one of the most delicate supersensitive recording instruments in our poetry. He has been training himself to hear and feel his way back in touch with distant places, ages, epochs. Like some stones, there are men "too quiet for these days," and a part of themselves hangs back, lingers, dreams its way to other eras, universes. But it's not bodiless imagination, pure enchanted spirit, that negotiates the leaps across thousands of years, billions of miles. It is, rather, an act of the senses, a superkeen listening, a reaching of the hand via its magical powers of touching for immanent—but deeply buried—crypts of reality hidden in the rock, the walls of a cave:

Touches

> Late, you can hear the stars. And beyond them
> some kind of quiet other than silence, a deepness
> the miles make, the way canyons
> hold their miles back: you are in the earth and
> it guides you; out where the sun comes
> it is the precious world.
> There are stones too quiet for these days,
> old ones that belong in the earlier mountains.
> You put a hand out in the dark of a cave and
> the wall waits for your fingers. Cold, that stone
> tells you all of the years that passed without knowing.
> You think of caves held in the earth, no mouth,
> no light. Down there the years have lost their way.
> Under your hand it all steadies,
> is the world under your hand.

It is the transcendent grace of the hand's gentlest touch, and of the listener's marvelously intense hearing, that achieves penetration into spheres of reality the mind cannot enter. The hand's touch can recover any lost world.

Touches. The shocks of a normal hand. In our homes and families, by common daily routines, we connect with the spirit of all that lives across the planet ("At the sink I start / a faucet; water from far is / immediate on my hand"), the whole world rescued and transmitted in each natural human gesture, and these are the events most worth publishing to a readership; the simple motions of our body's saying them at home are the true miracles, the noteworthy headlines of each day's life. The poem aspires to catch the exact uniquely marvelous twist of each never-to-be-repeated human event of watching this bird now, glimpsing the moon between buildings at a special new angle, improvising a new story to a child at bedtime, seeing the light (" . . . any light. Oh—any light.") come on again in the child's eyes, or in his late father's intricately remembered words. These occurrences, then, are Stafford's alternative to what newsprint "an eighth of an inch thick" offers as world news (from *Allegiances):*

> That one great window puts forth
> its own scene, the whole world
> alive in glass. In it a war happens,
> only an eighth of an inch thick.
> Some of our friends have leaped
> through, disappeared, become unknown
> voices and rumors of crowds.
>
> In our thick house, every evening
> I turn from that world,
> and room by room I walk, to
> enjoy space. At the sink I start
> a faucet; water from far is
> immediate on my hand. I open our
> door, to check where we live.
> In the yard I pray birds,
> wind, unscheduled grass,
> that they please help to make
> everything go deep again.

Stafford chronicles *his* global highlights in the form of lean verses, messages offered to the world for minimal daily unction, so many "small acts of honesty, to use like / salt pills, one at a time, at need." Stafford always localizes himself by starting from the small indigenous happenstance whereby he feels solidly anchored and centered in his person (from *Allegiances):*

> Like a stubborn tumbleweed I hold,
> hold where I live. . . .
> We ordinary beings can cling to the earth and love
> where we are, sturdy for common things.

If the poem always stays within hand's reach of pedestrian daily events, it finds its life mainly in collecting the inner resonances. How quickly and adroitly Stafford can step back from the life of action, himself the tree abruptly engulfed in fog, given over completely to the inner storm of mirrorings and reverberations ("that far flood / Inside"), without losing his grasp of the bare, plain, earthy quantities—mortal or inanimate particularities—that touched off the inner chain of correspondences (from *Allegiances*).:

In Fog

In fog a tree steps back.

Once gone, it joins those hordes
blizzards rage for over tundra.

With new respect I tell
my dreams to grant all claims;

Lavishly, my eyes close between
what they saw and that far flood

Inside: the universe that happens
deep and steadily.

Stafford's calm, mild-mannered voice dances lightfootedly, the nimble steps half-masking the scrupulous rigor of his thought and toughness of his vision. Many readers fail to grasp how much concentrated force of mind—a shrewd, energetic intelligence—is mobilized to support his mild soft-spokenness, those lines that would "breathe a harmless breath." Stafford would make his lines imitate the effortless floating ease and drift of the falling snowflake ("what snowflake, even, may try / today so calm a life, / so mild a death?"). Words and phrases, as in a dance by Fred Astaire, swish and glide and float across the page—lightest footfalls, a delicate, thin, relaxed saying that approaches a condition of pure breath, all easefulness:

This whole day is your gift:
hold it and read a leaf at a
time, never hurried, never waiting,
Step, step, slide; then turn,
dance on the calendar,

> reach out a hand, give lavish
> as anyone ever gave—all.

The lines imitate the smooth, easy gestures of a dancer, or those of any great musical performer whose instrument—violin, piano, cello, his own body or voice—seems to vanish, to disappear, to melt away into the serene flow of pure, entranced rhythm. There is a quality of relaxed arbitrariness by which Stafford lazily coaxes—or coaches—so many of his best lines and images out of the depths of his solitude, such that the lines seem to lean backward, half-clinging still to the lovely voiceless silence of his frequent late-night strolls. By a most rigorous artifice, he establishes the fleetingly accidental human impulse, the feeling of this moment, as *the* viable human occasion most tractable for grafting into his art; he celebrates, above all, each accidental next passing fancy, notion, hunch, guess, chance remark. He must learn to be always on the alert, on his mental toes so to speak, to select fertile items from the always available and swiftly unfolding agendas of sensory and cerebral data that flicker upon the screen of his rich imaginative life, and he proceeds with an unprecedented good faith that the inexhaustible stockpile of such treasures of information is readily accessible to the poetry-making process at any moment of our waking lives, and it will be fully replenished every next moment. Luck is a helpful catalyst that we can train ourselves—always on the run, in the midst of flow—to seize upon as an indispensable ally to creation, and some moments are inherently more propitious to the creative eye than others.

We are persuaded by the sheer weight of swiftly mounting evidence, as we move from poem to poem, that William Stafford's day-to-day life is perennially aglow with constellations of tiny momentous events, meetings, exchanges, transferrals of mystical energies between Stafford and the world. We witness in him a chosen person whom the world makes thousands of careful moves daily to reward:

> Oh, I thought, how hard the world has tried
> with its wind, its miles, its blundering
> stumbling days, again and again, to find my hand.

To receive the many gifts, he need only restore in himself daily the condition of availability and receptiveness.

In the Staffordian psychic Elysium, it appears that anyone who simply cultivates the spirit of lowliness, one who trains daily the faculty of bowing down before the world's delicate beauties ("'A great event is coming, bow down.' / And I, always looking for something anyway, / always bow down"), enhances the world's power to bestow them. Stafford is not, as might appear to some, offering himself as a candidate for sainthood; speaking for the common chosenness in us all, he locates and canonizes a site in himself that is shared by all of common humanity, and perhaps this is why William Stafford, to a keener pitch than any other American contemporary, raises in his voice the accents of a statesman's speech. He would reendow our poetry with a Frostian vernacular, a level directness of delivery of sufficient plainness to win back to the reading of verse a wide readership of unsophisticated caring humans. He is a civic manager legislating urban renewals of the heart. Stafford is our poetry's ambassador to the provinces.

On nearly every page of Frederick Morgan's *Book of Change,* I feel that I come into touch with a lively, warm human being through the poetry. Although in some sections of this ambitious and expansive poetic sequence the pressure of human feeling overtakes the formal structuring of lines and stanzas, how refreshing it is to read a premiere volume in which the sheer quantity of erupting life overwhelms the literary boundaries, at times, after so many recent first books of verse in which the self-conscious stylistic mannerisms of this or that school squelch the sense of self.

Morgan, who, as founding editor of the *Hudson Review,* has been regarded for many years by William Stafford, A. R. Ammons, and other central poets of our day as being a profoundly influential guiding mentor to contemporaries, has shifted the focus of much of that energetic brilliance—in midcareer—from the editorial platform to the swift unfolding of a full-fledged mature poetics of his own. Although for some twenty-odd years Morgan had written, intermittently, successful—if undistinguished—original verse and some passable translations, his poetic art has taken a breathtakingly sudden upswing in the last few years, and he leaps into prominence in this first collection as an important writer in the current scene. Perhaps following the lead of the senior poet Stafford in the richly human articulateness and candor of his style, Morgan's zest and unguarded forthrightness of delivery ensure the distinctiveness of his voice and measure. He appears to have assimilated an impressive blend of influences and orthodoxies without strain: so many ideas and presences, epiphanies and personages and beings—demonic, angelic, and mortal—are falling all over each other in the struggle to be born, any derivative elements of Morgan's style are burned away as he amplifies his medium and stretches the skin of the work to contain so much eruption of newly awakened life:

> At this fresh dawn in the middle of my life—
> [Oh Lord] . . . steady my steps along the road,
> help me abate my rage and fretfulness,
> this energy of yours, help me control it!
> Strong and in order let the good words sound.

Morgan's outburst of creativity—which appears to have taken its author by surprise with the unforeseen violence of a seizure or a visitation—was evidently prompted by the sudden tragic death of his son, John, followed mercifully by the birth of the revitalizing love relation with Paula, Morgan's present wife:

> Dear son, you died three years ago today.
> I died too, and have risen from the dead
> and take you with me in my blood and bones
> through a new life.—Poor boy, what was there left?
> Your corpse, part-decomposed when it was found
> sent home for burial; your clothing, books,
> letters, snapshots—a suitcaseful shipped home.
> Sad remnants, John. . . .

In "The Smile," as in a number of the other best love poems to Paula, Morgan achieves a rare discipline, the power to step back far enough into oneself—during moments of profound intimacy—to pass through the self and move beyond into a condition of spirit in which even the beloved may be witnessed purely, freshly, and accurately. At such moments, a supernatural radiance lifts the usual film of haziness from the lover's eyes, and all is seen with a final clarity—even those humans closest to us—such as we suppose may be afforded only to ghosts returning from the dead. Our eyes seem to pass through themselves into another life, beyond sight into a second seeing:

> Your hands were deft. Your face, intent
> above that work you do so well,
> took on a gentle, abstract smile.
> . . . the true beauty, grace of one
> at home with her desires and powers.
> I treasure it, and always shall,
> that smile of yours above the flowers.

His abstracted vision is half human, half transhuman, modeled after the smile described. Second sight has sprung up within love, but passes beyond into a solitary and lonely life of its own. The poet has witnessed this capacity for purely independent self-possession in the beloved, of which her smile is both manifestation and emblem. The poem had begun by ridiculing Byron's betrayal of his true affections in poetry by a heavy-handed submission to convention. Dante's adoration of Beatrice is the closest prototype in literature for the exalted love portrayed, but for all Morgan's struggle to escape the falsities of convention, he establishes a more subtle artifice in which the relation between lines of verse and human moments they mirror approach photographic realism. However, his warring against the inbred artificialities of the medium infuses most of his poetry with the quality of utmost ingenuousness.

Morgan's plain, lucid style—all openness and transparency—endues the infrequent occasions of modest stylistic glamor with surprising power and resonance. His relaxed highlighting is always suavely compatible with the prevailing forthrightness of voice, virtues of a kind that the density and compression of a grand style could never support:

> In last extremities of pain and fear
> when you are all alone with nothingness
> and clench your teeth on it and taste despair,
> if you remember this is each man's fate
> and God's fate, too, as far as we are he,
> and let your inner substance rest on it
> and merge with it as with a summer sea—
> then comes the Change. You have become the pain
> and all at once attained the further shore.
>
> from "Pain Poems"

How much power he gets from the inescapable hard-earned honesty of these plain findings—the language not invented, adorned, reveled in muscularly, but simply received and guilelessly transmitted to the reader. His many poetic forms, like his style, approach the purity of a natural expressive instrument superbly well synchronized with the widely varied dimensions of his mind and art.

Although Morgan has a strong predilection for condensed nuggets of wisdom—the axiom, the adage, the proverb—his comic spirit saves him from any leanings toward pedagogy:

> The wise old man said, "He's a fool
> who tries to live his life by rule,
> but if you think to get to heaven
> by rules, I'll gladly give you seven.

> First, *be healthy:* because, you know,
> your body's you, it's where you grow
> and meet the real world, opening.
> Don't treat it like a foreign thing. . . ."

This poem exhibits a cunning of self-parody. Much of the thematic content of the book is presented in the form of refined epigrammatic thought-capsules, but Morgan always escapes self-conscious didacticism, since his philosophic baggage is lightly held. His voice has, unfailingly, the authentic ring of a man thinking on his feet, soliloquizing in the heat of passion, or conducting a sensual wrestling bout with his god, displaying all the tactile intimacy of Donne's *Holy Sonnets:*

> Letting go into God is almost physical . . .
> like letting your body slide into a quarry pool
> deep in the woods. It's summertime—hot sun, green trees—
> but the water is dark and chill, and there is no one watching.
> You slip from the edge—a shock of cold—and then you're free!
> Indeed, if you died that instant, free for ever
> because you've given your self . . . But the heart stops at last.
> The truth is in the shock and the surrender.

Throughout *A Book of Change,* Morgan's late-blooming youthful exuberance, surging as if for the first time in a man of fifty, combines freshness with reserve, lighthearted optimism with an earned austerity of command in drawing upon his prodigious reservoir of neglected intellectual resources: he both achieves an attractive synthesis of wisdom of the ages—extracted from classical works of theology, philosophy, and mythology—and produces a full-scale self-portrait. But the work is not diaristic, after the fashion of *Notebook* or *The Dream Songs,* though the four-part structure is punctuated with recurring confessional motifs. The book's overall design unfolds by such a natural rhythm of disclosure of key moments and upheavals, selected from the flux of ongoing human experience, that the seminarrative episodic form wears the guise of conventional autobiography. But the thin veneer of chronological narration masks a consistent grasp of inner spiritual cycles that truly dominate the vision, and that are skillfully reinforced by the internal arrangement of poems within each of the four sections.

The slow, irreversible growth of a second mental life—the fruition of a totally new sensibility—hiddenly evolving within the dried-out husk of a middle-aged man's former collapsed identity is the remarkable adventure recounted in *A Book of Change*. If the book's formal design seems scattered, from time to time, with each rereading of the work one is inescapably struck by the cumulative power of a sustained vision of human regeneration. This is a book of awesome metamorphosis.

Postscript

Hold the Audience

A Brief Memoir of John Berryman

In the middle of the winter of 1969, shortly following the announcement of the awarding of the National Book Award in poetry to John Berryman's volume *His Toy, His Dream, His Rest,* the University of Illinois invited Mr. Berryman to visit the campus for a few days and present a couple of readings from his work.[1] The letter of invitation was sent some months before the suggested date for the readings, but we received no reply from Mr. Berryman. Finally, a couple of weeks before the date scheduled for his arrival, we phoned the poet, and he warmly agreed to be our guest. Apparently, he had misplaced our letter and then had forgotten about the matter, thinking he had already replied in the affirmative.

I had for many years been an ardent devotee of the poet's work, and since I was to act as his host at the university, I looked forward to our first meeting with great enthusiasm. I strongly advised Mr. Berryman to plan to arrive a day or two before his first reading, because bad weather in midwinter between Minnesota and Illinois often interrupts jet traffic. But he arranged to reach Urbana just a few hours before the reading. There was some snowfall on the day of his arrival, not heavy enough to ground the planes but sufficient hazard to delay his shorter flight—the notoriously unreliable Ozark shuttle plane—between Chicago and Urbana. I drove to the airport to meet the late Ozark plane, and when Mr. Berryman failed to appear among the deboarding passengers, I panicked, since his first scheduled performance was just hours away. I phoned his home in Minneapolis, and his young daughter assured me that he had flown by jet to Chicago. Then began the marathon wait.

Mr. Berryman's first performance was scheduled for 8:00 P.M. and by 7:30 P.M., most of the audience of several hundred had already assembled in the lecture hall. I hurriedly composed a speech of apology, but just before I reached the speaker's podium to send the audience home, I was called to the phone. Mr. Berryman was calling from a public phone

---

1. This memoir first appeared in *Eigo Seinen [The Rising Generation]* 118 (May 1972): 68–70.

booth at some point along the highway between Chicago and Urbana—he wasn't sure of the distance—and his first words to me were, "Lieberman, hold the audience!" He sounded in very high gay spirits, saying he had found a cabdriver at O'Hare Airport in Chicago, a lovely, talkative man, who had agreed to taxi him 140 miles to Urbana for a reasonable price. He expected to be about one hour late, and I should kindly ask the audience to wait. Nearly everyone in the crowded auditorium was happy to wait. I delighted to imagine the dialogue between Mr. Berryman and his cabdriver, which I assured the audience jokingly must resemble the wonderful repartee between Henry, the autobiographical persona of Berryman's famous *Dream Songs*, and his friend and counterpart who refers to Henry in the poems as Mr. Bones. A student carrying a guitar mounted the stage and began to play folk songs; then a number of other students followed the first, and all spontaneously began to sing—so the time passed quickly and happily for all.

Shortly after 9:00 P.M., some of the audience became fidgety, and a slow stream of those who had lost patience and were tired of waiting began to trickle out of the lecture hall. At 9:15, the phone rang again. Mr. Berryman, his voice now at fever pitch, repeated "Hold the audience!" In the background, I could make out a jukebox and jangled voices: Clearly, Mr. Berryman was phoning me from a bar, and no doubt he would be treating his chauffeur to "a couple for the road." At 10:00, when the phone rang for the third time, half of the audience had left. Mr. Berryman was calling at last from the registration desk of the Illinois Union, his place of lodging for the night. He had arrived safely, paid his cabdriver, and wished to rest for a short while in his room to get ready for his performance. I elatedly reported the news to the audience, and we all moved from the auditorium to a very spacious private home. We settled in for a late meeting with our poet, in which we anticipated the intimacy of a small, informal—if crowded—gathering would compensate for the long delay.

At 11:00 P.M., I met Mr. Berryman at his room, as agreed earlier, and he rose to greet me, while covertly replacing a whiskey flask in his satchel. He was shaking from head to foot, and I distinctly remember him saying as we shook hands, "There's nothing wrong with me that a completely new nervous system wouldn't fix." (I'm reminded of those words by a line in one of the poems in *Love and Fame*, "When all hurt nerves whine shut away the whiskey.")[2] When we arrived at the large home at which the remains

---

2. John Berryman, *Love and Fame* (New York: Farrar, Straus and Giroux, 1970), 88.

of the audience were gathered, Mr. Berryman was quickly accosted by a somewhat deranged young ex-GI poet. I was amazed at Mr. Berryman's extreme kindness toward this ill-mannered fellow; he exercised infinite patience toward a man who was obviously very unbalanced mentally and perhaps dangerous. Mr. Berryman's astonishing compassion for troubled young people was unmistakably demonstrated by this incident. I can hear his words of sympathy for this young man echoed in the many poems in *Love and Fame* dealing with agonized patients of the psychiatric ward in which Mr. Berryman apparently was a patient for a short while.

Another revealing exchange preceding the performance was Mr. Berryman's meeting with John Shahn, the son of the famous artist Ben Shahn, a dear friend of the poet's who produced the superb drawings for the first edition of Mr. Berryman's book *Homage to Mistress Bradstreet.* Ben Shahn had recently died, and his son, John, was the first to give Mr. Berryman the terrible news. Mr. Berryman's instant outpouring of grief for his friend gave me a firsthand glimpse into the poet's great talent for friendship, a major theme of so many of his best poems—laments over the deaths of his friends. In the course of his reading, he interrupted the actual flow of his poems often to comment on friends living or dead, and I particularly remember that he frequently sang the praises of Robert Lowell. He tried to convince the audience that Lowell deserved the Nobel Prize in literature, and evidently he felt there was a good chance that Lowell would win the award later that year.

The performance itself was surely one of the most electric and memorable poetry readings I have ever attended. Mr. Berryman felt a great affection for his audience, so many of whom were seated in ardent adulation at his feet in the large front-room parlor, and he easily established a communion with a couple of the prettier girls in the front rows. He often seemed to address the lines of his poems, as well as the wonderful flow of anecdotes and reminiscences between poems, directly to those individual faces. And this quality of personal involvement and exchange gave more life to the experience for us all.

In the next few days, during which I was honored to act as Mr. Berryman's host, he often exhibited the same instant surging of warmth and affection for attractive females, including my younger daughter Deborah, who was seven years old at the time and probably reminded him of his own daughter of about the same age. Contrary to the legend of Mr. Berryman as an impetuous seducer of women, his expressions of affection for females of all ages took the form of a spiritual, loving kindness. As I think back to his genuine fondness for every lovely young lady he met while in my company, the memory gives a special ring to my ear as I read the following lines from perhaps the loveliest and most moving of the "Eleven Addresses to the Lord."[3]

> Sole watchman of the flying stars, guard me
> against my flicker of impulse lust: teach me
> to see them as sisters & daughters. Sustain
> my grand endeavours: husbandship & crafting.
>
> Forsake me not when my wild hours come . . .

---

3. Ibid.

About the Author

Laurence Lieberman is professor of English at the University of Illinois and author of many books of poetry and criticism, including *New and Selected Poems: 1962–1992*, *The St. Kitts Monkey Feuds*, and *Unassigned Frequencies*. Editor of the Illinois Poetry Series since its inception in 1971, Lieberman is also the advisory/contributing editor to *The James Dickey Newsletter* and an advisory editor to *The Caribbean Writer*.

Photo by William Wiegand, Illini News Bureau